SAVING OUR SURVIVORS

THE MODERN JEWISH EXPERIENCE

Marsha L. Rozenblit and Beth S. Wenger, editors
Paula Hyman and Deborah Dash Moore, founding coeditors

SAVING OUR SURVIVORS

How
American
Jews
Learned
about the
Holocaust

RACHEL DEBLINGER

INDIANA UNIVERSITY PRESS

This book is a publication of

Indiana University Press
Herman B Wells Library 350
1320 East 10th Street
Bloomington, Indiana 47405 USA

iupress.org

© 2025 by Rachel Deblinger

All rights reserved

No part of this book may be reproduced or utilized in any form or by
any means, electronic or mechanical, including photocopying and
recording, or by any information storage and retrieval system, without
permission in writing from the publisher.

First printing 2025

Cataloging information is available from the Library of Congress.
ISBN 978-0-253-07269-6 (hdbk.)
ISBN 978-0-253-07270-2 (pbk.)
ISBN 978-0-253-07271-9 (web PDF)
ISBN 978-0-253-07272-6 (ebook)

For Aya.

CONTENTS

Acknowledgments	*ix*
List of Abbreviations	*xiii*
Introduction: In a World Still Trembling	1
1. Heartstrings and Purse Strings: Fundraising and the Battle for Jewish Survival	20
2. Voicing Survivor Narratives: Postwar American Radio and Refugee Policy	49
3. Translating Postwar Europe: American Jewish Aid Workers as Secondary Witnesses	75
4. Sending Hope, Securing Peace: Volunteerism and Direct Aid in the Early Cold War	101
Conclusion: Toward a Longer History of American Holocaust Memory	129
Notes	*137*
Bibliography	*179*
Index	*195*

ACKNOWLEDGMENTS

I want to start by thanking David Myers, Sarah Stein, and Todd Presner, who have been supportive of this project since its earliest days, when I had only the vaguest research question about how Holocaust survivor voices were first heard in America. Over the past sixteen years, their support has remained strong. They have each served as readers, advisers, collaborators, and mentors. I am so grateful for their guidance and encouragement over so many years.

In those early days, as I continued to refine this project and identify sources, I benefited from working with scholars within and beyond the field of Jewish history who helped me narrow my questions, hone my writing, and expand my thinking. Thank you to Hasia Diner, Peter Baldwin, Geoffrey Robinson, and the late Richard Hovannisian. I am also grateful for the many fellow graduate students who offered feedback, support, and encouragement over the years. Thank you to Leslie Waters, Anat Mooreville, Jason Lustig, Alma Heckman, Carrie Sanders, Chris Silver, Ronit Stahl, Shayna Weiss, and Rachel Gross.

Since finishing graduate school, I have been lucky to build a career launching spaces and programs that support the creation of digital knowledge and provide global access to archival collections. The last decade of work in libraries and university research support has greatly impacted the final direction of this project, and I am grateful for Elizabeth Cowell, Irena Polic, Sharon Farb, and Todd Grappone. I have been so lucky to learn from each of you and build things alongside you. Thank you for your trust in me. I also want to thank Elliott Shore and the team at the Council for Library and Information Resources for smoothing my transition into the world of academic libraries and for seeing that I could bring something valuable to the field.

ACKNOWLEDGMENTS

The work of writing and editing this book has happened alongside my professional growth. It has ebbed and flowed, fit in beside professional and personal commitments. As someone who has never been on a traditional academic track, the generosity of so many scholars has felt even more rewarding and meaningful. Thank you to Paul Jaskot, Lila Corwin Berman, Barry Trachtenberg, Libby Garland, Sharon Oster, Kierra Crago-Schneider, and Anne Gilliland for reading drafts, offering feedback, and providing ways for me to remain engaged in the field. Perhaps without even knowing it, you have offered me advice, reassurance, and inspiration precisely when I needed a little extra boost. I also want to thank the incredibly generous community of scholars I worked with at UC Santa Cruz for recognizing my research and creating opportunity for intellectual exchange. Among many others, I want to thank Alan Christy, Deana Shemek, Tyrus Miller, Katie Trostel, Kyle Parry, Fabiola Hanna Miriam Greenberg, and Amanda Smith. In particular, thank you to Nathaniel Deutsch for providing structure and funding for my work and for your ongoing, consistent support and encouragement.

I also want to acknowledge Rachel Kranson's helpful editing and strategic insight through the revision process. And thank you to Deborah Dash Moore, Beth Wenger, and Marsha Rozenblit for supporting this manuscript and offering such a close review near the final stages.

This work has been supported by many grants and fellowships, and I have been lucky to receive support throughout the research process. Thank you to Eric Sundquist, who first supported this research with a UCLA/Mellon Fellowship through the Program on the Holocaust in American and World Culture in 2008. This fellowship affirmed the direction of the research that grew into this book. In the years that followed, my research was also supported by a Skirball Fellowship in Modern Jewish Culture (UCLA), a 1939 Club Pre-Dissertation Fellowship (UCLA), a Monkarsh Graduate Fellowship (UCLA), a Rabbi Joachim Prinz Memorial Fellowship at the American Jewish Archive, a Charles H. Revson Foundation Fellowship at the United States Holocaust Memorial Museum, a Samuel and Flora Weiss Research Fellowship at YIVO Institute for Jewish Research, a UCLA Dissertation Year Fellowship, the UCLA Center for Jewish Studies grant, and the Ross Endowment for Jewish Studies at UCLA.

I have so many friends and family members to thank for supporting me over the many years this book has been in progress. First, thank you to Allen Loeb, my earliest reader, who applied every ounce of his lawyerly training to consistently tell me that each sentence and paragraph was far too long. Thank you for never saying no when I needed a second set of eyes and for willingly becoming an expert on David Boder after reading so many early drafts. I want to thank Caroline Luce and Leah Hiller for being the best, most reliable cheerleaders. You have helped me see this work as meaningful in the moments when I needed it most.

Let me thank my family for continually asking why it was taking so long for the book to be published. Your constant questions always felt like support instead of criticism, and I am grateful to have had so many people invested in the success of this work. Thanks to Jonathan, Josh, Molly, Judy, and Ron for being in my corner. And a huge thank-you to my parents, Ronald and Rebecca Deblinger, for their truly unending belief that I can do whatever I set my mind to do.

I began the research that became this book before I met my husband, Adam, and before we welcomed our daughter, Aya, into the world. And yet, I cannot imagine this book coming into the world without them. Adam, thank you for every home-cooked meal and for reading each draft of the introduction. Thank you for helping me figure out what I wanted to say and offering edits that helped me say it better. Aya, you inspired me finish this book. Thank you for being the brightest light and showing up in the world with joy and enthusiasm and empathy.

LIST OF ABBREVIATIONS

AJC	American Jewish Committee
CCDP	Citizen's Committee on Displaced Persons
DP	displaced person
HIAS	Hebrew Immigrant Aid Society
IIT	Illinois Institute of Technology
IRO	International Refugee Organization
JDC	Jewish Joint Distribution Committee
JLC	Jewish Labor Committee
JNF	Jewish National Fund
JPS	Jewish Publication Society
NCJW	National Council of Jewish Women
NCRAC	National Community Relations Advisory Council
NRS	National Refugee Service
ORT	Organization for Rehabilitation through Training
OWI	Office of War Information
UCLA	University of California Los Angeles
UIA	United Israel Appeal
UJA	United Jewish Appeal
UN	United Nations
UNCC	United National Clothing Collection
UNRRA	United Nations Relief and Rehabilitation Administration

UPA	United Palestine Appeal
USHMM	United States Holocaust Memorial Museum
USNA	United Service for New Americans
WJC	World Jewish Congress

SAVING OUR SURVIVORS

Introduction

In a World Still Trembling

IF YOU HAD BEEN listening to station WMCA on the radio between 1:30 and 2 p.m. on Thanksgiving Day 1947, you would have heard Raymond Massey, a prominent actor of the time, welcome an audience of Jewish immigrants to a celebratory dinner. The radio broadcast, titled "Delayed Pilgrims Dinner," was sponsored by the United Service for New Americans (USNA), a Jewish organization founded the year before to support Jewish refugees from Europe after the Holocaust.[1] On the broadcast, Massey referenced his own ancestors who had landed at Salem, addressing the audience of new immigrants as "fellow pilgrims." Massey was followed by New York City mayor William O'Dwyer, who had recently ended his work as director of the War Refugee Board. O'Dwyer also addressed the gathered immigrants, saying, "I greet those who so recently arrived from the Displaced Persons Centers of Europe . . . to start new lives in America . . . a country which itself started as a refuge for those who needed shelter."[2]

The broadcast was a recorded version of a live dinner sponsored in part by Mr. D. Beryl Manischewitz (owner of the well-known B. Manischewitz Company, manufacturer of kosher food and wine). During his turn at the microphone, Manischewitz similarly evoked America's past as a haven from religious persecution to address the refugee crisis following World War II, which displaced over ten million people. He connected the plight of Jews under Nazi persecution to the struggle of the Pilgrims: "Like their predecessors who came on the Mayflower, these later day pilgrims have wandered for thirteen years, seeking a place where they might live in peace."[3] For Manischewitz, the survivors featured in the broadcast exemplified the best of America—the optimism and potential of the land of opportunity. Manischewitz introduced one of these survivors, saying, "I want you to meet Israel Burkenwald, survivor of Auschwitz concentration camp, age 20. Israel has been learning English, rapidly, in evening school. He said to me, 'Every word I learn makes me feel more and more American.'"

Once given the microphone, Burkenwald said, in accented English, "I have many reasons to be thankful on this Thanksgiving. I was only 14 when I was taken to Auschwitz. After years of forced labor, you can understand what it means for me to have a home, a job, a country that I can call my very own." Burkenwald reinforced the framing set up by Massey, O'Dwyer, and Manischewitz. He referenced his time in Auschwitz only to highlight the bounty and wonder of America, looking ahead rather than dwelling on the past.

If you had heard this broadcast in 1947, somewhere near New York City, perhaps while cooking a turkey dinner or sitting with your family around a large radio set, how would you have understood these voices? How would you have understood the story of Jewish immigration layered on top of America's founding myth? What would it have meant to hear Auschwitz survivors called "fellow pilgrims," to hear them celebrated as they worked to become "more and more American"?

"Delayed Pilgrims Dinner" was not the only broadcast to feature Holocaust survivors and their experiences on the radio. Nor was it the only broadcast to explicitly employ American ideals to tell stories about the Holocaust. The next year, another live event, the *Herald-Tribune* Forum, was recorded and broadcast by the Citizen's Committee on Displaced Persons (CCDP), an organization launched in 1946 to lobby and advocate for more expansive immigration laws following the end of World War II.[4] The recording, broadcast as "An American with a Mission," highlighted the work of William Sudduth (the titular American). Sudduth left his job in 1945 to volunteer with the United Nations Relief and Rehabilitation Administration (UNRRA) and, while in Europe, became scholarship director at Heidelberg University. "An American with a Mission" featured nine young refugees who had survived Nazi Europe and secured scholarships and visas to come to the United States through Sudduth's efforts. The young people—some Jewish and some not—talked about their experiences coming to America and celebrated the opportunity of their new lives. Like Burkenwald, they juxtaposed the horror and loss of their lives in Europe with the joy, optimism, and possibility of life in the United States. Sudduth offered the most direct example of this narrative strategy, describing the young survivors as "youngsters who escaped the gas chambers, and who are now breathing the free air of America."[5]

Introduction

These radio broadcasts demonstrated how foreign victims of Nazism could become Americans—not only by learning English and breathing free air but also by enacting the story of Thanksgiving. They were pilgrims arriving in America to build a life free from religious persecution. This was true for Burkenwald and even more for young Peter Forshee. Featured on "An American with a Mission," four-year-old Forshee sang "My Country, 'Tis of Thee" on air. Without irony, the broadcast included a young orphaned European refugee singing about the "land where his father died" and "land of the pilgrim's pride."[6] The host, Anthony Ross, ensured that listeners understood this central transformation, rendering European refugees, including Jewish Holocaust survivors, Americans: "His voice, a thoroughly American voice. For Peter is an American now. He sounded like your own child. Or the youngsters of the people next door. That's the wonderful thing about this American melting pot. People from all over the face of the earth are welcomed and absorbed into our heritage and culture."[7] In this broadcast, the CCDP portrayed European refugees as capable Americans and "excellent citizens for the United States."[8] Radio became a medium through which survivors could be transformed from foreign victims of Nazi terror into future American citizens full of generosity, gratitude, and optimism.

Similar narrative transformations occurred across the landscape of Jewish communal organizations in brochures, posters, fundraising speeches, filmstrips, and campaign paraphernalia. While many of these materials echo the forward-looking optimism of the "Delayed Pilgrims Dinner" and "American with a Mission," this book highlights a range of narrative strategies employed by Jewish communal organizations in the wake of the Holocaust. In response to the unprecedented needs of surviving Jews in Europe at the end of World War II, American Jewish communal organizations crafted and disseminated stories and images about Holocaust survivors that drew on American ideals and pulled at the heartstrings of American Jewish donors. How did American Jews make sense of these stories in the immediate aftermath of the war? And how did they understand their own relationship to the experiences of European Jews under Nazism?

Drawing on material produced and circulated by Jewish communal organizations in the aftermath of the Holocaust, *Saving Our Survivors* proposes a way of expanding our understanding of Holocaust discourse in America. These narratives reflect how stories about the Holocaust and its survivors were first adapted for and distributed to American audiences. They offer a way to expand the timeline of collective knowledge about the Holocaust in America and challenge our understanding of what Holocaust narratives should look and sound like.

These early, communal, ephemeral narratives are largely absent from historical studies about Holocaust memory and representation. We have been told, repeatedly, by historians, journalists, and museums that American Jews did not respond—or did not adequately respond—to the Holocaust.[9] We have been told that silence followed the Holocaust, that American Jews turned their backs on their brethren—that in pursuit of comfort and acceptance in American suburbs, they ignored the needs of Jewish survivors. Hasia Diner traces the idea of silence back to the 1960s, when young Jews argued that the "Jewish establishment" had "blotted out the memory of the Holocaust because it jarred with the communal agenda of accommodation and assimilation."[10] By the 1980s, these accusations had found their way into scholarly discourse, and we can begin to cite criticism of American Jewry's manipulation of Holocaust memory in Leon Jick's 1981 essay "The Holocaust: Its Uses and Abuses in the American Public."[11]

It is not coincidental that Jick's essay appeared just after the establishment of the Fortunoff Video Archive for Holocaust Testimonies at Yale University, a breakthrough moment for the creation and collection of videotaped survivor accounts, which have become the primary means of preserving survivor testimony as sacred sites of memory.[12] Such institutional efforts to collect and preserve Holocaust survivor memory, which began in the late 1970s and surged in the 1990s, sparked attention to cultural production about the Holocaust. Scholars sought to explore and address the ethical ramifications of public engagement with Holocaust history and memory.[13] Scholars including Norman Finkelstein, Peter Novick, and Alan Mintz sharply criticized the popularization of Holocaust memory, arguing that American Jewish communal leaders were responsible for pronounced silence after the Holocaust only to deploy Holocaust memory for political purposes in the 1980s and beyond.[14]

Mintz summarizes the assumptions behind this school of thought in his introduction to *Popular Culture and the Shaping of Holocaust Memory in America*: "In the depths of the 1940s and 1950s, at a time when the term Holocaust as we now use it had not been invented, when survivors were silent and stigmatized, and when the destruction of European Jewry did not figure in public discourse, who could have predicted that the Holocaust would move so forcefully to the center of American culture?"[15] The "orthodoxy" of this perceived silence spread across America and Europe, in both scholarly and public circles.[16] As David Cesarani summarizes, scholars promoted the "notion that after the war there was a 'silence' about the attempted annihilation of the Jews until it was in the interests of the organized Jewish community in America to break it by

Introduction 5

'constructing' what we know today as the historical event and cultural subject called 'the Holocaust.'"[17]

Despite the persistence of this popular perception, *Saving Our Survivors* follows in the wake of abundant scholarship combating the idea of failure and silence.[18] In fact, scholarly attention to the postwar period has revealed "the sheer volume of talking, recording, writing, representation in various media, and publishing that went on from 1945 well into the 1950s."[19] I pick up the threads of this conversation by considering how Jewish organizations shaped Holocaust narratives through active communal response and how individual American Jews heard, saw, and viewed those narratives through all available media.

As Eric Sundquist suggests, acknowledging the ways Jewish communal groups crafted and shared narratives about the Holocaust at this time starts at "the point where we can dispense with the myth of silence without dispensing with the question of silence."[20] This shift invites us to take seriously the kinds of stories circulated about the Holocaust in the aftermath of the war and to recognize that they may not look the way we expect—like the kinds of testimonies now centered in discourse related to Holocaust memory. We can recognize, for example, that while there was pronounced attention paid to surviving Jews in Europe who needed aid from America, those survivors, on arriving in the United States, did not receive the kind of attention needed to address the trauma and grief of their experiences.[21] American Jewish organizations, focused on the immediate needs of Jewish survivors, did not collect or preserve detailed eyewitness accounts, instead designing narratives to generate aid for the most urgent suffering: postwar hunger, disease, and displacement.

Let me return to "An American with a Mission" to underscore this idea. Among the nine young survivors featured on the broadcast, Irene Hass stands out. While the other young refugees echo Forshee's optimism and Burkenwald's earnestness regarding his free life in America, Irene is sarcastic and bitter. Where the other refugees sound young and cheerful, Irene sounds sad: "I am a graduate of three concentration camps. Three very pleasant places. Auschwitz, Buchenwald, and Belsen. My parents were killed in a gas chamber, and I have my diploma on my arm. The Nazis tattooed a number on my forearm. I'm working as a stenographer now and I managed to get a scholarship at Hunter College, where I'm studying biology and I'm a graduating senior. I know I speak now for all of us when I say how grateful we are for the chance to come here and for the chance we continue to have now to be here."[22] Irene clearly understood the story they wanted her to tell; she touted her academic scholarship and gratefulness to be in America. Yet she rejected the framework that so many sponsored postwar Holocaust narratives tried to impose, the notion that the future could somehow allow her to forget the past. Here, the friction between expression and intention is audible. Irene did not tell a universal story; her story was hers alone. We see this tension again and again throughout this book—between broad, universal stories that had purchase for American audiences and more individual ones that rejected a tidy framework of optimism and resiliency.

Irene reminds us that awareness and knowledge of the Holocaust were not silenced and then activated; rather, awareness changed, and narrative norms shifted in relation to the needs of surviving Jews, the broader context in America, and the politics of Jewish communal life. As Annette Wieviorka has written, "testimonies, particularly when they are produced as part of a larger cultural movement, express the discourse or discourses valued by society at the moment the witness tells their stories as much as they render an individual experience."[23] So, too, these early narratives reflect their moment of creation. In recognizing not silence but gaps and narrative transformations, we can understand how the Holocaust has acquired different meanings in American Jewish life over the past seven decades.

I apply the term "narrative" broadly, referring to slogans, speeches, scripted performances, still and moving images, and more, to address the full scope of storytelling formats and methods employed by Jewish communal organizations. Approaching a range of materials as narrative calls attention to the constructed nature of organizational communications that adapted and reimagined stories about Holocaust survivors for their constituencies and for American audiences beyond organizational members and donors. This method favors close reading, which allows me to draw connections between early postwar Holocaust representations and more contemporary survivor accounts as well as scholarly discourse around Holocaust testimony.

Even as I draw on contemporary interpretations, it is essential to note that the survivors depicted in the pages that follow are not the survivors of the Shoah Foundation; they are not the survivors you may have heard in middle school or high school; they are not the tour guides you may have met at a Holocaust museum; they are not the survivors walking up the hill at the end of *Schindler's List*. The survivors in these pages have not yet become essential witnesses to the Holocaust. Their accounts have not yet been transformed into "a privileged mode of access to the past."[24] Rather, the stories, faces, letters, and voices examined in this book were employed to represent the precarity of the postwar period and convey the urgency of humanitarian aid that "could only come from America."[25]

This is to say that the narratives in the chapters ahead are likely to be unfamiliar to contemporary readers accustomed to testimony collections from

Introduction

the 1980s and '90s. Nevertheless, they demand our attention. Why? Before the effort to collect testimonies, before communal and institutional investment in archival collections of survivor voices through oral histories, video recording, and 360-degree capture, these narratives were powerful drivers of how Americans understood the experiences of Holocaust survivors. These narratives help us confront how collective understanding of world events is shaped by humanitarian efforts built in response to those events and how participants in campaigns come to understand themselves within broader historical narratives.

Expanding the Holocaust Archive

Saving Our Survivors examines a broad range of archival objects, including fundraising letters, pamphlets, speeches, and slideshows; membership brochures; program guides; bulletins; newsletters; annual reports; instruction guides for speakers; campaign posters; newspaper articles and advertisements; promotional films; and radio broadcasts (beyond "Delayed Pilgrims Dinner" and "An American with a Mission"). The breadth and range of materials rebuff the simple narrative of postwar silence. And these varied materials reflect how initial representations of the Holocaust circulated through different mediums for different audiences. All of these ephemeral materials are well preserved in Jewish archives, dispersed across organizational records, personal papers, and miscellaneous collections. For the most part, they are not classified or labeled explicitly as Holocaust related. The use of ephemera—defined in archival practice as noncommercial, nonbook publications including bulletins, newsletters, posters, and other kinds of printed materials—as the central source of analysis for this book invites a new, more expansive look at what we consider to be the Holocaust archive.[26]

Since the 1980s, we have come to identify survivor eyewitness testimony as the key transmitter of Holocaust memory. Collections held by the Yale Fortunoff Video Archive, the USC Shoah Foundation Visual History Archive, and the US Holocaust Memorial Museum (USHMM) preserve thousands of eyewitness Holocaust survivor testimonies.[27] These videotaped accounts center survivor bodies and focus on unique, individual stories of Jewish experiences under Nazism. They were recorded and cataloged with long-term preservation in mind, meant to capture eyewitness accounts, act as a bulwark against forgetting, and ensure that survivor testimony would be accessible after survivors died. The materials explored in this book served a different function. They were ephemeral—not only in the archival sense but also in that they were meant to be discarded. (How many fundraising brochures do you hold on to today?)

These pamphlets and posters, letters and speeches were not created as historical documents or intended to be held and preserved as Holocaust records.

In this way, they are categorically different from voices of Jewish Holocaust survivors that were recorded, collected, and archived in the decades after the war but also from diaries, written testimonies, and other records of Jewish experiences written during and immediately after the war. Consider the wartime eyewitness accounts preserved in the Underground Archive of the Warsaw Ghetto—popularly known as the Ringelblum Archive—discovered in milk cans dug up from under the Warsaw Ghetto. These recovered materials remain preserved at the Jewish Historical Institute in Warsaw and are now accessible online via Yad Vashem.[28] Eyewitness testimony written and documented by survivors, captured in diaries hidden during the war or through the efforts of historical commissions after the war, were also organized and cataloged.[29] Many have since been published and included in both scholarly and public discourse.[30] These records of Jewish experiences under and after Nazism reflect immediate attention to survivor accounts as meaningful documentation requiring institutional care. Efforts to collect these survivor accounts were part of what Jason Lustig has described as an "archive fever" that resulted in the creation of new Jewish archives from Jerusalem to Cincinnati after the end of World War II. Lustig notes that the impulse to collect "gained heightened urgency after the Holocaust, when Jewish leaders looked to gather survivors and cultural remnants."[31] However, these materials—testimonies of survivors written in Yiddish, French, German, and other European languages, diaries of Jewish victims—did not circulate in postwar America.

This is not to say that the organizational materials examined in this book were the only form of Holocaust narratives available for American audiences. On the contrary, Yiddish media, including newspapers, books, and radio, contained accounts about the Holocaust and survivor experiences, and dozens of books and memoirs published in the years after the war garnered attention from American readers, both Jews and non-Jews.[32] We need only acknowledge the popularity of *Anne Frank's Diary* in the 1950s to recognize that Holocaust narratives were part of popular American discourse in the first decade after the war.[33]

It is precisely the work of this book to expand our view of the Holocaust archive so that it includes narratives explicitly created in the service of communal efforts to raise funds and activate communal engagement. These materials push against our expectations of what Holocaust narratives look and sound like. But by adding them to our understanding of Holocaust representation, we are better able to see the structures and mediating factors that informed how American Jews first encountered stories about the Holocaust and formed

Introduction

relationships to it. Importantly, we are invited to recognize that stories about the Holocaust have been and will continue to be mediated and constructed for new audiences and changing communal needs according to the ever-evolving technological possibilities of the moment.[34]

This approach allows us to recognize Jewish communal activity as a meaningful site for knowledge creation and dissemination about the Holocaust—one that defined narratives about survivors in the immediate aftermath of trauma, crisis, and war. We can reimagine a history of Holocaust representation in America that better accounts for the commitments of American Jews in the wake of the war and considers the way narrative tropes and patterns echo through more contemporary approaches to telling stories about the Holocaust. We also gain insight into contemporary organizational practices that shape our understanding of world events through humanitarian aid and fundraising campaigns.

Recognizing the Precarity of Liberation

Saving Our Survivors calls attention to the transitional moment when World War II had ended but the future of Jewish life around the world remained in question. The chapters ahead explore public narratives, slogans, and images that made up organizational campaigns between 1945 and 1953, after which time most displaced person (DP) camps in Europe were closed and American Jewish communal attention shifted to needs in other geographic areas.[35] Survivors reflecting on their Holocaust experience often minimize this period in recorded testimonies. Testimonies from the USC Shoah Foundation in particular follow a narrative structure that jumps from liberation to resettlement.[36] Seriously considering organizational materials during the period when survivors had been liberated but were not yet resettled offers us an understanding of Holocaust survivors different from that provided by testimonies or diaries. We see survivors in relation to American Jewish philanthropy, as recipients of humanitarian aid, as refugees or "Delayed Pilgrims." They were in a period of waiting and uncertainty—not yet in control of their own narratives.

By focusing attention on the years 1945–1953, *Saving Our Survivors* explores the construction of Holocaust narratives in that particular postwar moment, recognizing the work of American Jews to respond to changing boundaries of Jewish life, global politics of the emerging Cold War, and cultural norms of postwar America while grappling with the devastation of the Holocaust. These factors shifted—even during this short period—and American Jewish communal organizations focused on postwar aid altered campaign narratives accordingly. No single, static representation of survivors emerged during this transitional period. Instead, most of the stories in the chapters ahead reflect the challenges of DP life—from the administrative struggles Jews faced in Allied-run camps to the need for emigration routes to urgency around material needs.

And the challenges were significant. As liberation spread across Europe, the number of DPs, defined by UNRRA as all individuals displaced by the war, rose to nearly ten million by most estimates.[37] Of these, Jews made up only a small percentage, even after millions were repatriated in the second half of 1945.[38] Those who refused to be repatriated were declared refugees and protected by international law enforced by UNRRA (and later the International Refugee Organization). By August 1945, roughly 1.5 million DPs remained in occupied territories as refugees. Many of them were housed in makeshift DP camps fashioned in former concentration camps, like Bergen-Belsen, and abandoned Nazi spaces, like the Landsberg DP camp that occupied former Wehrmacht barracks.[39]

In the first months after liberation, as UNRRA assumed management of DP camps, Jewish survivors remained stateless, without enough food, clothing, housing, or means of finding lost family members. At the same time, Jews were not recognized as a unique and designated group of refugees.[40] This resulted in Jewish survivors being classified by nationality, which meant they might be boarded alongside Nazi collaborators or forced laborers whose wartime experiences differed vastly from their own. Jews did not become a distinct group within the DP administration until September 1945, when Earl Harrison, American representative to the Intergovernmental Committee on Refugees, published a scathing report of the treatment of Jews under US military command.[41] Harrison's report received widespread coverage and attention in the US, and it was damning. He declared, "As matters now stand, we appear to be treating the Jews as the Nazis treated them except that we do not exterminate them."[42] This criticism marked a turning point for Jewish DPs, who were thereafter recognized as a distinct group within camps, and for Jewish organizations in America, which were able to distribute aid directly to Jewish survivors.

In the early months following liberation, some Jewish survivors chose to travel back to their prewar homes, while hundreds of thousands chose to stay in DP camps across the British, French, or US zones of postwar Europe. In doing so, they sought (and later demanded) immigration paths out of Europe.[43] Yet there remained a lack of immigration options around the world, preventing Jewish survivors from leaving Europe. The British White Papers limited immigration to Palestine, and restrictive quotas prevented Jewish immigration to the United States at the scale needed to accommodate DPs.[44] Jews sought

Introduction

immigration routes to both the US and Palestine despite these limitations, waiting years for quota numbers or following illegal routes to Palestine through Czechoslovakia, Yugoslavia, and Italy.[45]

In December 1945, President Truman issued a directive to utilize existing quota numbers for DPs (paying particular attention to orphaned children), but the US remained slow to open the doors for increased immigration.[46] This was true for both Jewish and non-Jewish DPs. In fact, while Jews accounted for two-thirds of DPs who entered the US under the Truman Directive of 1945, they accounted for only 16 percent of DPs who arrived under subsequent DP acts.[47] Leonard Dinnerstein estimates that between May 1945 and December 1952, 137,450 Jews arrived in the United States. After 1948, immigration to Israel provided another way out of Europe for Jewish survivors. Ben Shephard estimates that in 1948, 141,608 Jews arrived in Israel, and in 1949, another 141,608 arrived. Of this total group, he estimates roughly 198,000 were Holocaust survivors.[48]

Saving Our Survivors does not detail the political negotiations related to the passage of the 1948 or 1950 DP acts. Rather, I focus on public discourse related to political advocacy and the kinds of narratives Jewish organizations crafted to shift public perception of DPs. In this regard, the prolonged period of policy debate in the United States is of particular relevance to the narratives explored in the chapters ahead. Jewish communal leaders asked donors to give in extraordinary amounts in 1946, proposing to solve the Jewish refugee crisis in one year. As the crisis continued year after year, fundraising narratives underscored a perpetual urgency, prompting donors to give at ever greater "one time" amounts. Additionally, Jewish organizations constructed narratives that minimized Jewish particularity under Nazism to "emphasize the 'non-Jewish' nature of the European refugee problem."[49] During this period, the community of Jewish survivors in Allied DP camps increased. Jews who had survived the war in the Soviet Union made their way back to their prewar homes, then fled further west with the goal of smuggling themselves into US-administered camps.[50] For many, this continued flight west was provoked by antisemitic pogroms like the violence in Kielce, Poland, where forty-two Jews were killed on July 4, 1946.[51]

The fundraising and communal narratives written for American audiences at the time—meant to inspire unprecedented action in response to these concerns—reflect this period as one of continued threat and uncertainty, echoing the ever-changing conditions on the ground across Europe and beyond.[52] Postwar antisemitic violence, malnutrition in DP camps, and mistreatment by Allied forces featured in postwar campaigns by Jewish organizations like the Joint Distribution Committee (JDC). In other words, in these early representations, the postwar was not a distinct period that followed the Holocaust. Rather, it was a continuation of persecution. The precarity of the postwar is evident across the campaigns explored in the chapters ahead, as American Jews were called to support an evolving set of programs that met a changing list of urgent needs for Jewish survivors.

These calls accompanied increased circulation of narratives and images about the war and Nazi crimes that Americans encountered with greater frequency. Newsreels created by the Office of War Information (OWI) captured moving images of US soldiers liberating concentration camps, celebrating America's role as the hero of World War II.[53] These short films were distributed by the OWI and aired before main feature films in theaters across the country to boost support for the war as battles continued in the Pacific theater. Representations of global war victims called on Americans to help ensure postwar peace through campaigns to collect used clothes, donate canned foods, and maintain victory gardens. Images circulating in newsreels portrayed German crimes, including the use of crematoria, dehumanization through numbered tattoos, and starvation of emaciated victims, without specific attention to Jewish victims as a designated group. These narratives echoed across newspapers and magazines promoting America's role as a global leader in the postwar world. For example, the *Saturday Evening Post* story "World Relief Is America's Job" explained that America was "the only country still capable of producing in quantity what the world needs"; it needed to act as "Santa Claus" and "Clara Barton" at once—sending material goods, medicine, and good cheer around the world.[54]

Working across the Jewish Communal Landscape

Jewish communal organizations augmented these national narratives as they sought to engage their constituents as Jews. Across a diverse landscape of political, religious, and cultural affiliations, Jews acted—individually and in community—to offer aid, build relationships, support immigration, and advocate for political change. The chapters ahead explore differences in organizational campaigns, recognizing that Zionist organizations, including Hadassah, the World Jewish Congress (WJC), and the United Palestine Appeal (UPA), depicted survivors and the tragedy of their wartime and postwar lives as justification for a Jewish state. These Zionist groups represented the displacement of Jews during and after World War II as an existential danger and defined the creation of a Jewish state as the only solution to ensure Jewish safety. In contrast, the JDC prioritized the immediate needs of survivors, stressing access to food

Introduction

and medicine and arguing that funds should be directed to provide essentials to those who had survived the Holocaust. For religious organizations, like Vaad Hatzala, rebuilding Jewish life in Europe following the war was the priority. Their leaders called on donors to fund kosher kitchens and support Jewish orphanages where young Jews who had been hidden in Catholic spaces during the war could be cared for and educated.[55] Other organizations—most notably the USNA, Hebrew Immigrant Aid Society (HIAS), National Refugee Service (NRS), and CCDP—concentrated on aiding Jewish immigrants in America and advocating for more expansive immigration policy in the United States.[56] These organizations championed stories of "New Americans" like Israel Burkenwald and Peter Forshee, relying heavily on American tropes to tell stories of Jewish survivors and depicting them as Delayed Pilgrims in search of freedom from religious persecution.

Other Jewish groups offered additional portraits of survivors, appealing to different audiences and aligning with different political affiliations. The Jewish Labor Committee (JLC) and Organization for Rehabilitation and Training (ORT), for example, created survivor narratives connected to the American labor movement. In so doing, they transformed narratives about Holocaust survivors into recognizable stories of hardworking Americans pulling themselves up by their bootstraps.[57] Jewish women's organizations shaped narratives about survivors by focusing on Jewish children and appealing to Jewish women as mothers.[58] Consider an appeal from the American Committee for the Rehabilitation of European Children directed at Jewish women featuring an image of DP children and asking, "Who will mother them on Mother's Day?"[59] Jewish women represented an essential constituency for postwar aid as women's organizations responded nimbly and quickly to overseas material needs.

These varied communal activities and campaigns took place within a broader context of transformation in American Jewish life. Historians have generalized that from the end of World War II through the 1950s and '60s, American Jews, buoyed by the GI Bill and the optimism of postwar American life, moved to the suburbs, built new synagogues, and integrated into mainstream America.[60] Some have argued that the integration of Jews into white spaces resulted in a turn away from the needs of Jews in Europe after the war.[61] However, as Lila Corwin Berman details regarding the Jewish community in Detroit, broad social and political changes related to "white flight" did not take place overnight.[62] Rather, individual Jews negotiated postwar racial politics alongside economic and cultural politics in different ways throughout this period.[63] Institutionally, as Barry Trachtenberg notes in *The United States and the Nazi Holocaust: Race, Refuge, and Remembrance*, race was an especially important criterion for Jewish organizations negotiating refugee policy and immigration advocacy during and after the war.[64]

How did racial, geographic, religious, and political concerns of Jewish communities across the country impact early representations of Holocaust survivors? One answer is that American Jews responded to each of these shifting concerns through communal organizations. Local Jewish federations launched campaigns to address citywide or regional issues while national communal activities sought to address the needs of Jewish survivors in Europe. Joint fundraising campaigns throughout this period integrated appeals so that narratives about the Holocaust would share space and priority with local discussions. Focusing on communal ephemera—fundraising materials in particular—allows us to see that while organizations were focused on Jewish survival overseas, they were also working to meet the changing needs of American Jewish communities at home. Within this institutional context, we can look at the record of campaign materials that reached nearly every Jewish home during this postwar period and see that American Jews took seriously their role in saving European Jews alongside their responsibility to confront local political and social conditions.

Survivor Voices in the Postwar World

Saving Our Survivors explores the narratives that drove American Jewish action and philanthropy at a moment when there was no collective understanding of the Holocaust and its meanings had not yet crystallized. As such, I refer to narratives and representations, leaving the term "testimony" to stand for survivor accounts intentionally and consciously constructed between a listener and an interviewee.[65] I recognize testimony as a distinct genre that emerged later in the history of Holocaust memory in America. As Henry Greenspan explains, "Eyewitness accounts were created and collected in the midst of the destruction and by the historical commissions that followed liberation. But the role of 'witness' or 'bearer of testimony' as generally understood is a more recent phenomenon."[66] Terminological distinction serves as a reminder of the many ways early communal narratives defied not only a set genre but also contemporary expectations of Holocaust witness accounts.

It is precisely because the narratives in the pages ahead differ from the kinds of Holocaust narratives that came later that I offer such close readings. In "Catastrophic Mourning," Marc Nichanian reflects on *Among the Ruins*, a 1911 book that documented the Armenian Genocide while it was ongoing. He asks: "Is it a testimony? A reportage? A chronicle? A call for justice? Is it a solicitation—for

Introduction 15

aid, for action?"[67] I hear the echo of his question here. There was an urgency to *Among the Ruins* that demanded attention; it did not matter whether the accounts are called "testimonies" or "solicitations." There is a similar urgency in these Holocaust narratives. They do not fit the definition of testimony because there was no discrete space to have these conversations. There were few intentional listeners and no "general affirmation of truth."[68] Nonetheless, they offer evidence of how American Jews learned about the Holocaust and point to the ways Americans continue to learn about ongoing global crises—through participation in and affiliation with communal organizations.

At the time, a range of terms was used to define the experiences of Jews under Nazism as well as their experiences in the wake of the war. Attention to the range of terms and the fluidity with which terms were interchanged points to the context in which these narratives were created. For example, the term "holocaust" was in circulation as early as 1945, when Rabbi James G. Heller, national chairman for the UPA, wrote in support of its 1945 campaign: "Disillusionment and despair threaten the Jews who have survived the Nazi holocaust . . . unless American Jews take heroic measures to assure a permanent and secure future for the vast majority of them in the Jewish National Home in Palestine."[69] Heller used the term to point to the experience of Jews under Nazism. And yet, Alan Mintz was right when he noted in 2001 that "the term Holocaust as we use it now had not been invented" in the 1940s and '50s.[70] No, the term did not yet signify the specific and well-documented annihilation of Jews under Nazism. As Hasia Diner writes, American Jews "had no single word to encapsulate the event, no single metaphor that stood for the phenomenon. Rather, they tried out words and images on their own as they made remembering the Holocaust a fundamental part of their public Jewish lives."[71]

Similarly, survivors used a range of terms to describe themselves, and American Jews used yet more terms to reference the community of Jewish survivors. Survivors living in DP camps gave themselves the name *She'erit Hapletah*, translated as "the surviving remains," "the remnant," or "the surviving remnant." From inside DP camps, this term defined a community of Jews who had survived Nazism in Europe.[72] Additional terms used at the time illuminate how American Jews understood the Holocaust and its survivors, recognizing Jewish survivors as DPs, refugees, and New Americans in universal stories about displacement and migration, as well as "liberated Jews," "the remnant," and "remaining Jews" in stories that more specifically addressed Jewish suffering. Terms like "survivors of Nazi terror" or "victims of Hitler's cruelties" expose early conceptions of Nazi crimes and speak to the suffering across Europe that sparked American aid after the war.

I use both the terms "Holocaust," with a capital H, and "survivor" throughout the book. This decision is meant to extend our understanding of the Holocaust in America, proposing a new starting point for conversations about Holocaust memory and collective understanding of survivor experiences. In this way, I draw from Gary Weissman's assertion that the term "Holocaust" "suggests not only the Jewish genocide but its Americanization, not only the event but the attempt to name or represent it."[73] These terms also reflect the fundamental premise of this work: that historians have missed the opportunity to ask what initial narratives looked and sounded like. We have failed to ask how the demands of the postwar world—including immediate relief and aid, international limits on immigration, the founding of a Jewish state, and the shuffling of global alliances that defined the initial years of the Cold War—shaped initial understanding of the Holocaust.

Saving Our Survivors takes up this challenge, centering organizational ephemera as a significant site of knowledge formation and dissemination about the Holocaust and its survivors. Through campaign materials, public speeches, appeal letters, brochures, posters, radio broadcasts, and short films, all of which reflect organizational strategy, American Jews were urged to act heroically, saving Jewish lives and ensuring a Jewish future.

Saving Our Survivors

The chapters that follow chart the multiplicity of images and voices that transmitted narratives to American audiences for communal engagement, fundraising, and political advocacy. They urge us to reconsider the idea that American Jews turned their backs on their brethren abroad and, instead, see how they—through the organizations they supported—faced the reality of Jewish destruction in Europe and wrote themselves into the story of Jewish survival after the war.

This narrative starts in late 1945 as Jewish communal organizations embarked on an unprecedented joint fundraising campaign. Chapter 1, "Heartstrings and Purse Strings," explores United Jewish Appeal (UJA) fundraising campaigns from 1946 through 1953 as well as fundraising efforts by Hadassah, Pioneer Women, HIAS, and other Jewish organizations. I ask how American Jews raised the funds that, as Yehuda Bauer has argued, "had [they] been found in 1936–1942 might have saved many, many lives."[74] As such, this chapter draws attention to the stakes of postwar fundraising, understood by American Jewish leaders and Jewish donors across the country as nothing less than essential to Jewish survival. A close reading of ephemeral campaign materials reveals

Introduction

narrative strategies that allowed disparate organizations to tie their fundraising priorities to the experiences of Jewish survivors. The result is a variety of survivor representations rendering survivors as American Pilgrims, Jewish pioneers, desperate victims, and hearty freedom fighters. Fundraising materials also circulated a set of symbols that continue to resonate today, including number tattoos forced on Jewish concentration camp prisoners. Fundraising brochures, posters, and films, in particular, used recognizable symbols to motivate American Jews.

Chapter 2, "Voicing Stories of Hope," considers how American Jews and their non-Jewish neighbors first heard survivor voices even as the majority of survivors remained in European DP camps. As "Delayed Pilgrims Dinner" and "An American with a Mission" suggest, radio was an important medium that allowed Americans to hear survivor narratives for the first time. This chapter examines the use of radio to narrativize the experiences of survivors while employing foundational American myths, including the Pilgrims and Founding Fathers, to advocate for changed immigration policy and to shift public opinion about refugees. The chapter examines "Displaced," a CCDP-sponsored radio drama about musician Kurt Maier, who survived Theresienstadt, Buchenwald, and Auschwitz, and "Case History #20,000," a scripted drama about a young survivor named Hannah that was sponsored by Hadassah. These two radio broadcasts illuminate communal effort to communicate narratives about survivors to a national audience. They also depict the process of giving testimony, foreshadowing the central mode of Holocaust memory that eventually gave survivors more agency over how their own stories are told and their voices preserved.

At the time, most Jewish survivors did not have a platform for sharing their own narratives with American audiences. Chapter 3, "Translating Postwar Europe," examines witnesses in postwar America who did—focusing on narratives about postwar Europe told by American interlocutors including Cecilia Razovsky, Rabbi Herbert Friedman, Leo Srole, David Boder, and others. Razovsky and Friedman—a social worker and a chaplain, respectively—serve as case studies of American witnesses not to the Holocaust but to the survivors and the aftermath of the war in Europe. These secondary witnesses translated stories about survivor suffering into American idioms, communicating the demands and needs of survivors to American audiences through the fundraising networks of Jewish communal organizations. Through these mediators, the immediacy of "being there" and "having seen" conveyed not the tragedy and loss of the Holocaust but the urgency and precariousness of the postwar period. At a time when survivor testimony had not yet found the potency it would later command, these secondary witnesses became essential mediators and advocates for surviving Jews in Europe.

Finally, chapter 4 explores a different role for Americans—that of volunteer. While only a small number of Americans participated directly in postwar humanitarian aid work in Europe, many engaged in efforts domestically to collect clothing and canned foods, knit layettes, and facilitate material aid. "Sending Hope, Securing Peace" examines the nationwide clothing drive campaign Supplies for Overseas Survivors (SOS), a JDC-sponsored effort that collected over twenty million pounds of clothing, canned foods, and medical items, as an example of how American Jews responded to the Holocaust and the urgent needs of Jewish survivors. In postwar America, renewed consumerism intersected with early Cold War rhetoric to send freedom abroad. Cleaning out closets was promoted as a form of patriotism that facilitated new purchases and contributed used goods to postwar humanitarian efforts. SOS invited American Jews to become "lifelines" for surviving Jews, reflecting a particularly Jewish approach to national postwar efforts that sent material goods abroad to war victims. Seen alongside the United National Clothing Collection, a federally supported clothing drive, SOS gave Jews a way to act both Jewish and American at the same time. The narratives generated through these efforts underscore how American Jews perceived themselves as heroes in the postwar period, reshaping American Jewish life and impacting the stories survivors continue to tell about their experiences under and after Nazism.

Each of the individuals featured in this work responded to the Holocaust in its immediate aftermath and worked within established networks and systems to address the unprecedented loss and tragedy. The exigency and uncertainty of the postwar period is an essential context for understanding American Jewish communal response to the Holocaust. As Gisela Wyzanski and Lola Kramarsky wrote to all members of the Advisory Council of the Hadassah National Youth Aliyah Committee on July 27, 1945, "In a world still trembling with the impact of evils let loose upon the world by our enemies and the enemies of mankind, let us resolve to snatch the children from the site and memory of their martyrdom, and to give them what they so desperately need—a home, love, and hope."[75] Philanthropy became a meaningful way for American Jews to respond to the shock of the Holocaust: Jews were in dire need around the world, and American Jews were empowered, encouraged, and determined to help.

By taking seriously the ephemera of American Jewish communal life in the immediate aftermath of World War II, this book depicts how the work of humanitarian aid contains within it the practice of narrativization that creates memory. In other words, early representations of survivors of Nazi persecution are inseparable from the work of American Jews to respond to the Holocaust—to raise funds, collect clothing and food, deliver medicine and toys to DP camps, and advocate for changed immigration policies. To better contend with the full breadth of Holocaust memory, we must reinsert these expressions into the archive that has crystallized so narrowly around survivor testimony. If we expand what we understand to be the archive of Holocaust narratives, we can better trace how knowledge about Holocaust survivors has been, and continues to be, crafted and circulated.

This approach reveals how the words, voices, and images of survivors and aid workers who spent time in postwar Europe mobilized American Jewry to act. As American Jews participated in efforts to save survivors, they also reimagined their own role in the changing borders of the postwar world and redefined what it meant to be Jewish in America in light of the Holocaust.

1

Heartstrings and Purse Strings

Fundraising and the Battle for Jewish Survival

IN OCTOBER 1936, A year after the Nuremberg Laws removed citizenship from German Jews and just months after the Berlin Olympics put Nazism on full display to the world, Mr. R. Cohen sent a letter to Koppel Pinson in response to his article "The Jewish Spirit in Nazi Germany," published in the *Menorah Journal.*[1] The letter stated, "So much of what is nowadays written about the Jews in Germany is intended to wring our hearts and touch our purse-strings—which is, I suppose, necessary."[2] Cohen's voice, preserved in Koppel Pinson's personal papers but not published in the journal, offers us a way back to 1936, before American Jews knew where the story of Nazi Germany would end, before millions of Jews across Europe were murdered. Through this letter, we get a peek into how American Jews received information about Nazi persecution of German Jews and understood the necessity of American Jewish fundraising. At the same time, Cohen reveals a cynicism held by at least some American Jews about the practice of employing emotionally evocative narratives to drive fundraising campaigns.

The focus of this chapter starts almost a decade later, in 1945, when American Jews were first grappling with news of the horrors only suggested in 1936. Cohen's letter reminds us that American Jews were already familiar with narratives from Nazi Germany and that these narratives were directly tied to fundraising. We can thus identify a certain continuity in the fundraising strategies of Jewish communal leaders who sought to wring the hearts and touch the purse strings of American Jews through stories of Jewish suffering and survival before and after the war. These are exactly the kinds of narratives this chapter explores, and I invite us all to understand this narrative construction not with Cohen's cynicism but with the urgency of 1945, when American Jews were called to respond to unprecedented loss and need around the world. Let us hold the tension of Cohen's letter as we consider how survivors of what we now call the Holocaust were represented in fundraising campaigns by Jewish communal organization across political, cultural, and religious spectrums. Yes, Jewish organizations crafted and disseminated narratives specifically meant to motivate financial giving, and yes, these narratives reflected real and urgent needs of Jews in Europe at the end of World War II.

Recognizing both truths allows us to take seriously the material record of Jewish communal fundraising efforts as a meaningful driver of Holocaust knowledge creation and dissemination and, at the same time, to acknowledge that Jewish communal engagement defined postwar American Jewish response to the Holocaust. This chapter tracks Jewish communal fundraising campaigns from 1946 through 1953 and brings to light ephemeral materials that introduced American Jews to representations of survivors, inspired meaningful connections between American Jews and their European brethren, and raised unprecedented amounts of money to define a Jewish future in the wake of the Holocaust. It considers public campaign materials—including brochures and pamphlets crafted according to annual themes, speeches, films, and slideshows—as well as internal marketing memos and campaign reports shared with volunteers and lay leaders.

An exploration of public-facing and internally focused materials reveals how organizations across the landscape of American Jewish communal life adapted narrative strategies that framed surviving European Jews according to organizational priorities. Each organization employed narratives about Holocaust survivors in the service of its particular work. As a result, American Jews received fundraising requests—through knocks at the door, in mailed letters, or at communal events—depicting a multiplicity of images of Jewish survivors in Europe.

This chapter is not an exhaustive study of Jewish communal organizational fundraising across America in the second half of the 1940s. I do not dive into all corners of communal activity or demographic differences of organizational donors. Rather, I focus on the United Jewish Appeal (UJA) and its constituent organizations, primarily the American Jewish Joint Distribution Committee (JDC), United Palestine Appeal (UPA) / United Israel Appeal (UIA), and the United Service for New Americans (USNA). UJA organized joint fundraising for these institutions, coordinating American Jewish philanthropy across political and communal interests. After its reconstitution in 1939, UJA drove fundraising for material relief in Europe through JDC, for development and settlement in Palestine through UPA (UIA after 1948), and for immigration and refugee aid in the United States through USNA.[3] These three fundraising priorities reflect communal efforts that connected American Jews with Jews around the world. Focusing on UJA offers an opportunity to assess how different objectives were represented alongside one other in fundraising campaigns sent to nearly every Jewish home in the late 1940s. The goal, then, is not a comprehensive catalog of every postwar fundraising campaign. Rather, this chapter explores fundraising campaigns from 1946 through 1953 that addressed a core set of Jewish concerns, tracing the way survivor representations were shaped and reshaped during this precarious early postwar period.

I start in 1945 before the end of World War II, when American Jewish communal leaders were strategizing their postwar response and articulating opposing priorities for postwar rehabilitation. For Jewish leaders, fundraising in the wake of the Holocaust was a life-and-death pursuit, and the stakes of annual campaigns remained high throughout the postwar period. As such, the chapter introduces joint fundraising in 1945, laying out the tense relationship between JDC and UPA as the primary organizations benefiting from UJA campaigns. This section describes the stakes of fundraising at this time as UJA raised ever greater sums, surpassing $100 million each year from 1946 through 1950. Considering UJA raised roughly $100 million over the full course of the war (1939–1945), the postwar figures are remarkable and speak to the seriousness with which American Jews took up the task of postwar fundraising as a meaningful response to the Holocaust.[4]

The chapter then offers a close reading of UJA campaign themes in 1946, 1947, and 1948 to consider how American Jews encountered Holocaust survivor narratives through the frames of survival, sacrifice, and destiny. These three themes defined more than just the titles of fundraising events; they informed which photographs were taken and disseminated, which films were produced, and how narratives about both Holocaust survivors and American Jews were crafted. Exploring the brochures, speeches, and films that made up campaigns uncovers the narratives that invited American Jews to participate in a communal response to the Holocaust.

In the final section of the chapter, I zoom out, returning to joint fundraising as a site of integrated Zionist and Diasporist concerns as well as immigration and domestic Jewish interests. We see how Jewish survivors in Europe were imagined as victims of Nazism, pioneers in Palestine, and New Americans all at once. In each capacity, survivors of the Holocaust were at the center of post-war Jewish philanthropic activity and recipients of urgent American Jewish aid. As the conclusion pushes forward into the 1950s, we see how the images of survivors became essential markers for American Jewish philanthropy into the 1950s.

This chapter explores how American Jews encountered the stories that wrung their hearts and touched their purse strings. How did the changing needs of survivors, shifting boundaries of the postwar world, and organizational priorities of Jewish groups shape survivor representation? What kinds of images, terms, and narratives about survivors resonated for American Jewish donors at the time?

In answering these questions, R. Cohen is a starting point to assess how American Jews understood themselves in the story of postwar Jewish life. A close reading of fundraising materials offers a challenge to scholars who have criticized the malleability of the Holocaust and its role in American Jewish fundraising as signs of the impoverished spirituality of American Jews. Consider the anecdote Hilene Flanzbaum wrote in the 1999 *The Americanization of the Holocaust*: "It became a crass joke in the American Jewish community in the 1960s that when a synagogue or a congregation needed money, all the rabbi had to do to get a bundle was to mention the Holocaust."[5] Flanzbaum's critique came at a moment when "the Holocaust has become an artifact of American culture."[6] By 1999, Holocaust survivors had resettled (in the US, Israel, and elsewhere), and the Holocaust had become a recognized historical event perpetrated against Jews. For the Jewish leaders and American Jewish donors reflected in this study, conditions were different. In the immediate postwar period, no cohesive narrative about the Holocaust had found purchase in American life. The needs of Jews in Europe were urgent, and the success of postwar aid depended on American Jewish fundraising. The narratives reflected in this chapter—which relied on images and descriptions of Holocaust survivors in order to "get a bundle"—were essential for meeting the unprecedented demands of the postwar Jewish world.

Following the decimation of European Jewry, American Jewry was the largest and wealthiest Jewish community in the world. American Jews took seriously the work of raising funds in service of Jewish survival, defining a new role for the American Jewish community as savior of Jewish life, a Jewish future, and in some instances, Judaism itself. As the chapter reveals, ephemeral materials of Jewish communal fundraising document not only early representations of Holocaust survivors but also a collective anxiety about Jewish survival that prompted competing visions for American Jewish aid abroad.

The Stakes of Joint Fundraising: Defining a Jewish Future after the Holocaust

In March 1945, two months before the end of World War II in Europe, Rabbi Jonah Wise, national chairman of JDC, published a letter in the monthly membership journal, *JDC Digest*, writing, "German hate has decimated Europe's Jews, but today from the ruins of devastated towns and villages, wan skeleton-like wraiths are emerging. Weakened by their privations and destitute of all possessions, they stand helpless. They need food, clothing, medicines."[7] Wise championed American Jews as the only solution to the problem: "We American Jews—the only large body of Jews who have not suffered physically the source of German bestiality—we are the one hope of these destitute unfortunates." One month earlier, in February 1945, Rabbi James G. Heller, national chairman for UPA, had written in support of the organization's separate 1945 fundraising campaign in the UPA monthly journal, *UPA Reports*: "Disillusionment and despair threaten the Jews who have survived the Nazi holocaust." As quoted in the Introduction, he argued that, " unless American Jews take heroic measures to assure a permanent and secure future for the vast majority of them in the Jewish National Home in Palestine."[8]

These two letters reached Jewish homes across America at the tail end of World War II, articulating two competing visions for American Jewish response to the Holocaust. Since 1939, these organizations had joined efforts to fundraise under the umbrella of UJA.[9] But in 1945, the united effort failed as leaders of JDC and UPA could not agree on how to split funds raised in a joint campaign. JDC, founded in 1914 as the first organized Jewish effort to provide funds for international relief, focused on aiding surviving Jews in Europe with immediate, short-term needs like medicine and clothing, while UPA, founded in 1925 to fundraise for a Jewish homeland, articulated the need for long-term immigration solutions and a permanent, secure future in Palestine.

Of course, Jewish survivors in Europe needed both immediate attention and long-term emigration pathways. But in 1945, the plan for a broad, communal response was not yet clear, and Jewish organizations like JDC and UPA communicated opposing response plans, defining each as most urgent. It was precisely this urgency that fueled Wise and Heller as they battled for the attention and funds of American Jews. By May 1945, following Victory in Europe Day, JDC and UPA had reconciled and agreed to a goal of $80 million, of which they raised approximately $45 million.[10] Of that, 57 percent was to be distributed to JDC and 43 percent to UPA.[11] From 1946 forward, UJA sustained an annual campaign for funds with increasing goals that allowed individual Jews to anticipate one annual campaign and give without apportioning loyalties or priorities.

How is it possible that as the doors to Europe finally reopened, as news and images from liberated concentration camps made their way to the United States, American Jewish leaders failed to define a cohesive vision for American aid and collect the necessary funds? Some scholars have argued that American Jewish communal leaders, including Wise and Heller, failed, that they deserted European Jews.[12] However, we might consider that at the heart of this dispute was not a turn away from collective relief but tension over how best to respond to the very real needs of Jewish survivors. For the leaders of JDC and UPA, the stakes of UJA allotment were nothing less than the survival of Jewish life. Rather than a failure of American Jewish response, the dissolution of UJA in 1945 reflects a moment of internal discord driven by opposing commitments to aid Jews around the world. American Jews were debating, publicly and within their communal institutions, how best to respond to the tragedy of the Holocaust and battling over competing possible futures for Jewish lives.

From 1945 through 1948, even after the reconstitution of UJA, JDC and UPA did not mediate these ideological differences. The tension that undermined the 1945 campaign persisted through this precarious period as American Jews, European survivors, and Jewish communities around the world sought to define a Jewish future. While JDC's efforts eventually (after 1948) aided immigration to Palestine, its work also supported revitalization efforts for Jewish communities in Europe. It set up microloan programs in Czechoslovakia, Hungary, and Poland and worked with surviving Jews to define a Jewish future without emigration. At the same time, UPA and Rabbi Heller maintained that Palestine was the "only real chance for the survival of the Jews in Europe."[13] Even as the two groups jointly sought funds from American Jews, their differing visions for a Jewish future remained. As seen later in this chapter, these ideological differences had narrative and representational consequences, and images of survivors were adapted to reflect organizational initiatives.

But, for communities across the country, united appeals eased fundraising efforts. As Yehuda Bauer has argued, "Jews in the organized communities did not want to have dozens of agencies knocking at their doors."[14] National leaders also recognized the importance of a combined appeal. Henry Montor, executive vice-chairman of UJA from 1946 to 1950, "understood the potential rewards in dollars for Israel" if Zionist efforts were aligned with non-Zionist appeals.[15] Montor recognized that Jews across the country were more likely to give to a combined appeal than to a specifically Zionist one. The ability to promote local interests alongside national and international ambitions pushed Jewish communal leaders to support joint fundraising throughout the postwar period. This arrangement ensured that the organized Jewish community met

26 SAVING OUR SURVIVORS

the immediate needs of Jews in Europe and Jewish life at home while anticipating the future of a Jewish state.

The split between JDC and UPA in 1945 marks a moment of disjuncture between wartime and postwar philanthropic engagement and points to the way campaigns throughout the postwar period continued to grapple with tension between supporting short-term needs in Europe and long-term needs in Israel. Subsequent UJA campaigns applied stories and images about Jewish Holocaust survivors to illuminate different organizational choices, inviting American Jews with different philanthropic priorities to jointly participate in the work of securing a Jewish future. The precarity of these years meant that stakes were high, and fundraising campaigns—not only of UJA but also of Hadassah, Vaad Hatzala, the National Council of Jewish Women, and many other organizations—translated the life-and-death circumstances of the postwar years for American Jews across the country.

Following the truncated 1945 campaign, the joint fundraising efforts of UJA succeeded: American Jews responded to stories of Jewish suffering in Europe and around the world with unprecedented generosity.[16] When UJA declared an audacious goal of raising $100 million for the 1946 Year of Survival campaign, there was little reason to believe it would succeed. Montor is quoted as calling the 1946 goal "ridiculous."[17] Consider that the Red Cross, a nationally supported organization with a membership of more than eighteen million in the 1940s, also set a goal of raising $100 million in 1946.[18] In fact, UJA exceeded its 1946 goal, raising nearly $103 million.[19] In 1947, UJA surpassed its goal again, raising over $150 million, and totals remained above $100 million through the next five years (hitting over $200 million in 1948 after the founding of Israel).[20]

At the time, Jewish fundraising ran counter to the deflation of humanitarian philanthropy across America, and the success of Jewish appeals in the postwar period was recognized as a "bright spot" in the field of postwar philanthropy.[21] In 1960, historian Robert Bremner acknowledged that American Jews, "numbering less than five million," had raised a stunning amount of money that facilitated "European Jews out of Displaced Persons Camps, assisted Jewish emigration and resettlement, and helped the new state of Israel in its fight for life."[22]

What motivated such unprecedented giving? In *Out of the Ashes*, a study of JDC philanthropy during and after the war, Yehuda Bauer lists several reasons for the postwar success of American Jewish fundraising: better, "more accurate, and frightening" information, developed fundraising techniques, and "the general war atmosphere in which people were expected to make sacrifices."[23] Yet he lands on guilt as the primary factor driving the increase in Jewish philanthropy after the war, arguing that Jews gave in greater amounts after realizing they should have done more during the war.[24] We cannot discount guilt as a motivating factor in the increased and sustained giving that followed the end of the war. But certainly, we must also consider the work of Jewish organizations in creating channels for meaningful, annual, sustained giving Let us now look closely at campaign materials to understand how narratives about the Holocaust were translated for American donors.

Defining Survivors, Defining Saviors: Fundraising in the Wake of the Holocaust (1946)

Jewish survival, long a theme in communal work of American Jews, took on new relevance in the aftermath of the war.[25] The 1946 UJA Year of Survival campaign generated speeches, brochures, chapter events, films, and other materials—all of which articulated the responsibility of American Jews to save the lives of the remaining European Jews through fundraising. This narrative strategy invited American Jews to join the battle for Jewish survival explicitly by donating funds. The campaign speaker's bureau manual instructed volunteers to say: "Any failure on our part to provide the help needed will condemn the survivors to the fate of the 6,000,000 who perished in the death camps and gas chambers."[26]

In this way, American Jewish communal organizations defined American Jewry as central to the story of Jewish survival. Without the humanitarian intervention of American Jews, European Jews would again face certain death. To aid volunteers in drawing connections between American Jewish fundraising and Jewish survival, the campaign manual scripted the following key phrases: "The remnants have been saved from extermination. They have not yet been saved from hunger, disease, homelessness and suffering. . . . The $100,000,000 UJA Campaign is our strongest weapon in the battle for survival."

This script called attention to the liminality of the postwar moment, when the life-and-death immediacy of wartime persisted. Although Jews had been liberated from concentration camps, the years between liberation and resettlement were defined by upheaval, displacement, and uncertainty for most survivors. The fear and violence of the war continued in some parts of Europe, and Jews across the continent struggled to secure housing, food, and clothing. As American Jews took up the challenge of alleviating these postliberation problems, they constructed narratives that highlighted Jewish postwar anxieties more than wartime tragedies and defined a central role for American Jews as postwar leaders of world Jewry.

Toward this end, UJA leaders communicated the need for unprecedented levels of giving, asking Jews and non-Jews across the country to give onetime gifts through local and national campaigns. They activated networks created during the war by setting regional quotas that doubled or tripled previous goals and established a "Big Gifts" level for contributions over $10,000 in February 1946. The Big Gifts effort was an immediate success, and a kickoff meeting for Big Gifts donors was declared "the greatest outpouring of generosity ever witnessed in the history of American Jewry, or perhaps America."[27] Individual gift increases were publicly celebrated, as one man who had given $2,500 in 1945 gave $10,000 in 1946, and one man "from Philadelphia who gave $1,500 in 1945 gave $15,000 at the Washington meeting." Public commitments came to define UJA appeals, and throughout the postwar period, social pressure inspired continued and increased giving.[28] As Lila Corwin Berman has shown, US tax law also facilitated increased giving as organizations like UJA helped American Jews understand that "a larger gift could carry tax benefits that outweighed the difference between it and a smaller gift."[29]

Despite these successes, the 1946 campaign reveals a certain naivete on the part of UJA leaders, who believed that the crisis facing displaced persons (DPs) in Europe could be solved in one year. By October 1946, only eight months after the first optimistic Big Gifts meeting, Edward M. M. Warburg, chairman of JDC, announced that JDC would have to ask people to continue giving at onetime gift amounts into 1947. Warburg said, "American Jewry might well ponder the feeling of the Jews in DP camps whom we had anticipated releasing this year and who now find, instead, that they will be sitting there two years after 'liberation.' The promises made to them have not been fulfilled."[30] In this speech, Warburg articulated the failure of liberation to grant Jewish survivors access to new lives and, in so doing, reaffirmed the urgency of a strong—and sustained—American Jewish philanthropic response.

While communal leaders like Warburg focused their efforts on securing big gifts through in-person solicitation, UJA relied on printed campaign materials sent to constituents and mass media technologies, such as radio and film, to spread the word for smaller donations. These materials communicated a coordinated campaign strategy, articulating the organizational vision for Jewish survival after the Holocaust and identifying American Jewish financial support as essential for executing that vision. Film technology, in particular, allowed Jewish organizations to narrate compelling stories and highlight the pressing needs of postwar Europe alongside the success of communal projects. Jewish leaders from a range of organizations employed film technology for publicity, sponsoring one or two short films per year to reach a Jewish and a wider non-Jewish audience. For example, the Organization for Rehabilitation through Training (ORT), an organization dedicated to vocational training and education, sponsored a short documentary described as follows: "In about 15 minutes we want to contrast the demoralizing idleness and lack of purpose among vast numbers of adult Jews in Europe . . . with the constructive forward-looking work of schools, workshops, and farming projects of ORT."[31] By creating documentaries, organizations could tell their story, highlight the success of their work in Europe, and challenge stereotypes of Jewish survivors for American audiences. ORT's theme of looking ahead echoes other campaigns at the time, as seen in the next pages.

Only a few organizations, namely UJA, JDC, UPA (later UIA), and Hadassah, had the resources and vision to use the new medium extensively.[32] Mostly, these organizations produced short documentary films (usually fifteen to thirty minutes) distributed from national offices to local chapters or rented out with film projectors or other necessary hardware, generally at a rate of one dollar per film.[33] While the film technology was new, the infrastructure for circulating films was adapted from previous strategies for sharing organizational messaging; filmstrips with coordinating scripts and skits to be performed at membership meetings were circulated through the same networks. National communications and membership offices created tool kits, circulars, program guides, and more to send to regional chapters across the country.

Organizational leaders believed that these kinds of films could help raise funds with relative ease, but the films were also created for the purposes of spreading knowledge about the plight of survivors through the frame of American intervention.[34] The JDC Community Services Department, for example, marketed its 1946 film *Report on the Living* as a way to "broaden American Jewry's understanding of the hopes, plans, and dreams of the 1,400,000 Jewish men, women, and children in Europe."[35] At chapter meetings and local events, films depicted a cohesive and consistent narrative about not only survivors in Europe but also ways American Jews could help.

Some films had a wider distribution, spreading stories of survivors around the world. Among these was the Hadassah film *They May Live Again*, which depicted "harrowing experiences of Jewish refugee children in Europe."[36] The film was shown at the Lugano Film Festival in July 1947 and met with "great success," expanding its audience internationally.[37] The HIAS-produced short film *Placing the Displaced*, which featured the story of DPs arriving in America, premiered on CBS Television on June 14, 1948, and narrated the success of

Jewish survivors who had assimilated into American life for a large American audience.[38] Outside the Jewish communal world, short documentaries similarly disseminated stories about postwar Europe and worked to inspire philanthropic giving. *Seeds of Destiny*, produced by UNRRA, won an Academy Award for Best Documentary Short in 1947 and is said to have raised over $200 million dollars for war relief.[39]

These three films point to the diversity of postwar films about DPs and the refugee crisis of postwar Europe. Each film represented survivors of Nazi atrocity through a story that celebrated its organization's postwar priorities. Hadassah highlighted the journey of child survivors brought to Palestine, HIAS depicted the ability of survivors to adjust to an American way of life, and UNRRA warned of postwar dangers by asking, "What seeds of destiny will sprout from within these ravaged ranks . . . new Führers or new lovers of liberty?"[40] Through narrative films, each organization communicated its own vision of a safe and secure future to a broad audience. Hadassah asserted that child survivors could live again in Palestine just as HIAS proclaimed America to be the land of possibility for Jewish survivors. UNRRA's film championed the potential of American aid to determine the future of Europe and the world.

I want to examine one specific film from the period to illuminate how Jewish organizations crafted and disseminated blended stories of survivors and organizational intervention. UJA produced the film *Battle for Survival* to document its historic 1946 campaign and convey the potential of American Jewish organizations to alleviate the suffering of Jews in Europe. The film is narrated by Orson Welles and juxtaposes footage from the December 1945 Atlantic City conference announcing the $100 million UJA campaign with shots of ragged Jewish DPs of Europe. The film, distributed across the country and internationally through UJA-affiliated Jewish organizations, offers a way to consider visual and narrative representations of survivors crafted by UJA according to the 1946 theme of survival. *Battle for Survival* also illustrates annual campaign mechanisms, documenting meetings and events that defined and communicated the needs of survivors to American Jews.

Battle for Survival opens with a shot of feet, barefoot or wrapped in rags and walking on a dusty road. Welles's dramatic, deep, and recognizable voice narrates, "Once, long ago, these feet were shod. Once, long ago, they turned homeward every evening." As the camera pans out, the viewer sees people wrapped in rags walking slowly down the road. Welles continues, "These are remnants of a people, let them represent the 1.5 million European Jews incredibly alive, hardly a fraction more alive than when their six million brothers were starved and burned to death."[41] This introduction depicts survivors on the brink of death and suggests that the answer to the devastation is American Jewish aid: "For these, there is but one hope, the United Jewish Appeal." The opening also reveals how, already in 1945, the number of six million had found a central place in talking about and understanding the Holocaust as a Jewish story.

The film jumps from Europe to the UJA campaign kickoff meeting in Atlantic City, and images of ragged survivors are replaced by shots of well-groomed American men—the leaders of UJA and members of the military and political establishments. Among the parade of men is William Rosenwald, cofounder of UJA and one of its three national chairmen between 1942 and 1946; Edward Warburg, cochairman of JDC from 1939 to 1965; Joseph Schwartz, JDC European director; Earl Harrison, author of the Harrison Report, which documented the treatment of Jews in European DP camps; and Col. Judah Nadich, Eisenhower's adviser on DPs.[42]

Joseph Rosensaft, a survivor of Auschwitz and Bergen-Belsen and elected leader of the Central Committee of Liberated Jews, is seated alongside the community leaders and national representatives.[43] In the film, Rosensaft is described as a "frail flame of a man," and the film's audience is asked to consider the weight of his speech by imagining his experience of having had "all loved ones murdered in battles of Polish ghettos, then the ingenious tortures of six concentration camps."[44] Yet the image belies the description of Rosensaft as frail. He appears alongside the other men, standing tall and equally well dressed. The visual representation of Rosensaft better supports the assertion that the losses of the war years "have not defeated him."

What should we make of such narrative inconsistencies? The 1946 UJA campaign represents survivors as frail and skeleton-like, yet Rosensaft is as polished and powerful as any of the other speakers. In these fundraising campaigns, survivors could be—and in some ways, were required to be—both. They were simultaneously in need of urgent aid and capable of becoming American citizens. The film also depicts Jews more clearly as victims of Nazi crimes, showing skeletal survivors still dressed in striped camp uniforms and languishing behind barbed wire fences. We see in Rosensaft how multiple representations of survivors coexisted. He was, at once, a victim of Nazism, a recipient of American aid, and a polished future citizen.

In 1946, as *Battle for Survival* was shared across the country in support of UJA, these initial stories and images of Holocaust survivors informed how American Jews began to make sense of a Holocaust experience. Significantly, these narrative elements remain central to cultural understandings of the Holocaust today. We recognize the six million killed in ghettos and concentration camps, those who were starved through Nazi policy, and those whose bodies were burned in crematoria. (Of course, we also recognize survivors as well-dressed and well-spoken Americans from thousands of survivor testimonies.) In 1946, these images were intertwined with demand for Jewish intervention. American Jews were not given these narrative elements as a memorial practice; they were asked to be part of the story—to secure survival.

In *Battle for Survival*, the role of American Jews as heroes is both affirmed and complicated. Toward the middle of the film, Welles's voice commands, "We are survivors too . . . of Buchenwald, of Bergen-Belsen, of Nordhausen, Dachau, but for some accident of birth or lucky migration, we might have a role in this wretchedness." Who are "we" here—the survivors depicted in the film? The American Jewish audience? What is the role "we" play? Is the film addressing American Jews who might also have been victims in Nazi Europe? Or is it speaking to Americans of European descent who might have been perpetrators in "this wretchedness"? Perhaps the film seeks to recognize the essential humanity and innocence of the victims, urging all audiences, both Jewish and non-Jewish, to identify with them. Certainly, the film is meant to build empathy, to recognize survivors not as others but as brethren.

Yet *Battle for Survival* does not end on a note of unity, compassion, or empathy. Rather, Welles narrates an idea that has echoed continually in relation to engaging with the memory and the history of the Holocaust, stating, "You from your safe vantage may never comprehend."[45] We can hear the echoes of Primo Levi's "If This Is a Man," which starts: "You who live safe / In your warm houses, / You who find, returning in the evening / Hot food and friendly faces."[46] Levi asks the reader to see the victims of Nazism, to "carve them on your hearts," even as he defines a chasm between the world of hot food and that of a fight for a "crust of bread." Levi's poem was first published in his memoir, *Survival in Auschwitz*, in 1947 (as "If This Is a Man") and not translated into English until 1958, yet the resemblance with *Battle for Survival* is clear.

Battle for Survival also references the distance between those who experienced the Holocaust and those who did not in 1946. Like Levi, the film suggests that those who only hear about, read about, or see representations of the Holocaust "may never comprehend." We heard the same idea from Elie Wiesel throughout his career—that the world of the Holocaust cannot be understood. It is well articulated in his 1985 essay "Why I Write: Making No Become a Yes," published in the *New York Times*: "If I write, it is to warn the reader that he will not understand either. 'You will not understand, you will never understand. . . .' All I know is that Treblinka and Auschwitz cannot be told."[47] This gap between the world of the concentration camp, of the Holocaust, and of an audience that cannot fathom it was articulated in 1946. Did American Jews recognize, at that time, this gap between the world of the Holocaust and the world outside? Were they concerned, like literary scholar Lawrence Langer, about having "the courage to stare into the abyss" of that gap?[48] Or would this awareness only come later?

For UJA and American Jewish audiences in 1946, the film's abyss was not metaphorical; they sought to inspire donations to meet the needs of Jewish survivors. To do so, the film built empathy by tugging at heartstrings, as R. Cohen, quoted in the opening of this chapter, reminds us. For Jewish communal leaders—and for the surviving Jews in Europe—the stakes were tremendous. Welles narrates, "Once Hitler had the decision of life or death. Now, that decision is ours."[49] In this way, *Battle for Survival* presents its titular battle; DPs had survived liberation but continued to struggle, and only American donations and generosity could save them. The urgency around fundraising that builds through the film reaches a crescendo in the final appeal, made at the Atlantic City meeting by the only female speaker. Adele Levy, chairman of the UJA National Women's Council, shames the assembled leaders—and in turn, the film audience—for not having sacrificed enough for the cause of Jewish survivors. She passionately delivers the core of her speech to big applause: "Unless you care enough, and unless I care enough, we cannot succeed in this great undertaking. . . . Not one of us, including myself, has ever made one real sacrifice for this cause. Some of us have felt very good. Some of us have felt that we have given generously. . . . Has one of us sacrificed something that we really wanted in a material sense? For these are suffering, bleeding, starving, persecuted people. And I think the answer is no."[50] Following this call to action, Welles asks, "Can we spare it?" With its ending, the film explicitly appeals for American Jewish donations by demanding a "real sacrifice," a theme picked up in the 1947 UJA campaign: the Year of Sacrifice.

Jews around the world heard this call.[51] *Battle for Survival* aired in Canada with a new ending. Samuel Bronfman, leader of the United Jewish Relief Agencies of Canada, made a direct appeal to the Jews of Canada in an addendum to the film. He sat stiffly behind a desk, looked straight at the camera, and read "We were spared the horrors of war, and the pictures we have seen must rend the heart of every thinking and feeling Jew in this country. They bring within our vision the plight of our wandering people, still wandering the face of Europe, still homeless. Those impoverished children's bodies little more than living skeletons . . . cry out to us for help. Seeing is understanding, understanding is feeling. And to feel is to open our hearts and purses."[52] For Bronfman, the power of film was in its ability to disseminate images of children and other survivors, to evoke emotional responses and financial giving from its viewing audience. He overtly connected the representation of surviving Jews as "living skeletons" with the opening of hearts and purses.

Other organizations similarly relied on the moving images of survivors to motivate giving, using other technologies, such as slides and filmstrips, to evoke an emotional response from audiences. The Hadassah slideshow "Look at Their Faces" was distributed to local chapters with an accompanying script to generate a "moving and powerful fundraising push."[53] As images of young child survivors were projected at local meetings, chapter leaders were instructed to say, "You have heard what children endured in Europe.... You have hoped and laughed with them in Palestine. Before you go, I want you to LOOK AT THEIR FACES." Such an appeal was rooted in the power of children's faces to inspire empathy and generosity.[54]

Similarly, a slideshow at the December 1945 fundraising dinner for Vaad Hatzala used photographs of survivors to encourage giving. The accompanying script explicitly details the tortures of Buchenwald, narrating, "The gates of Hell close on the living.... These to the gas chambers, these to slave labor and shame ... these to be made into fat and blood ... these to dig their own grave."[55] The climax of this performance echoes Adele Levy's call to UJA leaders as the narrator asks, "In God's sight, can we say we have done all we could? Vaad Hatzalah speaks to the purity of your hearts! ... Jews of America ... for mercy and help and love, to save, to keep alive, and bring hope, and warmth and light."[56] In other words, have we sacrificed enough?

Sustained Urgency: Sacrifice, Destiny, and the Future (1947, 1948)

The 1947 UJA campaign picked up this exact question, turning the lens of the campaign from the suffering of European Jewry to the work of American Jews. As a 1947 Year of Sacrifice campaign booklet declares, "The years between 1933 and 1946 were years which witnessed the Jews overseas making sacrifice after sacrifice—they lost their homes, their hopes, their lives. Now 1947 has come— *our* year for sacrifice."[57] UJA national chairman Henry Morgenthau Jr. echoed the need for sacrifice and more explicitly expressed the identification American Jews should have with their European brethren, writing, "You and I—we cannot rest, we cannot enjoy the good things of life as long as we know that our brethren are wandering across the face of Europe, homeless and without permanent roots."[58] The assertion of American Jews as the "only hope of survival" continued to resonate in 1947, even as postwar reality in Europe began to shift.

The needs of Jewish survivors were no longer for immediate medical aid and shelter but long-term resettlement and moral support to withstand continued displacement. A 1947 UJA campaign brochure articulates this shift for American donors:

The Jewish crisis has not only grown in its proportions, but changed in its nature since December 1945. The Jewish survivors were considered the victims of war and the remnants of savage Nazi persecution which brought about the death of six million of their kin. Today these Jewish survivors are the greatest sufferers from a universal crisis which has had its most serious impact on Europe. Whatever hopes were had last year that the non-Jewish world would participate substantially in the work of relief, rehabilitation, and resettlement are not being realized, at least in the measure required by the urgency and tragedy of the Jewish position. In 1947, as in 1946, the support—financial and moral—which the Jews of Europe need must come from American Jews as their last and almost only hope of survival.[59]

The changing realities of the postwar world, including anti-Jewish violence in Poland, political upheaval in Poland, Czechoslovakia, and Hungary, and weather patterns that produced low crop yields in Europe, increased the number of stateless Jews in American-run DP camps and increased pressure around emigration.[60] In the wake of these changes, Jewish survivors (and Jewish organizations like JDC) largely abandoned hopes of rehabilitating Jewish life in Poland and Czechoslovakia. As a result, the financial demands for supporting DP camps increased. The hopes of 1946 to quickly bring about resolution to Jewish displacement were dashed, and UJA urged American Jewish sacrifice for increased and continued giving.

This call for sacrifice resulted in pledges of over $125 million to UJA, although it did not quite manage to meet its stated $170 million goal.[61] Renewed intensity for fundraising gained momentum as the Jewish world shifted following the November 29, 1947, United Nations (UN) vote to partition Palestine. The real possibility of a Jewish state and the end of the British mandate resonated with American Jews and American Jewish leaders, particularly those who had long been fighting for the Zionist cause.

By 1948, narratives of sacrifice gave way to narratives of destiny as the possibility of a Jewish state became a reality. The UJA campaign was designated the Year of Destiny, and the idea reverberated in all campaign materials: UJA's 1948 film *Dollars for Destiny* explicitly demanded cash from American donors to realize the State of Israel; an oversized booklet, *Maps of Destiny*, set maps of the new Jewish state alongside appeal language; and speeches of UJA leaders from throughout the year referred to the destiny of the Jewish people, connecting the fates of American Jews with those of survivors and Jews around the world.[62] These appeals continued to promote American Jewry as the only answer to challenges facing world Jewry in the postwar period, including the historic challenge of Jewish statehood: only if American Jews gave beyond their capacity could a Jewish state be realized. In this way, the focus on sacrifice continued.

UJA set an audacious goal of $250 million to support the creation of the new state, the military necessities to defend it, and the stream of emigration out of Europe. Could American audiences once more give at onetime levels? Would American Jews sacrifice even more?

Fundraising efforts across the country (and around the world) were reenergized by the possibility for the creation of a Jewish state. Although UJA failed to raise $250 million, total estimates range from $150 million to $200 million, an incredible amount considering American Jews (and non-Jewish partners) had already raised over $100 million each of the two previous years.[63] To bolster Jewish efforts in Palestine, UJA shifted the allotment agreement so that UPA received the majority of UJA funds for the first time.[64] The shift in priorities was permanent; UPA received between 60 percent and 70 percent of totals raised from 1949 to 1955.[65]

The spirit of the 1948 campaign cannot be understated. The Jewish press reported that the 1948 campaign reflected gifts from more than one million individual donors, including community leaders who took out loans to respond to the desperate calls for cash.[66] Survivors from Nazi Europe remained central to the communications strategy of Jewish communal organizations even as the attention of Jews around the world turned toward Israel. The Jewish state was often portrayed as the happy ending survivors required and deserved.

This narrative was particularly resonant for JDC, which continued to manage Jewish aid in DP camps and across Europe throughout this period. The 1948 JDC film *The Future Can Be Theirs* exemplifies the way survivors were represented in the new Jewish landscape and how the story of Jewish tragedy was transformed into one of rebirth.[67] Like *Battle for Survival*, *The Future Can Be Theirs* is twenty minutes long and jumps between scenes in America and in Europe, weaving together stories of survivors with the story of American aid. It begins at a meeting of JDC leaders Edward M. M. Warburg, Herbert H. Lehman, Harold Linder, and Moses A. Leavitt, who discuss the success of past JDC work and the efforts still underway to rehabilitate Jews in Europe.[68] These leaders narrate the rest of the film as scenes cut to DP camp footage where JDC aid is seen in action.

Considering the previous two years of extraordinary giving and the dramatic shift in Jewish philanthropic attention to Israel, the film seems to address donor fatigue for European aid, depicting both ongoing need in DP camps and on-the-ground success. The film features JDC workers striving "to heal, to council, and to save fellow Jews" and trucks loaded with packaged food, described as "a huge defensive against hunger." The past generosity of American Jewish donors is quantified as JDC leaders narrate, "In three years, JDC has put 165 million pounds of supplies into Europe. Enough to put food on the plates of three-quarters of a million people."[69] These figures account for the successes of JDC and justify its continued importance; as the narrator declares, survivors were "still alive *because* the JDC was there."

That American Jews were solely responsible for the future of Jewish life and the survival of Europe's remaining Jews is clearly communicated in the film's final scene. The film ends inside a DP camp as the camera sweeps across a large, crowded Passover Seder. The room is filled with hundreds of people at long tables, and the narrator employs the story of Passover to describe the journey of Europe's surviving Jews during and after the war: "We have helped bring them out of bondage. We have helped deliver them from death. We have promised them a future. Now we must help them still so that the future can be theirs."[70] In this way, the film casts American Jewry as Moses, the ultimate savior, who can bring fellow Jews out of bondage and into the Promised Land.

Hasia Diner cites the 1948 Seder Ritual of Remembrance as an example of the Holocaust in early postwar American Jewish culture, including a Haggadah that declared Hitler "a tyrant more wicked than the Pharoah who enslaved our fathers in Egypt."[71] But how did the story of Passover resonate for survivors of the Holocaust in 1948, with the promise of a life in Israel, when they had been denied the right to sit together, to recite the story, to recline for so many years? *The Future Can Be Theirs* does not explore the meaning of the event for the Jews gathered in that large, communal room. Rather, the film employs the central Jewish story of freedom to frame the experiences of Jewish survivors. For JDC, the story of Passover offered an opportunity to again cast American Jews as heroes responsible for saving Jewish lives in Europe and preserving the continuity of Jewish life as it had existed since the exodus from Egypt.

Unlike past fundraising efforts, *The Future Can Be Theirs* portrays vibrant life in DP camps. Extended footage of a soccer game and children running on a beach by the ocean evoke life, vitality, and health, depicting the rebirth of Jews in Europe. Nowhere is this transformation better visualized than in an image of a young girl sewing. The girl is first seen from far away, sitting at a sewing machine, surrounded by other women at sewing machines. As the camera zooms in, viewers see a tattoo on her arm. The voice-over reports that this young woman is "working towards the future while blotting out the past."[72] The visible tattoo represents her past, and the sewing workshop (sponsored by JDC) ensures she will have a productive future.

Already in 1948, number tattoos served as symbols of the Holocaust, becoming a repeated visual motif in brochures, journals, newsletters, magazines, and newsreels. The tattoos recalled the inhumanity of the concentration camps and visually evoked Nazi crimes against the Jews. *The Future Can Be Theirs* does not need to describe the crimes against this young girl or the suffering she has lived through in detail. In the context of the film, the tattoo serves as signifier for a larger story of victimhood and depravity. It allows the past, present, and future to coexist in one frame that conveys the tragedy of the war, the revitalization of the DP period, and the future in a Jewish state. Thus, even as the young woman works to "blot out the past," she evokes both the horrors of the Holocaust and the promise of the future.

The connected stories of past and future found expression throughout the Year of Destiny campaign—a theme palpable in campaign materials for non-UJA organizations as well. As part of a proposed 1948 Pioneer Women's Passover event, From the Old to the New, Labor Zionist women across the country performed a skit shared in a chapter program calendar titled "From the Warsaw Ghetto to the Gates of Hope."[73] The script calls for two chapter members to perform as friends at their settlement in Israel, musing about Passovers missed during the war. One friend asks, "Dear friend, dear sister, do you recall what we were doing a year ago at this time?" The second friend responds, "No, don't glance backwards to our greatest despair. Must we always remind ourselves of how we slept in the woods and ran at the sounds of a human footfall?"[74] After recalling Passovers with their families many years ago, they count themselves lucky to have fulfilled the promise of Passover, to be in Israel. The skit ends with the friends declaring, "Let us look forward—to many Passovers here—to holidays that shall spell new freedoms."[75] It depicts a hopeful journey of young Holocaust survivors to Israel and the fulfilled promise of JDC's film: that those free from bondage can find a future in the Jewish state. According to the script, the transformation of these young survivors into Israelis requires looking forward instead of backward. Nonetheless, one young woman continues to remember, defining the joy of her present in light of the past.

The success of American Jewish communal fundraising during the short but volatile period of 1946–1948 hinged on an overall communications strategy that invited American Jews to participate in the urgent work of postwar aid. The images and narratives that drove each annual campaign, whether sent in direct mail, articulated in speeches, drafted in program guides, promoted in volunteer training manuals, narrated in films, or scripted for a slideshow, brought stories of survivors into American Jewish homes across the country. Through these campaigns, American Jews encountered a set of visual and textual motifs—including survivors as skeletal or skeletons, number tattoos on survivors' arms, and concentration camps and ghettos as sites of both loss and survival—that informed their understanding of the Holocaust. Through interconnected themes of survival, sacrifice, and destiny, American Jews began to fashion their own relationship to the Holocaust as saviors not only of Jewish survivors but also of a Jewish future.

Heartstrings and Purse Strings 39

Figure 1.1. Drawing of three individuals huddled together on the cover of the 1945 Joint Distribution Committee annual report. "So They May Live Again," 1945 Annual Report, Joint Distribution Committee. *Courtesy of the American Jewish Joint Distribution Committee.*

Representation and Joint Fundraising: Survivors as Victims, Pioneers, and New Americans

With the themes of survival, sacrifice, and destiny in mind, let us return to the question of joint fundraising. How did the commitment to joint fundraising shape representations of Holocaust survivors? Consider these two images (figs. 1.1 and 1.2). A drawing from the 1945 JDC annual report depicts a group of Jews huddled together with the slogan "So they may live again"; the other image, a photograph from the March 1945 UPA report, shows a young man smiling and raising up a small child with the caption "Freedom in Palestine for Passover." The juxtaposition is striking: one image depicts survivors as destitute unfortunates in need of saving, and the other offers a hopeful portrayal of survivors who have found freedom and light in Palestine.

These images stand in contrast, representing a battle over short-term needs versus long-term security as Jewish leaders solicited financial support for one over the other in 1945. During the few months in 1945 when JDC and UPA

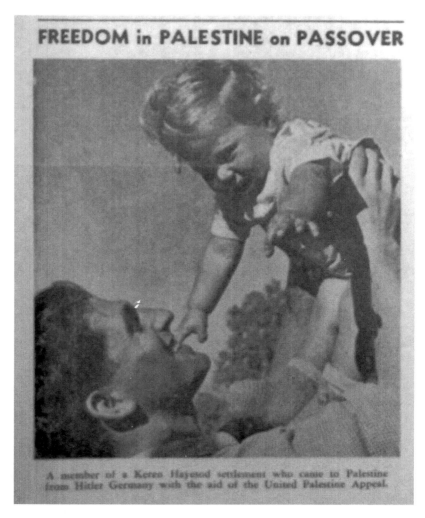

Figure 1.2. A close-up photograph of a young man playfully holding a small child represents the opportunity for freedom for Jews in Palestine. "Freedom in Palestine on Passover," UPA Report, March 1945, 1, Nearprint UJA/AJA.

fundraised separately, these images and the vision for postwar aid they represented were in opposition. Once UJA reconstituted, such images were placed in dialogue rather than in conflict—Jewish survivors needed *both* short-term survival and long-term security; they were both desperate victims and hopeful pioneers in Palestine. Public materials of each annual campaign bring together threads already examined, including immediate need for material aid, support

Heartstrings and Purse Strings 41

Figure 1.3. The cover of the 1948 Los Angeles Jewish community yearbook juxtaposes the strength and vigor of an Israeli pioneer with the despair of young Jewish survivors. Cover of the 1948 yearbook from the Los Angeles Jewish Community Council.

for emigration and resettlement, state building in Israel, and the assertion of American Jews as the saviors of world Jewry.

The 1948 Los Angeles United Jewish Welfare Board Yearbook illustrates the visual intersection of these narratives (see fig. 1.3). The yearbook cover features a photograph of a strong young man looking out toward the future, wearing a light-colored uniform with a Jewish star. He makes a fist with his left hand in a display of strength, while his right hand is wrapped around the shoulder of a young girl wearing a dark dress and clutching a young boy cloaked in a blanket. The caption declares, "They *must* live—in FREEDOM!" The image constructs a visual symbol of immigration to the Jewish state—the strong, lightly clothed young Jewish soldier in Israel acts as protector for the children, draped in dark colors, who have survived Nazi persecution. This scene of freedom, attainable only through the generosity of American donors, also repurposes the symbol of the Jewish star, not a mark of shame but a symbol of strength.

Inside, the yearbook makes a more local appeal, assuring donors that not all their funds will be sent abroad: "Here in America, your Welfare Fund dollars support the fight against anti-Semitism and meet the growing expenses of your Los Angeles Jewish community. Your Welfare Fund contribution assures the increasing spread of Jewish education, helps in the establishment and maintenance of Jewish centers, supports hospitals and welfare institutions."[76] This messaging, both visual and textual, appealed to donors interested in any of these philanthropic priorities: Zionism, aid for Europe's surviving Jews, Jewish immigration to the US, and Jewish education at home. Each of these efforts was supported through the joint fundraising of local welfare campaigns, connected nationally through UJA.

Representing local, national, and international Jewish concerns unified UJA campaigns. As a result, campaign materials preserve the multiple and disparate representations of survivors employed to reflect the distinct geographic spaces of postwar Jewish aid: America, Europe, and Israel. These Holocaust narratives fit multiple visions for the future of Jewish life; they are malleable, indeterminate, and unhindered by expectation and taboo. They are also generic instead of particular, representative instead of individual. While some fundraising materials from the late 1940s and early 1950s feature images of survivors as destitute, hungry, and skeletal, others characterize them as resilient, capable, strong, and powerful. How else could these organizations have insisted that Jewish survivors would make successful future citizens in both Israel and the United States?

Jewish survivors were thus cast not only as victims but also as DPs, refugees, pioneers immigrants, and New Americans to promote the work of JDC in the DP camps of Europe as well as the need to fund infrastructure in Palestine, housing in Israel, and immigration to America. These distinct identities also reflected the liminal status of survivors as persecuted victims of Nazism, stateless individuals, and potential emigrants.

A 1948 campaign booklet sent to potential donors from the UJA of Greater New York exemplifies the use of multiple survivor identities to appeal to Jews across the political spectrum and reconcile its diverse campaign goals. The

Figure 1.4. A young girl squints at the camera while cradling a sleeping child. "The Survivor," 4 Tasks, 1 Answer, pamphlet, Box 206, Folder 2, USTC/YIVO. Courtesy of YIVO.

booklet outlines "four tasks" that demand support from American Jews: "the needs in Palestine"; "the needs in Europe"; "the needs of those who wish to enter the United States within quota limits"; and "our own needs here in America."[77] To render these needs in human terms, the booklet depicts "the Pioneer," "the Survivor," and "the Newcomer," all dependent on American aid. In this context, "the Survivor" is defined as "those remaining in Europe, and those who have fled to the ends of the earth . . . to escape persecution" and depicted by a picture of young people slumped together (see fig. 1.4).[78] One young girl looks directly at the camera, squinting her eyes against the sun while holding a sleeping child in her lap; in the background, another small child nods his head in sleep.

As the booklet indicates, the Survivor was a recognizable figure in postwar aid efforts, one that American Jews were told was hanging between "survival and extinction." At the same time, the Newcomers, those "seeking haven in our own land," were also survivors. The booklet describes them as "European Jewish men, women, and children . . . from the graveyard lands of the old world" and explicitly identifies them as the "thousands of survivors of Nazi

Figure 1.5. A young woman holds up a small baby in the sunlight. "The Pioneer," *4 Tasks, 1 Answer*, pamphlet, Box 206, Folder 2, USTC/YIVO. *Courtesy of YIVO.*

persecution." These Newcomers needed aid to adapt to American life and integrate into society, work performed by the USNA.[79] The needs in Palestine following "the immigration . . . of 75,000 European Jewish D.P.s" also demanded attention from UPA.[80] The Pioneer represented in the booklet is not explicitly identified as a survivor. The image of a strong, smiling young woman hoisting up a small baby corresponds to the idea of the Pioneer as laborer on the land: with "their labor" and "our money," UPA could "build the homeland" (fig. 1.5). These multiple identities reflect the diversity of survivor experiences in the postwar period: some survivors were trapped in Europe while others were able to immigrate to Palestine or the United States. Yet the brochure reveals more than a range of experiences—it conveys a diversity of representation in which Jews struggling in postwar Europe were depicted as DPs or Survivors, those who made their way to Israel as Pioneers, and those in America as Newcomers or New Americans. That UJA could present each of these distinct survivor identities within one appeal underscores the narrative significance of joint fundraising.

Outreach and publicity materials from ORT (also part of the UJA joint fundraising efforts starting in 1947) similarly complicated the depiction of Jews as victims, presenting them as productive future citizens through images of work and job training. The appeals are similar to those of USNA and UPA in projecting emigration as a solution to the DP crisis but offer yet another priority for postwar intervention. ORT opened schools across Europe after the war to allow DPs to develop skills they could take with them to their new homes. ORT was not ideological about where Jews should immigrate; rather, the organization focused on enabling a better future for survivors and asked donors who "saved them from dying" to "train them for living."[81] The images in such appeals show well-dressed men and women sitting at sewing machines or standing beside large industrial instruments. These Jews are not helpless or distraught but focused and productive.

Through fundraising materials of this kind, organizations like ORT not only solicited money from American Jewish donors but also waged an important publicity campaign in support of expanded immigration. As part of what Shandler describes as an "extensive public relations effort made during the early postwar years by a variety of agencies," these kinds of images sought to "promote the acceptance of DPs as citizens."[82] While UJA materials, and USNA efforts in particular, defined survivors as Newcomers and New Americans, ORT materials employed a more nuanced strategy by highlighting the spiritual strength and technical skills of Jewish survivors.

A February 1948 exhibit in New York, sponsored by ORT, showcased the handiwork of Jews in Europe and allowed the material production of ORT students to speak for survivors.[83] The exhibit brochure states, "Every single exhibition article has been produced by the hands of former concentration camp inmates and persecutees. Though they are silent, their work speaks for them, and says: 'Am Jisroel chai'—the Jewish people live! / In this work the Jewish people show that they can create from dead matter valuable contributions for the world."[84] This message directly challenged the notion at the time (and thereafter) that survivors were weakened by or powerless because of their wartime experiences. In fact, the ORT brochure declares, "through the darkness to a brighter future," suggesting that Jews could emerge strong from years of persecution.[85]

Pursuit of a secure Jewish future motivated organizations across the political spectrum after the war and resulted in a multiplicity of survivor representations conveying the fundraising urgency of organizations. The realities of postwar immigration as the answer to DP suffering necessitated a layered identity for survivors—one that reflected their status as refugees while simultaneously

46   SAVING OUR SURVIVORS

projecting their capacity to become citizens. This kind of multiplicity invited American Jews to donate without differentiating their political affiliations or divvying up their financial contribution. Survivor narratives were thus molded to fit multiple frames that reflected American Jewish interests more than specific experiences of survivors.

Conclusion

By 1949 and 1950, the pressure for emigration and sustained material support for DP camps had waned. The establishment of Israel had provided most Holocaust survivors with a pathway out of Europe. Relatedly, the Displaced Persons Act of 1948 allowed for increased immigration to the United States. The extraordinary crisis in Europe had eased.[86] However, crises threatened Jewish lives in other parts of the world as national boundaries and politics continued to shift. Beginning in 1949, American Jewish fundraising campaigns centered around threats facing Jews in Yemen, Iraq, North Africa, and the Eastern Bloc countries. Jewish organizations conducted a series of programs to facilitate mass migration to Israel. In 1949, Operation Magic Carpet brought forty thousand Yemenite Jews to Israel; Operation Ezra in 1950 transported Jews from Morocco and Egypt to Israel; and in 1951, one hundred thousand Iraqi Jews were flown to Israel through Operation Open Sesame.[87]

In support of these initiatives, UJA joint fundraising campaigns employed a series of annual themes focused on migration, resettlement, and life in Israel. In 1949, the Year of Deliverance, the narrative theme was homecoming, celebrated as the "Greatest Homecoming in History." The next year was defined as the Year of Emergencies, as thousands of Jews were transported from North Africa to Israel. The Year of Progress took place in 1951, and 1952 became the Year of Homemaking, as campaign materials urged American donors to "turn the homecoming into homemaking."

These campaigns reflected the dramatic changes to world Jewry following the end of World War II and defined a "new battle of survival"—not in Europe, but for Jews of North Africa. As the 1951 High Holiday appeal manual for UJA of Greater New York noted: "Throughout North Africa—in the slums of Casablanca, in the hovels of Marrakech, in the ghetto of Tunis—every day constitutes a new battle for survival against poverty and disease."[88] Yet even as the focus of Jewish communal aid and joint fundraising shifted, symbols and motifs established in the late forties persisted. As the High Holiday appeal script continued, "In war-shattered Europe, where privation is the rule, children are the worst sufferers." Through fundraising rhetoric, European Jewish survivors, and orphaned children in particular, remained potent symbols of Jewish need around the world.

The 1950 film *UJA Report from Israel* reflects how Holocaust motifs remained central even as humanitarian aid and activities shifted beyond Europe. The film opens on an image of a ship pulling into a harbor as Albert Grobe narrates, "They are coming home. Home from the DP camps, home from the hovels of North Africa and the ghettos of Europe. They are coming home to Israel."[89] The camera then follows people getting off the ship, sorting through luggage, blankets, and strollers, and entering a sprawling tent city as Grobe asks, "Where will they go?" Like earlier films, *UJA Report from Israel* asks American Jews to sacrifice more as lack of permanent housing in Israel forced new immigrants to live in tent cities. Following the 1949 rhetoric about the "Greatest Homecoming in History," the film narrates broken dreams of homecoming and the failure of American Jews to provide enough support to the exploding population of the new state.

As the camera zooms into the tent city, Grobe's narration references the experience of Europe's Jews, saying, "What diabolical turn of fate, they are now in camps that are worse than the camps in Germany" and "Once, Hitler was the enemy, now it was the sun . . . burning through the thin piece of canvas covering the tent."[90] Even as the film highlights the needs of North African Jews, the language of the campaign continues to evoke the tragedy of the Holocaust.[91] Midway through *UJA Report from Israel*, the viewer sees a woman holding a small child. She is recognizable as a Holocaust survivor by the number tattoo on her arm. In 1950, this symbol continued to resonate for an American Jewish audience even as the primary community of refugees was no longer made up of those who had survived concentration camps.

The resonance of these symbols—of concentration camps, of tattoos— serves as a reminder that even as narratives about Holocaust survivors were malleable, American Jews were forming a shared understanding of the Holocaust in the wake of the war. These motifs evoked the tragedy of Nazi oppression, of the six million Jews lost. At the same time, they inspired unprecedented action that channeled American Jewish philanthropy into not only humanitarian aid in postwar Europe but also support for emigration and Jewish life around the world.

It is easy to dismiss the ephemera of Jewish communal fundraising campaigns, to criticize the explicit goals of building empathy and raising funds (like R. Cohen did), or to overlook the collective anxiety that drove Jewish leaders and the seriousness with which they took up the battle for funds (as Hilene Flanzbaum did). But doing so erases the practices of communal life that introduced American Jews to Holocaust survivors. Acknowledging the connection between heartstring and purse string in fundraising appeals does not diminish the power of early narratives. Rather, it reveals that the American Jewish response to the Holocaust depended on established networks of communal organizations and that the practice of giving provided American Jews with opportunities to participate meaningfully in postwar aid while reimagining their own place in the Jewish world.

As we turn our attention away from the images that animated postwar Jewish fundraising efforts to radio broadcasts and the voices that first defined Holocaust survivors in America, we will continue to see the same themes and central motifs. American Jewish communal efforts introduced American audiences to survivors who were at once victims of Nazism, pioneers in Israel, and new citizens in America. The narrative strategies that highlighted concentration camps and arm tattoos as identifiable Holocaust symbols resonated on the radio as much as in fundraising brochures. We will see, in the chapter ahead, how these symbols resonated beyond the Jewish community for listening audiences around the country.

2

Voicing Survivor Narratives

Postwar American Radio and Refugee Policy

WHEN DAVID BODER, A Latvian-born psychologist at the Illinois Institute of Technology (IIT), traveled to Europe in July 1946, he carried with him an Armour wire recorder and two hundred spools of wire to record the "impressions still alive in the victims liberated from concentration camps and from slave labor . . . not only in their own languages but in their own voice."[1] Over a period of two months, Boder collected more than 100 interviews with Jewish and non-Jewish victims of Nazi atrocities in nine languages and brought over 120 hours of orally recorded material back to America.[2] Boder's are considered the earliest oral recordings of Holocaust survivor testimony.

Yet Boder was never able to make the audio recordings available for listeners and instead published them in print. In 1949, he published nine transcribed interviews in a book titled *I Did Not Interview the Dead*, and he self-published seventy interview transcripts between 1950 and 1957 as *Topical Autobiographies of Displaced People Recorded Verbatim in Displaced Persons Camps with a Psychological and Anthropological Analysis*.[3] As such, Boder's work first circulated in print, and the orality of the interviews was lost until the IIT found a misplaced box of his materials in 1990 and began digitizing his original recordings.[4] The IIT Voices of the Holocaust project launched its website in 2000, providing English translations of seventy interviews; by 2009, it had made all original language interviews available to listeners for the first time.[5] The website finally allowed Boder's work to be heard as initially intended.

Like Holocaust testimony collections from the 1970s, '80s, and '90s, Boder's recorded interviews capture the voices of survivors—eyewitness accounts from their own perspectives. Boder's ability to communicate in nine languages enabled him to capture testimonies from eyewitnesses in their native languages, including

German, Yiddish, Russian, Polish, Spanish, French, Lithuanian, Latvian, and English. The audio recordings also include noninterview content like speeches and songs. All of this is to underscore the unique nature of Boder's recordings and the value they hold as early audio records of Holocaust survivor witnessing.

Boder's project offers an introduction to the possibility of audio technologies to collect, preserve, and transmit voiced expressions of survivors in the immediate aftermath of the war. And yet, Boder's interviews failed to find an audience as audio recordings at that point. At the same time, however, American Jewish communal organizations were using radio to disseminate stories about the Holocaust and to share voiced Holocaust narratives. Groups such as the United Jewish Appeal (UJA), National Council of Jewish Women (NCJW), United Service for New Americans (USNA), Hadassah, and the Citizen's Committee for Displaced Persons (CCDP) used radio extensively to advocate for immigration reform, inspire financial giving, and spread awareness about the DP crisis in Europe.

These organizations produced dramatized radio plays, recorded live events, and wrote scripts to be performed live on local radio stations across the country. Sometimes, survivors were invited to speak, although more often actors or volunteers were engaged to perform as survivors. In this way, Jewish communal organizations used radio to create a voice for survivors before survivors could define what that might mean for themselves. As a result, American Jews and their non-Jewish neighbors first heard survivor voices that were, in fact, not representative of the majority of survivors still in DP Europe.

The first two sections of this chapter consider the use of radio as a communication medium that created opportunities and set limitations for how narratives were voiced. How did Holocaust survivors fit into the postwar American radio landscape? And how did Jewish organizations shape survivor narratives for this audio medium? American Jewish communal organizations relied on radio for more than fundraising; they employed the contemporary tools of radio broadcasting to harness the power of individual stories for political purposes. Through radio, American themes were integrated into voiced survivor narratives about the Holocaust in the immediate aftermath of the war. This strategy was particularly important for organizations working to change refugee policy and create immigration opportunities for Jewish survivors.

The chapter then examines two postwar radio shows in depth to explore the kinds of programs that provided American listening audiences with their first introduction to survivor voices: "Displaced," a radio drama produced by the CCDP that depicts the story of Kurt Maier, and "Case History #20,000," a Hadassah radio script that presents the story of "Hannah," the twenty thousandth child to immigrate to Palestine with Youth Aliyah. These programs showcase the role of audio technologies in shaping survivor narratives and reveal how Americans first heard the voices of survivors, before large numbers of them had immigrated to the United States. These broadcasts further demonstrate the centrality of American cultural motifs, including Thanksgiving and freedom, in constructing survivor narratives for American audiences. "Displaced" and "Case History #20,000" also offer opportunities to examine the role of the interviewer in the processes of making Holocaust memory.

Through the close readings of "Displaced" and "Case History #20,000" that follow, I call attention to shifting notions of authority related to survivor voices and the process of giving testimony. Who could speak for survivors? And why did organizations turn to actors to give voice to survivor accounts? One short answer is that organizational broadcasts required English speakers for American airwaves. By giving airtime to survivors who spoke English, organizations showcased how quickly European foreigners could become American. And by hiring actors to perform as survivors, they recast survivors as English speakers and transformed European stories into American idioms.

But the question of authority extends beyond language. Video testimony, which frames a survivor's face and preserves his or her voice, has been viewed as "sacred" and "privileged."[6] As we examine manufactured, mediated radio broadcasts produced by organizations in the late 1940s, we must acknowledge that video testimonies, too, are mediated—by the interviewer, the institution, and the camera. Considering the role of radio in the postwar period allows us to recognize how media technologies have always and will continue to structure and define survivor narratives.

Throughout, we must be mindful of the ways these postwar stories had real power for listeners. It was not the truthfulness or accurate representation of a survivor's experience that drove meaning. These radio shows inspired financial giving and political advocacy, shifting public opinion related to Jewish refugees. Radio became a key tool for organizations working to change American policy as organizations produced stories depicting European Jewish survivors becoming American. While Boder's interviews took decades to find a listening audience, survivor voices broadcast on the radio quickly became part of public discourse about immigration reform in postwar America.

Survivor Voices on Postwar Radio

In the late 1940s and early 1950s, radio drew in a wide audience that crossed economic, social, and ethnic boundaries. Families listened to radio dramas together, and World War II bolstered radio as a reliable source of up-to-date news.[7] As both a news and entertainment medium, radio featured stories about Nazi crimes and victims of Nazi persecution that, "unlike films or newspapers or even a good book, could both inform and entertain with no more effort on your part than simply listening, all in the comfort of your easy chair."[8] At the time, radio shows discussed Nazi atrocities in broad terms, referencing the diversity of DPs in Europe (including Catholics, Protestants, and Jews). Only some broadcasts recognized the specifically Jewish element of Nazi policies and focused on Jewish victims.

There was already a well-established Jewish space on the radio in English.[9] Beyond Yiddish radio, the weekly NBC radio drama *The Eternal Light*, sponsored by the Jewish Theological Seminary of America, drew millions of listeners each week.[10] The program featured dramatic readings and biographies of Jewish historical figures and aired multiple episodes about the events of Nazi Europe, the survivors of Nazi atrocity, and the postwar crisis facing the surviving Jews of Europe.[11] In the immediate postwar period, episodes ended with commentary about American Jewish aid work in Europe and directed audience members to organizations including UJA and the American Red Cross "to provide financial support for the DPs' immediate practical needs and political support for their desire to immigrate to Palestine."[12]

In addition to its popular appeal, *The Eternal Light* served an important role in the NBC broadcast calendar. The FCC Communications Act of 1934 mandated that radio stations play regular noncommercial programming as part of their weekly schedule, establishing space for educational programming on American airwaves. The 1946 report of the FCC guidelines, known as the Blue Book, reminded broadcast stations of this mandate and reinforced the need for all stations to air noncommercial, educational programming.[13] *The Eternal Light* was launched to fill this noncommercial air space. Religious and civic organizations also produced one-off shows to fill this mandate.

Of course, the FCC requirement did not guarantee that all noncommercial shows would air. In fact, public service airtime became competitive as stations fought for listeners and major sponsorships that did not want to follow "boring" programming.[14] Nonprofit groups sought to construct shows pertaining to DPs that were entertaining, informative, and appealing to local stations' producers and diverse audiences. A 1944 publicity guide of NCJW suggests this balance was hard to achieve: "The radio audience is the most casual of all to whom we tell our story. It is the one audience that can walk out on us without even an implication of rudeness."[15] The ease of radio, then, worked for and against organizations trying to convey important stories over the airways. Listeners could casually engage with narratives that were informative and entertaining, but they could also change the station. The NCJW guide continues, "If we do not give [the audience] what it wants, a flick of the knob may displace Council in favor of a popular crooner. Remember that on the air we are competing with the most experienced talent and showmanship."

Organizations across the Jewish communal landscape understood the importance of developing appealing content to take advantage of radio as an effective advocacy tool for reaching both Jewish and non-Jewish audiences. Nonetheless, each organization chose different strategies to appeal to the diverse listening audience. Hadassah preferred a direct, unimpassioned approach to its radio scripts because "as a rule, stations do not give time for controversial political issues as readily as they do for 'feature' material."[16] *The Eternal Light* similarly approached current topics of interest with the intention of reaching wide audiences. Markus Krah has detailed how *The Eternal Light* sought to impart different lessons to Jewish and non-Jewish audiences, writing that dramas, interviews, and other narratives on the show communicated to Jewish audiences how to be and act Jewish while simultaneously portraying the value Judaism brought to American society for non-Jewish audiences.[17] Listener mail suggests that *The Eternal Light* succeeded in reaching both audiences in a meaningful way, and records show that in 1946 and 1947, five to six million listeners regularly tuned in.[18]

Irregular programming, such as holiday specials or one-off reports, did not build audiences of this scale but allowed organizations to create and disseminate content that informed American listeners about the plight of DPs after the war. In broadcasts of this kind, survivors were represented as DPs in Europe, new immigrants in America, and victims of Nazism. Like the pamphlets sent to donors by UJA, radio scripts and broadcasts employed various terms and tropes to portray Jewish survivors in different contexts. Through interviews, scripted performances, and recorded live events, organizations called on American listening audiences to respond with action—either financial donation or political engagement.

Stories from Europe, often sent as reports from the ground, included interviews with survivors to give listeners a sense of being there. JDC produced a series of reports featuring JDC worker Sadie Sender. Sender was stationed in the Zeilsheim DP camp and regularly recorded interviews with DPs to communicate a range of Holocaust experiences with an American audience. These interviews, and others like them, allowed survivors to speak for themselves but framed their voices with the optimism of successful aid work. For example, the June 6, 1946, episode of *Sadie Sender for JDC in Frankfurt* features eleven-year-old Helen Opatovska, who survived two years in Bergen-Belsen. Having invited Helen to recite a poem in Yiddish, Sender introduces the poem, saying it "tells the feelings of the Jews that are still alive in Europe."[19] Helen's poem speaks of the "darkness coming" and the "children without their mother, murdered." Yet Sender enthusiastically declares, "That is the spirit that inspires the surviving Jews in Europe. It must inspire you." Sender transforms Helen's mournful poem into a symbol of hope for listeners who may not understand Yiddish. For American Jews who could understand Opatovska's poem, the despair and loss of the Holocaust were evident; for those listeners who could not interpret for themselves, Sender's optimism defined the survivor's voice.[20] We see how the truth and authenticity of survivor stories were secondary to their power to motivate attention and aid at the time.

Radio broadcasts about survivors as New Americans similarly featured survivor voices that celebrated American optimism.[21] "Out of the Wilderness," sponsored by the USNA, an organization that aided Jewish immigrants in adapting to American life, serves as one example.[22] The show aired on April 6, 1947, featuring five survivors of the Holocaust as part of a special Passover celebration.[23] One of the featured survivors was pianist Kurt Maier. I return to this broadcast later in the chapter to explore how Maier's voice was first heard by American audiences, but "Out of the Wilderness" also reveals how organizations employed American ideals, like the spirit of freedom, to align Jewish survivors with American history and values. David Timmons, announcer for "Out of the Wilderness," introduces the show as follows:

> We invite you to join us as the portrait of freedom grows upon our canvas. For tonight we celebrate the Passover. The Passover is the first holiday of freedom to enter into the conscious of modern man. The Passover is the first holiday of escape and deliverance. Yes, tonight we offer this celebration not as the recollection of a single freedom from the past, but as the warm thing in the hearts of those living and those present, as a reaffirmation of hope of these living for the future. The United Service for New Americans, a constituent agency of UJA, whose role is the care and settlement of those survivors of Nazi persecution who find haven on American shores, presents . . . a Passover celebration for this year, 1947, that equals the sound of freedom.[24]

Here, Timmons and the USNA rely on Jewish and American symbols to construct an integrated history of freedom. By layering the ideal of American life over the history of Passover, the broadcast defines a Jewish place in the American dream.

While interviews and specials allowed survivors to speak directly to the American listening audience, radio dramas scripted by Jewish organizations

Voicing Survivor Narratives

were performed by actors.[25] By the 1940s, scripted radio dramas had grown in number and reputation, a widely popular genre in the postwar period. Jeffrey Shandler and Elihu Katz argue that it "emerged as a 'high' art form" following the soaps and suspense shows of the 1930s and "could effectively present topics of serious social concern to the general audience."[26] The genre was influenced by the success of *March of Time*, a popular series in the 1930s and '40s that revolutionized the use of reenacted news events.[27] *March of Time* portrayed the news as an amalgamation of traditional announcements and dramatically reproduced scenes that broadly mixed fact and fiction. As seen later in the chapter, "Displaced" and "Case History #20,000" were made in the *March of Time* mode, as they reenacted historical events to call attention to the ongoing refugee crisis.

"Delayed Pilgrims" and the American Dream

In appealing to broad audiences, organizations focused on aiding DPs integrated archetypal American stories with the stories of Holocaust survivors. "Out of the Wilderness" recasts Passover, a Jewish holiday, in American terms, while "Delayed Pilgrims Dinner" (detailed in the introduction) applies Jewish themes and experiences to Thanksgiving.[28] As these broadcasts suggest, the USNA and CCDP associated the arrival of Jewish survivors in America with the history of the Pilgrims, who also sought freedom from religious persecution.

Thanksgiving in particular took on political dimensions in the postwar period as immigration reform, quota limits, and DP administration were debated in Congress.[29] By referring to Jewish DPs as Delayed Pilgrims, immigration advocacy groups like USNA and CCDP called attention to those still in need of saving and to America's historical imperative to act.[30] Timmons's introduction to "Out of the Wilderness" exemplifies this rhetorical strategy; the pursuit of freedom is a theme not only of American history but also of Passover, a story told across Jewish communities. This mutually enhancing value integrated Jews into mainstream American ideology.

Survivors featured in these broadcasts embraced the idea of Thanksgiving by expressing gratitude for America's freedoms and opportunities. They wove narratives of America into early discourse about the Holocaust. Consider Israel Burkenwald, quoted in the introduction, who claimed that he had learned English at night school to feel "more American," and young Peter Forshee, who sang "My Country, 'Tis of Thee."[31] These survivors enacted the promised narrative transformation by calling DPs Delayed Pilgrims.

Other programs similarly applied the trope of the pilgrim to frame survivor accounts: an episode of *The Eternal Light* titled "The Late Comers," which aired on November 23, 1947, the Sunday before Thanksgiving, tells the history of immigration to America beginning with the Pilgrims and ending with DPs after World War II. An episode broadcast in 1948, "The Arrival of Delayed Pilgrims," chronicles debates over the DP Act.[32] American Jewish communal organizations sponsoring these broadcasts relied on the rhetoric of freedom and the symbolism of Thanksgiving to appeal to non-Jewish American audiences, building emotional connections and arguing, implicitly, that European Jewish survivors would make successful Americans.

A majority of Americans at the time favored narrow immigration policies and feared that immigrants would take jobs and homes away from returning soldiers, draining the economy.[33] Referring to DPs as Delayed Pilgrims thus became a political strategy most often used by organizations working for immigration policy reform, like USNA and CCDP. The latter was founded in 1946 by the American Jewish Committee and the American Council for Judaism to advocate for increased American immigration as an alternative to Zionist-led immigration to Palestine.[34] The group sought improved conditions for DPs and urged America to take on a larger share of the world's problems after the war, declaring in a *Brief Statement of Aims* pamphlet, "After the nightmare of Nazism and Fascism, after the holocaust of World War II, we owe it to ourselves and to the world to be the guardians of freedom and peace. We owe it to ourselves and to the world to take action in solving problems which threaten the peace."[35] With Earl G. Harrison (author of the Harrison Report) as chairman, the CCDP advocated for suspended immigration quotas and temporary legislation to allow DPs to legally enter the United States. It sent brochures, published the *Displaced Persons Digest*—a newsletter of aggregated DP-related news from around the country—and sponsored a series of radio broadcasts, including "Displaced," designed to provoke Americans into action on behalf of DPs of Europe. Through these different forms of media, the group sought to shape public opinion about immigrants and focus the debate about refugees and DPs on America's role. To do so, the group appealed directly to non-Jews, often by minimizing the Jewish element of the DP story and marshaling Christian themes while evoking American ideals in entertaining radio dramas.

For example, a 1948 episode of *The Golden Door* titled "A Parable for Easter" employs the Easter story of death and rebirth to tell the story of DP #234, who dies in a DP camp in Germany and fights to enter the US zone of heaven.[36] Since DP #234 has no nationality, he poses a problem for the heavenly messenger. This story mirrors the experience of stateless DPs who had nowhere to go on earth

Voicing Survivor Narratives 57

and waited years for quota numbers and visas to become available. To address DP #234's dream of becoming American, the broadcast imagines a court made up of American Founding Fathers, including Thomas Paine, Thomas Jefferson, and Ben Franklin. They are appalled by the existence of US quota laws and, after hearing the struggles of DPs and the limitations of US immigration policy, admit DP #234 to the US zone of heaven because "he believes in the basic principles of freedom and liberty and if he had been admitted to the United States while mortal, he would unquestionably, have been a good citizen."[37]

This broadcast illustrates how familiar narratives from American history were employed to appeal to a broad American audience. While DP #234 is given a Jewish backstory, as shown in his assertion that "there are none of his people in his land and none of his people have a land," he is never described as Jewish or defined in religious terms. The actor playing DP #234 speaks with an American accent, so his voice matches the accents of Jefferson, Paine, and Franklin. These strategic choices affirm the potential of survivors to become strong, valuable, and productive Americans. Just as evoking the story of the Pilgrims connected postwar Jewish displacement with earlier moments of American immigration, the endorsement of survivors by the American Founding Fathers gave the contemporary refugee crisis mythic dimensions.

Kurt Maier, Paul Muni, and Postwar Broadcast Radio: Voicing Displacement and Haven

There is more to say about how the USNA-sponsored "Out of the Wilderness," which aired in April 1947, aligns the Passover celebration with a range of American values: optimism, opportunity, haven, generosity, and, of course, freedom. To do so, let me focus on one voice in "Out of the Wilderness." The broadcast features musical performances by survivors of Nazism (some Jewish, some not), including Kurt Maier, a Czech Jewish survivor of Auschwitz, Sachsenhausen, Ohrdruf, and Buchenwald. Announcer David Timmons presents him to American audiences, saying,

> You've surely heard of our next guest. His story has been published far and wide in the United States. . . . His name is Kurt Maier. Once his art was acclaimed, not only in his native land of Czechoslovakia, but throughout the world. Then the Nazis changed that world. The concert hall became the concentration camp. And the Nazis called upon Kurt Maier to play when they shipped him to that terrible place called Auschwitz. Today, Mr. Maier is here. He is the lone survivor of 86 persons of his family. Need we mention what his clean, free music means to him today?[38]

Like Massey and O'Dwyer in "Delayed Pilgrims Dinner," Timmons juxtaposes the freedom of America with the oppression of concentration camps to define America as a haven for Jewish victims of Nazism. Maier then directly addresses the audience, speaking clear and effective English but with an identifiably European accent. He says, "There are thousands of people brought here by the United Service, who, just as I, lost their mothers during the Nazi persecution. In memory, I want to play the old familiar song, 'My Yiddishe Mama.'" He goes on to play "My Yiddishe Mama" and two other songs, including "Ich hab kein Heimatland" (I have no homeland), of which he notes, "We have sung it in the darkest hours, in the various concentration camps . . . for all of us who went through the Nazi terror."

At that time, Maier's story—told "far and wide," in Timmons's words—consisted of his experiences in concentration camps and his survival, which had depended on his musical talent. Maier's story was also one continuous displacement, from Karlsbad to Prague, ghettos, concentration camps, and finally to a "homecoming" in America. This story of displacement, survival, emigration, and music was indeed told far and wide. In September 1947, just months after "Out of the Wilderness" aired, the *New Yorker* magazine featured a nine-page article detailing Maier's story, titled "Displaced." Written by reporter-at-large Daniel Lang as a personal profile, it detailed Maier's life from before the war in Karlsbad, Czechoslovakia, to his deportation to Auschwitz and his liberation from Buchenwald.[39] In the year that followed, Lang's article was adapted for a radio drama, also titled "Displaced."[40]

So Maier's story was represented at least three times between 1946 and 1947 for American audiences, in three different forms. First, Maier spoke to American audiences in "Out of the Wilderness" in his own voice—his piano skills were highlighted, his biography largely omitted. Then, he was interviewed by Lang, and a detailed version of his experience under Nazism was published in print. The article quotes Maier but expresses Lang's point of view. Finally, the CCDP transformed Lang's article into a thirty-minute radio drama. The radio piece includes Lang and Maier as characters, both portrayed by actors, and dramatizes the interview between Lang and Maier as well as Maier's experiences in Nazi Europe. Maier's story was thus adapted from a direct interview into a multitemporal and ruptured audio narrative that conveyed the horror of life under Nazism while asserting the need for American intervention in postwar problems.

As the title "Displaced" suggests, Lang's September 1947 *New Yorker* article tells the story of Maier's persecution and survival through the lens of his displacement and eventual immigration to America. Lang intertwines these narrative threads, asserting that Maier—and DPs like him—were America's latest pilgrims. The article begins, "One of the oratorical flourishes that almost every politician uses when addressing a group of foreign-born citizens is to hail America as the haven of the oppressed. He tells of the coming of the Pilgrims."[41] Lang continues by placing the DP into a long history of American Pilgrims: "In another year or so . . . the politician will be able to add a modern category, the DPs or displaced persons."

It is not surprising that the ideas of displacement and American immigration frame Maier's story both in the *New Yorker* and on the radio. The broadcast, like Lang's article, follows Maier's story from Karlsbad to Auschwitz and eventually New York, dramatizing multiple scenes from Maier's life under Nazism. Maier's story, like "Parable for Easter," served the purposes of the CCDP to highlight the potential for the United States to be a haven for strong, creative, and grateful refugees. The *New Yorker* article uses Maier's experience to open up a larger consideration of postwar immigration. It starts at Pier 86, where Maier's ship, the *Marine Perch*, has landed in New York.[42] Lang explains, "I was on hand in the hope of learning about what it meant to a person to be, in the cold language of our time, 'displaced.'"[43] From the beginning, then, Lang's story humanizes the conceptual category of DP. The radio piece echoes this language, keeping the title and beginning with the following announcement: "The word 'displaced' has a new and horrible meaning in our language when it is applied to a human being. This is the story of a displaced human being, one of hundreds of thousands. . . . What happened to Kurt Maier is neither more nor less horrible than what happened to thousands of other Displaced Persons. Perhaps that's why it's the best story to tell. Perhaps that's why Daniel Lang chose to interview Kurt Maier."[44] As the announcer makes clear, Maier is meant to be representative of hundreds of thousands of DPs. In this way, Maier's voice is both his own and speaks for all DPs. This echoes Maier's own reference in "Out of the Wilderness" to the thousands who lost their mothers.

While Lang does not elaborate on why he chose to feature Maier, his article describes an aid worker who introduced the two men; seemingly, the choice was not Lang's but arranged by the USNA, the group that sponsored Maier's transport to America. Certainly, it was not random. Maier spoke very clear English, and his skill as a musician made him an ideal public figure. As a well-known musician, Maier brought talent and creative energy to America.[45] That he was exceptional among DPs in Europe paradoxically allowed him to define what it meant to be displaced for Lang and American audiences that read and heard his story.

The *New Yorker* article and the radio drama depict Maier's experiences under Nazism chronologically. They begin in Karlsbad (Karlovy Vary),

Czechoslovakia, at the moment the Germans were awarded the Sudetenland in the Munich Accords and Maier fled to Prague.[46] He established himself and his mother there until the Germans invaded. Eventually, they were deported to Theresienstadt, where they lived for two and a half years. Maier's mother worked in the women's section, sewing uniforms for the Germans, until she was deported to Auschwitz. Soon after, Maier was also deported to Auschwitz, where he learned that his mother had been sent directly to the gas chambers.

At Auschwitz, Maier was assigned to the camp band, avoiding forced labor but witnessing the lines of victims sent to the gas chambers. Lang quotes Maier as saying, "The idea was for us to drown out their cries, but we never could." After two months at Auschwitz, Maier was sent to Ohrdruf, a slave labor camp where he worked on a V-2 launching site until he was again assigned to play music—this time for the camp commandant, Herr Stibitz. According to Lang, Maier recalled that as the Allies drew closer to Ohrdruf, the commandant became more erratic, making Maier polish his shoes and soap him while in the shower—degrading Maier to make himself feel more powerful.

In February 1945, Maier was sent to Sachsenhausen, where he worked in an underground airplane factory, and a few weeks later, in March, he was forced on a death march to Buchenwald, where, in April 1945, he was liberated by the Americans. In discussing liberation with Lang, Maier described his part in an effort at revenge. Lang writes, "The men in the Buchenwald underground broke out guns they had secreted, armed the other prisoners, including Maier, and went on a shooting spree of their own, picking off any Nazi they could find."[47] In the radio broadcast, this scene is narrated by Maier: "Then the Nazis fled and the men of Buchenwald underground, they brought out such guns as they had and they armed us. We prisoners went on a shooting spree of our own. Picking off any Nazi we could."[48]

The remainder of Maier's story accounts for his recovery and immigration to the United States. Following liberation, Maier fell ill with typhus and recovered for six weeks in a hospital the Americans had fashioned in a former SS barrack. On recovery, Maier was again asked to play music, this time for officers of the US Army, and he took the job with excitement and enthusiasm. He remained in Germany until he was able to contact his sister in New York, and she sponsored him to join her.

For American audiences, this was the kind of story that represented the Holocaust: a chronological progression from ghetto to camp to death march. Note that this story details much more of Maier's personal experience than any of the fundraising brochures explored in the previous chapter. The chronological structure remains central to contemporary narratives about Jewish experiences under Nazism. With that in mind, I want to highlight three elements that speak to the particular way American audiences heard these stories in the aftermath of the war. First, both versions of "Displaced" largely skip over Maier's time in Theresienstadt, notably focusing on his six or seven months in concentration camps as opposed to the two and a half years he spent in the ghetto. Despite early representations of the Warsaw Ghetto and commemoration of the Warsaw Ghetto Uprising, the concentration camp became an early symbol of Nazi atrocities.[49] Stories focusing on camp experiences signified the broader story of the Holocaust for American Jews.

Second, Maier articulates Jewish attempts for revenge at the very end of the war. This is a significant departure from how Jewish experiences were later represented in America. Sensitive topics were largely excised from public discourse about the Holocaust in the 1980s and '90s. In his history of the labor camp Starachowice, Christopher Browning writes, "Events of rape and revenge killing—obviously known to all Starachowice survivors but openly hinted at only by some and denied by others—began to become public memory some forty-five years after the event."[50] Naomi Seidman and Henry Greenspan both have identified this narrative shift, arguing that anger and the impulse for revenge were present in early Holocaust narratives and later minimized.[51] In Maier's story, we can see how this kind of experience was initially transmitted to American audiences, first in a secondhand report from Lang and then spoken by Maier as performed in "Displaced." It was not controversial or taboo—it was part of Maier's story from the first postwar years.

And third, Lang's article explains that older people were sent directly to their deaths in gas chambers while the young and healthy were not. This conclusion accompanies Maier's recollection that on arriving at Auschwitz, he learned his mother had immediately died in the gas chambers. The logic of this description—that the old and infirm were tagged for death while the young were forced to work—reflects a need to make sense of an incomprehensible past even if doing so requires departing from historical reality. To be clear, testimonies collected in the 1970s and '80s reflect the Nazi practice of sending older people directly to the gas chambers on arrival at Auschwitz. But survivor accounts—including one from Bela Fabian detailed in the next chapter—also reveal instances when these practices were undermined, when older Jews found their way into different lines or when younger people were also sent directly to the gas chambers. What I mean to highlight in Lang's article is not necessarily the accuracy of this statement but rather the framing of logic that Lang applies to this part of Maier's story—and in particular, how it is unclear from the article who articulated this understanding, Lang or Maier.

A gap between the way American audiences tried to make sense of Holocaust narratives and the reality expressed by survivors appears throughout this book. We see it in the UJA film *Battle for Survival* and again in chapter 3 in a speech made by social worker Cecilia Razovsky, who trained other social workers for assignment in postwar Europe. We also see this idea in the work of David Boder as he sought again and again to apply logic to the stories he heard from survivors, asking "why" repeatedly when survivors could offer no explanation for why some people were killed and not others.[52] Lawrence Langer addresses this gap in understanding, writing that we are "trained in the necessity of moral choice to preserve the integrity of civilized behavior."[53] He warns that we cannot attribute this sense of civility to an understanding of the Holocaust, where "belief in choice betrayed the victim and turned out to be an illusion."[54] In this way, Langer challenges attempts to apply moral logic or order to survivor testimonies in general and concentration camp experiences in particular. How did readers and listeners of Maier's story in 1947 seek to make sense of this new kind of narrative?

On radio, Maier's story served as an initial encounter with the Holocaust—but not through his own voice, as it was voiced by Paul Muni, Academy and Tony award-winning star of *The Story of Louis Pasteur, The Good Earth,* and the 1932 *Scarface.* A Hollywood star and Yiddish stage veteran, Muni was born in Lemberg, Galicia, and immigrated to America as a young child; he spoke English with an American accent.[55] Nevertheless, when Muni played Maier in "Displaced," he differentiated his voice from that of Lang (also portrayed by an actor) with a slight inflection. He sounded somewhat foreign but did not employ a heavy accent that would have indicated Maier's European roots. That is to say, Muni's portrayal is quite different from Maier's actual accented voice in "Out of the Wilderness" and certainly different from thousands of DPs who could not speak English at all.

Muni lent his voice to other radio and film productions about the plight of DPs in the postwar period, including multiple episodes of *The Eternal Light.*[56] Celebrity voices were popular in radio performances at large and in philanthropic appeals in the Jewish community. For "Displaced," Muni's famous voice and Maier's engaging story were a successful pairing. Maier's story was, in fact, an apt fit for radio as music played a central role in the narrative; Maier contributed the score for the final production.

"Displaced" relies on music to realize the story. An organ plays to signal transitions between scenes, allowing the story to jump through time and space. The collection of scenes depicted on the radio broadcast differs from the story written by Lang, and their ordering is one of the biggest transformations

Voicing Survivor Narratives 63

from print to radio. Lang's article is linear: he goes to the pier and meets Maier. Throughout the article, he conveys Maier's story with direct quotations. In adapting this story into a dramatic performance dependent on some level of entertainment, the radio version adds several layers so that multiple stories progress at once. The present action depicts Maier at the pier, waiting for his sister after the docking of the *Marine Perch*, talking to Lang. In performing this interview, the radio drama defines a second layer—the act of memory making, which dramatizes the process of giving testimony.[57] The audience hears Maier's story but also the process of narrating or creating that story; on top of the present action is a layer of narrative construction. And, third, the program depicts Maier's experience under Nazism. Some elements are depicted through the interview and others are reenacted, so the radio drama jumps back and forth between past and present, reimagining significant moments of Maier's life during the war.[58] Through these multiple layers of storytelling and imaginative reenactments, "Displaced" offers its audience a Holocaust narrative that Lang's print piece does not, shifting between years and representational modes.

What does it mean for "Displaced" to deconstruct Lang's article in this way? By making American listeners privy to the act of giving testimony (i.e., reading not just a constructed narrative but the questions and reflections that led to Maier's storytelling), the radio program makes listeners more than just donors or advocates; they became participants in the memory-making process. Lawrence Langer and Henry Greenspan have theorized the interdependent relationship between survivor and interviewer based on the practice of testimony collection from the 1970s, '80s, and '90s. According to Langer, the interviewer becomes witness to the survivor telling their story and, in this way, plays an essential role in creating testimony. He further argues that the audience of a videotaped testimony also becomes a witness, that both the interviewer and the audience take on the responsibility of understanding the survivor and the world of the Holocaust the survivor "reenacts."[59] Greenspan has similarly articulated how the interviewer, or partner in dialogue, must go on a journey with the survivor.

"Displaced" can be understood as a performance of this process. Lang's questions initiate dramatized flashbacks, as the show invites the audience to follow the journalist on the journey to Maier's past. In this way, Lang's character in the radio drama introduces key scenes and serves as a guide into testimonial experience. Transforming Lang into a central character makes him not just a reporter or observer but a precedent for the interviewer in Holocaust video testimonies, who is heard but not seen. The radio program complicates

64   SAVING OUR SURVIVORS

the printed article by dramatizing not only Maier's life under Nazism but also the process of giving testimony.

The transformation of Lang's story for radio involved the addition of sound effects to heighten the drama. For example, at Ohrdruf, before he was singled out by the commandant, Maier was forced to work hard labor. Lang writes in the *New Yorker*, "One afternoon, when Maier did not seem to be working fast enough, a guard wearing brass knuckles went to work on him and permanently scarred his chest."[60] The same scene in the radio version transfers the punishment from Maier to the man next to him, and rather than describe a beating, the show takes advantage of the audio capabilities of radio to add a poignant and shocking gunshot. The scene is played between two actors, both employing heavy accents. One portrays the German guard, who shouts that all the men should "get back to work." The other actor, portraying the prisoner with a heavy accent, responds, "Please, I must rest. Just for a moment. . . . I tried [to work] but I can't." His voice is shaky as he begs the guard. The guard has the strongest accent of all and barks with an aggressive tone: "If you can't work you are no use to us. So." A loud clap indicates that the German guard has shot the old prisoner, who is presumably, although not directly defined as, a Jew. The scene ends with the guard grunting, "Now, get to work!" and is immediately followed by dramatic organ music signaling a switch back to the present action.

The gunshot exposes a narrative leap from the article to the radio drama. There is no gunshot in the *New Yorker* article, suggesting it may have been entirely fabricated for radio. It is, certainly, a more dynamic audio moment, which may justify the change. It dramatizes the moment, revealing the ultimate consequence of the fear and danger Maier's beating provoked, but veers from Maier's story as he told it to Lang, multiplying the distance between his voice and the narration of his story. This change reveals succinctly how the practices and norms of radio dramas shaped survivor narratives at the time and defined how Holocaust stories became voiced in postwar America.

Additional changes from print to radio similarly reveal the consequences of constructing Holocaust narratives for postwar American listening audiences. Lang writes about the Pier 86 waiting area by noting the range of DPs arriving from the ship, the *Marine Perch*. He sees "an elderly Polish priest," "an even more elderly Austrian woman," and a "young handsome German woman holding a small girl by the hand" as well as the variety of aid workers, whom he describes as "representatives of Catholic, Jewish, and Protestant welfare groups."[61] In fact, a diverse population of European DPs sought immigration to the US after the end of the war, and the language of religious pluralism was widely evoked to remind Americans that this problem affected all religious groups—not only Jews. While Maier's story drives the primary emotional narrative of "Displaced," the DP crisis is the larger context for the broadcast, and the need for revised immigration legislation is built into the script. Even before Maier is introduced in the broadcast, a female aid worker tells Lang that she hopes the *Marine Perch* will make more trips back and forth to Europe "when Congress passes legislation admitting displaced persons."

The explicit mention of the need for legislation is echoed at the end of the broadcast. After Maier's story ends and the music flourishes, Paul Muni speaks as himself. He refers to DPs waiting in Europe as "helpless victims of tyranny and brutality" who are also "healthy, husky human beings." As in the fundraising campaigns of UJA, survivors were both helpless victims and healthy, capable citizens, ready to contribute to America. He urges listeners to care, saying, "Whether they live to breathe the air of freedom and health and happiness or sink into despair and death is for us to decide. The choice is ours." Muni argues that Americans can and must be the saviors of DPs. He invokes the New Testament story of the Samaritan, who stops to help a fallen stranger, as a means of provoking action among the American audience and ends by claiming, "It is for us to choose, remembering for that choice, we stand accountable to our conscious and to God."[62] Muni's appeal reiterates the idea that Americans (here, he speaks to all Americans, not just American Jews) are individually responsible for the lives and deaths of DPs, including Jewish survivors, and suggests that Americans have to choose between generosity and complicity.

Neither the gunshot nor the explicit plea for action is present in Lang's printed work. They were added by the CCDP and endorsed by Paul Muni. Radio programs like "Displaced" were used widely as advocacy tools among organizations concerned about DPs in postwar Europe. The CCDP produced not only "Displaced" but also numerous episodes of *The Golden Door*, including "I Am a Displaced Person," "Parable for Easter," "Joseph in America," and others that promoted temporary legislation for DPs.[63] Some of these productions feature explicitly Jewish survivors and represent the Jewish experience under Nazism; others, like "I Am a Displaced Person," which tells the story of Silva Maldist, an Estonian native, feature non-Jewish DPs.[64] The majority of CCDP productions, however, discuss the diversity of DPs and do not specify the religion of the protagonist. All of its broadcasts, meant to inform the American public about the problems facing DPs and depict immigration to America as the most viable solution, presented Americans with ways to help. These CCDP narratives show refugees as honest people eager to get to America to work hard and live in freedom, but they also depict the grave circumstances in DP camps and monumental challenges facing most DPs. They consistently portray DPs as enemies of tyranny, willing to fight for freedom.[65]

This framing is a reminder that radio programs sponsored by the CCDP must be read in the context of the organization's insistence on American immigration reform (as opposed to Zionist advocacy for a Jewish state) and the emerging Cold War. Many publications concerned with DPs at the time—including publicity and fundraising materials from Jewish organizations like the World Jewish Congress, ORT, UJA, and others—describe the vitality of survivors in an effort to represent them as prospective healthy members of American society. In trying to motivate Americans to care about DPs and support more open immigration, DPs had to be seen as capable of becoming successful, working members of society, not as desperate and destitute. These organizations managed a delicate balance, communicating the urgent needs of DPs while asserting that they could be active and healthy citizens. Muni's comments clearly articulate this balance—the DPs were "the helpless victims of tyranny and brutality" and still "healthy husky, human beings."

"Hannah" and Hadassah's 1947 Fundraising Campaign: Giving Voice to the Future

Hadassah's radio script for the drama "Case History #20,000" demonstrates how Zionist organizations, committed to DP immigration to Palestine and then Israel, similarly used radio to appeal to a diverse audience of donors and mimicked an interview style that portrayed memory making.[66]

Like "Displaced," "Case History #20,000" is an adaptation of a print story, one first crafted for use in the 1947 Hadassah fundraising campaign. The story of Hannah, a young survivor brought to Palestine by Youth Aliyah, is told in a brochure called *Ask . . . Hannah* and was later transformed into a radio script to be distributed to local Hadassah chapters.[67] While "Displaced" was prerecorded for broadcast, "Case History #20,000" was intended to be performed live; the printed script is the only extant record. The script was part of an annual programming guide that included general programming ideas, specific communications instructions, and templates for Hadassah chapter radio chairmen. The kit included radio scripts and an additional Youth Aliyah script of an interview between radio announcer and local chapter Youth Aliyah chairman.

After Hitler came to power in Germany, Henrietta Szold, founder of Hadassah, worked to provide sanctuary for as many Jewish children as possible in Palestine through a new program called Youth Aliyah.[68] The program grew throughout the prewar and war years and, following the war, expanded beyond Europe, bringing Jewish orphans from around the world to Palestine (and after 1948, to Israel). Youth Aliyah was administered by the Jewish Agency in Palestine, but in 1935, Hadassah negotiated the right to be recognized as the sole Youth Aliyah fundraising agent in the United States.[69] Hadassah took seriously its role as fundraiser for Youth Aliyah, a departure from its core work with the Hadassah Medical Organization. It enlisted celebrities, engaged other organizations, and inspired giving in the US and England throughout the war years. By the time the war ended, Hadassah had developed loyal donors to Youth Aliyah and established Youth Aliyah committees among Hadassah members and chapters.

Hadassah leaders recognized the importance of audiovisual media for publicity and fundraising purposes, using radio and film technology to publicize all programs and the Youth Aliyah project in particular. Films produced by the national office were rented out to local chapters, but the organization's radio strategy relied on local leaders to build relationships with radio stations and develop content that fit local efforts. NCJW similarly developed strategies that trained local leaders to take responsibility for radio publicity. As the 1944 radio manual announced, "Radio is becoming one of the most important media for transmitting ideas. Through a broadcast it is possible to create good will, win respect, and impart the information which is necessary for a better understanding and wider appreciation of Council."[70] Radio programs for local chapters aimed to achieve all these goals.

Hadassah employed radio to achieve a similar set of goals, relying on the potency of personal stories to expand understanding as well as inspire donations. Staff members in Palestine collected case histories about Youth Aliyah children and sent folders to the New York offices for publicity purposes.[71] A 1945 fundraising pamphlet titled *Escape to Life* features stories from the perspectives of young survivors, articulating the power of the first-person perspective in fundraising for Youth Aliyah.

> Have you read the eye-witness accounts of the extermination chambers, the death camps, the terror and disease which the fascists left behind them in Europe? Have you been shaken with anger and disgust? Do you want to do something immediately for the Jewish children who were among the first victims of this insanity? You can—through Youth Aliyah. Help us take thousands more of Europe's Jewish children out of this atmosphere of death and destruction, far away from the places where they were witness to murder and rapine. Help us teach them to laugh, to play, to study and work, to become upstanding men and women, good citizens of a democratic world.[72]

The voice of a survivor could inspire "anger and disgust," and Hadassah transformed anger into action through support for Youth Aliyah.

In 1947, Hadassah waged a campaign designed around the twenty thousandth child rescued by Youth Aliyah. One of a series of brochures that offer case histories, *Ask . . . Hannah* tells the story of twelve-year-old Hannah. The pamphlet calls attention to its own power in providing donors and members with access to the voices of young survivors by choosing to "let our Youth Aliyah children speak for themselves." Hadassah recognized the value of eyewitness accounts in its promotional campaigns, especially when the stories were by and about children. The simple, straightforward language of the brochure imitates the expression of a young person, even though Hannah is described as "wizened," "tense," and having a "hollow" voice.

Told from the first-person point of view, her story is accompanied by two pictures—one of Hannah in a hospital bed (fig. 2.1) and one of her healthy and smiling with a flower (fig. 2.2)—that, by themselves, convey the story Hadassah wished to tell, a story arching from despair and desperation to rebirth. Hannah's story begins, "I remember, I was nine when the Germans came with guns and tanks." She recalls living in a ghetto with her family for about a year after the German invasion. The story describes Hannah being taken to an open grave and forced to take off her clothes but somehow surviving a mass shooting. The brochure then states, "I was covered with dead people. When [the shooters] left I realized I was still living. I crawled over my daddy's body. I didn't even kiss him. I went up the sides and ran away." After running away from the mass grave, Hannah roamed from village to village until she was caught by police, who took her into a forest and intentionally allowed her to run away. Eventually, a Czech family took her in until she heard about children going to Palestine and joined them.

The end of the brochure switches perspective and addresses Hannah directly, assuring her that Youth Aliyah will "be brother and sister, mother and father to you." Still speaking to Hannah, the brochure appeals to generous American donors by saying, "We give your story to the great American public, certain that many will want to make $360 a year available to Hadassah to help regenerate and strengthen you, and the tens of thousands of others like you who still await salvation." Through this publicity, Hannah became representative of all twenty thousand children brought to Palestine by Youth Aliyah and those still "await[ing] salvation."[73]

While Hannah's story may have been representative of thousands of other Youth Aliyah children who found safety in Palestine, Hannah was not actually the twenty thousandth child. This misrepresentation was employed for

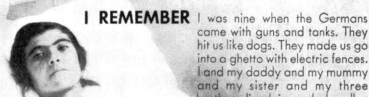

I REMEMBER I was nine when the Germans came with guns and tanks. They hit us like dogs. They made us go into a ghetto with electric fences. I and my daddy and my mummy and my sister and my three brothers lived in a dark cellar where it was always wet.

Maybe it was a year that passed. Anyway, we soon began to find dead Jews on the streets. And one day a bus came and they hit us and made us go on it, and they took us outside the town. Everybody screamed when we

my name is

Hannah

Hannah is the 20,000th child brought to Palestine from Europe under the auspices of the Youth Aliyah Movement. Her wizened face belies her twelve years. Her body is always tense. Her voice is hollow. She speaks in a monotone. This record comes from a report sent by the Youth Aliyah Bureau in Jerusalem to Hadassah, the Women's Zionist Organization of America which has been the official representative of Youth Aliyah in the United States for over a decade.

Figures 2.1 and 2.2. Hannah's image and story were the focus of the 1947 Youth Aliyah fundraising campaign in America that celebrated Hannah as the twenty thousandth Youth Aliyah child brought to Palestine. The two images visually represent the story of destruction and rebirth conveyed in Hadassah publicity materials. *Ask . . . Hannah*, brochure, Box 12, Folder: Presidents and Chairmen Circulates, 1946, Oct–Dec, OFPA/Hadassah. *Printed courtesy of Hadassah, Women's Zionist Organization of America.*

publicity purposes. A letter from August 29, 1946, sent from Lola Kramarsky, cochairman of Youth Aliyah, to Eva Michaelis, publicity director in Palestine, states, "We understand that the material for publicity on the 20,000th child did not actually refer to that specific child, as at the time you sent it to us the child had not yet reached Palestine."[74] This is not to say that Hannah's story does not reflect the experiences of a girl named Hannah or that it was fabricated, but the relationship between the survivor who lived through this experience, her voice, and the telling of her story is not straightforward. For Hadassah, the power of Hannah's story was disassociated from the person who lived it.

Nonetheless, Hannah's image and story were employed to celebrate the arrival of the twenty thousandth Youth Aliyah child in Palestine and became central to the 1947 fundraising campaign.[75] Through multiple media forms, Hadassah leaders intended for Hannah's story to reach a diverse audience, spread awareness of Youth Aliyah's mission, and raise funds to support ongoing work. Unlike "Displaced," the radio program "Case History #20,000" was not produced by Hadassah and then distributed. Rather, the script was created at the national office and sent throughout the country to be performed locally on radio stations.

The script follows the same story as the brochure, but in order to work as a radio drama, the story needed additional framing. Whereas the brochure features Hannah's story in the first person, without any dialogue, the adaptation sets the drama in the office of a Youth Aliyah worker who asks Hannah a series of informational questions; her story is revealed as she responds. Like "Displaced," this narrative construction presents a survivor's story through an interview. The interview presented in "Case History #20,000" depicts the kind of organizational setting in which many survivors shared their stories in the postwar period.

In "Case History #20,000," the character of the interviewer serves to break up and disrupt Hannah's account. Hannah, the character, narrates her experience being taken from the ghetto to the mass grave and forced to take off her clothes. When she comes to the part of her story where she finds herself lying among dead bodies, the aid worker character interrupts to say, "Yes?" and Hannah responds simply, "Well, I was the only one who escaped." The interviewer then asks, "How did you escape, Hannah?" The intensity of the brochure language that details her crawling over bodies and recognizing her father is edited out as Hannah answers, "I went up the sides and ran away." The story is otherwise the same, employing the same language and ending with the same assertion that "Youth Aliyah will be brother and sister, and father and mother to you." With this ending, Hadassah offers Hannah a home in Palestine, orienting her story toward home and the future. Yet the edit significantly minimizes the horror of Hannah's experience and diminishes the terror for a broader American audience.

The other main difference between the script and pamphlet is in the request for financial support. The print brochure asks directly for $360 per year, but the radio script ends by suggesting that listeners seek more information and leaves a blank space for the local radio chair to fill in with contact details. This was meant to follow a description of the entire campaign: "Hadassah is now engaged in a nationwide campaign to raise $1,400,000 for Youth Aliyah."[76] This difference reflected radio's reach to both Jewish and non-Jewish audiences. The print brochure was sent directly to members, former donors, or people who had requested more information—a constituency primed for immediate action. The radio drama, on the other hand, introduced the program to a wide audience, who could then contact a local representative for more information.

The blank space in the script underscores the local intentions for "Case History #20,000." Chapters were asked to approach their local radio stations for airtime, and the script was performed live. It was thus accompanied by stage directions such as "the story of Hannah is dramatic enough in its own words, the action should be underplayed rather than overplayed" and instructions on how to recruit actors, including the necessity of finding a "talented child, preferably working with a dramatic group."[77]

Scripts like "Case History #20,000" gave volunteers the power and responsibility to make the drama as compelling as possible to their community.[78] Local chapters found actors to perform and relied on the radio announcer to be part of the performance so that the voices were not those of national celebrities but instead (potentially) familiar. Such casting would have altered the accents of survivor voices, further dissipating the idea of a typical survivor voice. The local radio announcer plays a key role in the script, introducing Hannah as a young girl with "a concentration camp number branded into her skin in bright blue numerals."[79] Despite these local differences, "Case History #20,000" highlights key symbols of Holocaust narratives from that time. The power of the tattoo to serve as a marker of a Holocaust survivor is particularly interesting in this story about a young girl who escaped a mass shooting and hid in the woods in Eastern Europe. Since Hannah was never in a concentration camp, it is unlikely she would have had a tattoo at all. This symbol spoke to Hadassah's American audience rather than to the experience Hannah lived through.

In the immediate aftermath of the war, images of concentration camps were transmitted to Americans through newsreels played in every movie house across the country. Army film crews had captured footage of American soldiers liberating Buchenwald and other camps. These clips dominated the American imagination of Nazi crimes, evoking the depravity of the Holocaust and the devastation wrought on individual victims. By marking Hannah's experience with a tattoo, Hadassah evoked these familiar images and connected her story to the larger narrative of Nazi crimes. The CCDP similarly focused Maier's story on his concentration camp experience so that listening audiences could connect audio stories to familiar images. These attempts to connect the disembodied audio of radio to culturally resonant images shaped early representations of survivors for American audiences, establishing symbols that referred to the experience of Jews in general rather than individual experiences.

Conclusion

In the last thirty years, with the growth of institutional survivor testimony collections, scholars have theorized the way audio mediums disembody survivor voices. Langer has strongly argued for video testimony as the primary mode of memory making because the visual element captures meaning that is lost in written or oral forms of testimony.[80] Geoffrey Hartman has similarly asserted the primacy of video, declaring that removing the voice from the visualization of the speaker diminishes the "immediacy and evidentiality" of the account. Further, he notes, "The 'embodiment' of the survivors, their gestures and bearing, is part of the testimony. It adds significantly to the expressive dimension."[81] James Young similarly states that audio accounts without visual components weaken testimony because "the speaker in audio tends to be displaced from the words themselves."[82]

Hartman, Young, Langer, and others have created and approached testimony through video recording technologies available starting in the late 1970s and through the '80s and '90s, "unconsciously" linking the content to the medium.[83] Alan Rosen, on the other hand, asserts that audio technology offers unique value to Holocaust testimony and, in his study of Boder, finds that Boder felt audio could embody the experiences of his interviewees better than moving picture at the time.[84] In fact, Boder thought film in the late 1940s was too rehearsed and boring, and its technology made it too short and difficult to store.[85] In defending audio without any visual component as a valuable medium, Rosen cites Joan Ringelheim, former director of the USHMM Oral History Department, saying that interviews recorded only on audio have "a

Voicing Survivor Narratives

greater intimacy to the conversation than is typically developed in the video interview."[86]

Nonetheless, scholars debating medium in relation to survivor testimony tend to favor the visual, declaring video technology to be best for preserving Holocaust memory. How does this reflect back on early accounts like "Displaced" and "Case History #20,000"? It is essential to recognize that the radio programs explored in this chapter were not testimonies in the way Langer, Hartman, Young, and Rosen define them. They were not collected in a systematized way or organized to stand as witness to Jewish destruction under Nazism. Rather, the narratives considered here were created for radio, designed for consumption and entertainment—not historical preservation. They were intended as advocacy tools, not testimonies, even where we can see echoes of the testimonial process.

As transmitted on American broadcast radio, a survivor's voice was not necessarily tied to his or her story or experience, and performers had no relationship to the experience they enacted. "Case History #20,000" further fractures the relationship between survivor and voice by asking many actors across the country to perform as Hannah; as a result, Hannah's voice was reimagined in each town where it was performed. Without offering Hannah a last name, her story is disassociated from any young girl who perhaps lived through the performed experiences.

In many ways, the conceptions of survivor voice that permeate how testimony collections have been viewed since the 1980s do not speak to these early voiced narratives. Yet later ideas about testimony and voice offer a lens through which to think about the medium of radio and the available audio technologies of the day as essential tools for crafting, preserving, and disseminating stories about the Holocaust in the postwar period. The theoretical concerns of today also serve as a reminder that the authenticity and value of Holocaust testimony was not subject to the same kinds of critique in the immediate aftermath of the war. The stories of survivors in the postwar period were powerful in their own right—not representing historical truth or memory but justifying American aid for the ongoing refugee crisis and inspiring help for those who had lived through Nazi atrocity.

Employing actors and celebrities to dramatize experiences of the Holocaust and using sound effects to heighten the drama were common practices for broadcast radio, and organizations followed these methods of the medium to best appeal to a radio audience. The same was true for integrating American tropes into survivor accounts—making DPs part of the long history of American immigration was part of a strategy to sway Americans fearful of immigrants. Considering these broadcasts through the discourse of testimony and voice pushes us toward a richer understanding of how survivor narratives were disseminated after the war and who was called to speak for Holocaust survivors. The next chapter similarly considers narratives from the late 1940s alongside more contemporary concerns about Holocaust testimony, exploring questions of authority and witness as we turn to look at American aid workers who shared their own experiences working in postwar Europe.

3

Translating Postwar Europe

American Jewish Aid Workers as Secondary Witnesses

THUS FAR, WE HAVE seen how fundraising campaign materials—including pamphlets, brochures, and films—disseminated images and narratives about Holocaust survivors across America in the second half of the 1940s. We have also considered how Americans first heard survivor narratives through radio broadcasts sponsored by Jewish communal organizations, recognizing that those narratives were often voiced by actors or volunteers. In each case, institutional priorities and urgent postwar needs in Europe shaped survivor narratives so that American Jews first encountered stories about the Holocaust created for advocacy and fundraising purposes. This chapter continues to explore narratives about the Holocaust that resonated with American Jews and their non-Jewish neighbors by shifting focus to American Jewish aid workers who served as witnesses—not to the Holocaust but to survivors in postwar Europe. Letters, speeches, articles, and books written by chaplains, social workers, journalists, and organizational leaders informed friends, relatives, and broader networks about the state of Jews in postwar Europe.

How did these stories make their way from postwar Europe to America? How did they augment other kinds of Jewish communal narratives? And how did American aid workers take on the authority of witnesses in this period? Before survivors could become primary witnesses to their own experiences, the authority of having "seen" and "experienced" was attributed to chaplains, soldiers, and aid workers, who could readily convey the urgent need of Jewish survivors to American audiences.

Rabbi Herbert Friedman, a US Army chaplain stationed in Berlin, Germany, at the end of the war, serves as an example for thinking about the impact of this particular kind of witnessing. In June 1946, Friedman received an invitation to speak at a dinner launching the annual fundraising campaign of the Allied Jewish Council of Denver. The Denver council had a quota of $600,000 for the 1946 United Jewish Appeal (UJA) campaign (increased from the 1945 quota of $200,000), and its president, Charles Rosenbaum, knew that if Friedman could "tell the story, in your own words, based upon what you have seen and what you have experienced," the Denver community would "respond by giving in an unprecedented measure."[1] Yet again, we see how urgency for fundraising informed the shape of Holocaust narratives in postwar America.

At a time when survivors were largely still in Europe, Americans on the ground took on the role of witnesses, conveying narratives about Jewish survivors and the effect of American Jewish aid. Throughout the chapter, I employ the term "secondary witness" to define Americans who told stories about the aftermath of Nazi destruction. This term distinguishes those who witnessed the aftermath of the Holocaust from survivors themselves, who have become the key eyewitnesses to the Holocaust.[2] In using this term, I rely on Shoshana Felman's definition of a "second-degree witness" as "witness to the witness."[3] The term—and the distinction itself—would have been unrecognized at the time, when stories about the war and postwar naturally overlapped.[4] But such a distinction is essential for us, contemporary readers accustomed to viewing survivors as the primary witnesses of the Holocaust.[5] Drawing attention to contemporary survivor witness culture helps us interrogate authenticity and authority in regard to Holocaust narratives. We can consider not only how secondary witnesses activated American Jews in the postwar period but also what value these narratives might have now, as survivors have become the authoritative voices of the Holocaust. As the generation of survivors dies, we will once again become dependent on secondary witnesses to tell their stories.

To draw out this expanded story about witnessing and Holocaust narratives, this chapter looks closely at the work and words of Americans who spent time in postwar Europe and then joined UJA JDC, Hadassah, and other fundraising networks to inspire giving among American Jews. Consider Friedman, who could not be present at the Denver dinner. Instead, he sent a speech to be read in his absence, describing survivors as "the remnant left over from the concentration camps, the ones that were liberated by the victorious Allied armies."[6] He wrote, "They came out of Dachau and Buchenwald as skeletons. . . . You know that whole story—you've seen the pictures." In the remainder of the speech, Friedman told a different story—about Polish Jews who had returned home after the war and continued to live in danger. Hoping to "bring home" the urgency of American aid, Friedman reported, "Jews were being murdered steadily at the rate of two to three each day. Killing was taking place all over the land." He elaborated, "Men were forced, at the point of a gun, to take off their clothing, so that it could be seen whether they were Jewish or not. . . . It was Hitler all over again."[7] By describing the failure of liberation to free Jews from victimization, Friedman gave emotional potency to UJA campaigns. His appeal commanded the authority of his position as both rabbi and witness: "As your Rabbi and one who has spent almost a whole year working here I say one word. Please."[8]

Speakers like Friedman, including other chaplains, aid workers, writers, and communal leaders, became part of the vast network of fundraising established by UJA, its constituent organizations, and other Jewish communal organizations, shaping how American Jews understood the Holocaust, its aftermath, and their relationship to it. These Americans, including Cecilia Razovsky, Leo Lania, Leo Srole, Leo Schwarz, and David Boder, as well as countless others, toured the country speaking for UJA, JDC, Hadassah, and other groups, became political advocates for DPs, wrote articles, and published collected editions of survivor narratives. These men and women served as important intermediaries between survivors in Europe and American audiences, rendering stories in universal terms and through American ideals.[9]

This chapter again offers a close reading of two examples to illustrate a larger pattern. The first two sections explore speeches by Cecilia Razovsky and Herbert Friedman, respectively, to illuminate the construction of secondary witness narratives. Their work in postwar Europe provided them unique insight into Jewish experiences after the war and allowed them to narrativize the ongoing displacement and precarity of Jewish lives for American Jews. Then, I expand our scope of view, looking at a broader network of secondary witnesses, including journalist Leo Lania, sociologist Leo Srole, and Jewish communal leaders who become witnesses to the DP crisis and articulated the needs of survivors to American audiences. Back in America, these Jewish leaders brought their experiences to philanthropic as well as political spheres. In congressional hearings and other political settings, the authority of having "been there" helped secondary witnesses articulate a demand for immigration policy reform as part of a response to the refugee crisis in Europe.

Other secondary witnesses, including Leo Schwarz and David Boder, worked to translate their experiences working with Holocaust survivors for American audiences through curated collections, the subject of the final section of the chapter. Schwarz published a collection of edited accounts that celebrated American ideals and depicted individual survivors as symbols of Jewish survival. Boder translated and published survivor narratives that, in contrast, preserved the loss of the Holocaust through detailed accounts of Jewish experiences under Nazism, anticipating the testimonies we now know.

By the 1990s, survivors became definitive witnesses to the Holocaust, "bearers of testimony," but in the immediate aftermath of the war, when dangers persisted and survivors across Europe faced hunger, disease, cold, homelessness, and statelessness, American Jews served as witnesses.[10] American Jewish communal groups defined the way stories about the Holocaust were told and directed American Jewish attention not toward survivor witness accounts that memorialized and preserved Jewish experiences under Nazism but rather toward the most pressing needs of the postwar world. We can recognize the work of American secondary witnesses as essential transmitters of firsthand knowledge about the devastation of the Holocaust and the immediate needs of European Jewish survivors.

Cecilia Razovsky and the Imperative to Listen

Cecilia Razovsky began her career with refugees early in life, teaching English to immigrants at evening school in St. Louis before becoming an inspector in the child labor division of the US Children's Bureau from 1917 to 1920.[11] For the next two decades, Razovsky took on numerous leadership roles at the National Council of Jewish Women (NCJW), serving as secretary for its immigrant aid department and then as associate director for the department after 1932. Through these efforts, Razovsky became a leader in the field of refugee relief nationally and internationally; it is not surprising that she was enlisted to organize JDC's efforts with DPs at the end of the war and sent to Europe in the fall of 1944. Razovsky was only one of a network of women who managed JDC efforts around the globe during and after the war.[12]

Rebecca Kobrin has traced the importance of women in aid work during and after World War II through the impact of Laura Margolis, a JDC social worker stationed in Cuba and then Shanghai during World War II. As Kobrin describes, Margolis's success as a diplomat was, in some part, due to her gender: "NGO-led American internationalism was shaped by gender, as female NGO emissaries like Margolis both used and flouted gender norms to achieve their organization's philanthropic goals and spread progressive ideals."[13] Razovsky similarly recognized the important role social workers—a role dominated by women in the 1940s—could play in postwar Europe and fundraising at home in America.

From her office in Paris, Razovsky managed all aspects of DP aid: she served as chaperone for transports of child survivors from Germany to France, collected and organized lists of surviving Jews, communicated requests for lost family members between points across the continent, and juggled logistics for survivors who arrived in DP zones, crossed illegally into France, or needed medical attention. This work allowed Razovsky to meet countless survivors, learn about their experiences under Nazism, and recognize the challenges they faced in the postwar. Through her writing and public speaking after the war, Razovsky underscored the importance of relationship building in social work generally and in her work with Holocaust survivors in particular.

In addition to her ability to directly aid survivors through JDC, Razovsky understood the fundraising potential of the firsthand knowledge she gained through the relationships she built. In a letter dated June 12, 1945, she lamented to her husband, Morris, that her busy schedule kept her from serving as a better witness for friends and family "because they could have used the material for their fundraising."[14] Her conviction that she could help facilitate action at home came from a sense of being "right here, in the middle of things."[15] To underscore this point, she collected materials to be used in JDC publicity and hoped the stories of those she worked with would become well known at home.[16] Razovsky returned to the US later that month and took on the role of secondary witness in earnest. She was quickly employed by the United Nations Relief and Rehabilitation Administration (UNRRA) to speak on its behalf and was, by October 1945, officially transferred to the office of public information to give regular speeches.[17] In 1946, she also began speaking regularly for JDC, and she continued to address both Jewish and non-Jewish audiences throughout this period.

Among the countless speeches Razovsky gave between 1945 and 1950, one example reveals how her expertise on refugee issues and her position as a secondary witness shaped her representation of survivors for American audiences. This example provides a way to consider Razovsky's authority as a witness and, in particular, her understanding of how important it was that social workers serve as listeners to the stories of survivors, an idea still resonant in scholarship focused on contemporary testimony collection.[18] On July 24, 1945, Razovsky spoke to UNRRA staff members in Washington, DC, about the interaction between their organization and private agencies.[19] Her talk, tailored to her audience of future aid workers, addressed the chaos of postwar Europe, the struggle of DPs to return home and find lost family, and the limitations of UNRRA efforts. She tried to convey the value and urgency of working with DPs while recognizing challenges that could hamper success.

Razovsky built her speech from a number of stories about survivors she had met; her inclusion of a particularly long story about Bela Fabian, a former member of the Hungarian parliament, serves as a revealing entry point.[20] Fabian was fifty-four years old when he was deported; he was assumed dead because of his age, but as Razovsky described, he "was smart enough to say he was forty-four instead of fifty-four, and he was put in a work camp. Workers were sent out early in the morning and worked until late at night and beaten and harassed! It is remarkable that he lived."[21] Razovsky explained that because Fabian was well known, men in the camp helped him and covered for him— "they felt that if Fabian lived he could be their spokesman and therefore they must save his life." In this way, Razovsky highlighted the value Jewish victims of Nazism placed on living in order to bear witness. As Terrence Des Pres wrote in 1976, "survival and bearing witness became reciprocal acts."[22]

Much like the readers of Lang's article "Displaced" or the radio listeners of "Displaced," the audience of Razovsky's UNRRA speech had no way of knowing whether this explanation of Fabian's survival came from him or from her. They could not hear his voice. Rather, Razovsky's voice and experience were central to her speech, which she used to urge social workers to listen to survivors once in administrative positions in DP camps. To underscore this point, Razovksy recalled the first time she met Fabian: "He had to wait and he carried on terribly because I was keeping him waiting; the whole world should stop to hear his story and we were keeping him waiting. . . . After I talked with him for ten minutes, I thought he was justified in having us stop what we were doing to listen to him and his companions." Highlighting the importance of the stories survivors had to tell, she exclaimed, "They came like messiahs, they came from another world, and they have a message for us. We must, some of us, stop and listen to what they have to say." In calling on her fellow aid workers to stop and listen to survivors, Razovsky acknowledged her position as a secondary witness and emphasized the need for others to take up that position. Fabian could not tell his story directly to American audiences at the time, but he could tell it to Razovsky because she had listened. In turn, she could tell his story in America.

Razovsky identified the role of survivors as messengers and recognized the value of her role as a listener. She told the UNRRA audience, "Their hard-to-believe stories were nerve-racking, but some of us must listen. If UNRRA workers and workers [of] private organizations do nothing else but give the time and listen to their stories, we will have helped them and made a contribution and rendered a service."[23] Razovsky's commitment to listening as a service directly anticipates Henry Greenspan's insistence that survivors become witnesses through the process of retelling, a process he describes as unfinished. Razovsky seemed to anticipate Greenspan's assertion that "the essential truth is that survivors recount in order to be heard."[24]

Translating Postwar Europe

While Razovsky did not theorize about her role as a listener to survivors "from another world," she clearly understood the importance of telling for the survivors and listening for the social workers. Recognizing this early articulation of what later became a central component of testimony creation acknowledges that the process of witnessing and listening did not only develop with the use of video camcorders and the structure of institutional testimony collections. Rather, we can see how even when secondary witness accounts were employed to raise funds, American Jews took seriously their responsibility in amplifying the voices of survivors.

Razovsky noted that after hearing Fabian, she understood that "we can't ever let such a thing happen again."[25] Her work as a speaker across America was inspired by this belief. Des Pres articulated this recursive relationship between listening and telling decades later: "Having crossed a threshold of moral being by our reception of the survivor's voice, we are moved by a sense of obligation to pass it on, to transmit the survivor's testimony so that others may be likewise inspired and transformed."[26] Razovsky understood the importance of transmitting stories in this moral sense, in effect beginning the work of "never again." She saw it as her responsibility to talk about what she had seen and heard directly from survivors. It is clear from Razovsky's continued work that she saw a remarkable power in sharing the experiences of survivors to raise both funds and awareness so that something like the Holocaust would never happen again.

Toward this end, Razovsky took her story on the road, acting as a speaker for Jewish organizations. She toured the East Coast and the American South and went to Cuba and South America in October 1946, spending time in Havana, São Paulo, and other places with Jewish communities to meet with leaders and translate her experiences directly into fundraising appeals.[27] Razovsky traveled to Brazil with Rabbi Isaiah Rackovsky, a chaplain employed by JDC's speaker's bureau. Together they brought postwar perspectives to the Jews of South America. In the immediate aftermath of the war, this is what the work of "never again" looked like—seeking to end Jewish suffering by raising money on behalf of Jewish survivors in Europe.

The Postwar Adventure of Chaplain Herbert Friedman

Rabbi Herbert Friedman similarly traveled the country for UJA, telling stories about his experiences in Europe after the war. In different settings, for different audiences, Friedman told American Jews about what he had seen in Kielce, Poland, as briefly described above. Unlike Razovsky, Friedman did not focus on an individual survivor. Rather, he honed a story about his own experience, returning again and again to what he had seen in Poland in 1946. Friedman's papers preserve this story in four different letters and speeches that reveal how secondary witnesses crafted their own stories for the urgent task of fundraising.[28] Friedman's repeated use of this story in speeches underscores the continued uncertainty and fear survivors faced after the end of the war and the way their needs drove discourse about the Holocaust in the second half of the 1940s. As a witness to postwar insecurity, Friedman offered a first-person account of this liminal moment that has been largely minimized by later testimonial witnessing.[29]

How did Rabbi Friedman end up becoming such a witness? He left Congregation Emanuel in Denver, Colorado, to serve with the Ninth Infantry Division in the fall of 1945 and was transferred to Berlin on March 20, 1946, to coordinate DP centers in the US zone. For five months, Friedman served in this position, working with the leaders of DP communities and negotiating between the US military and survivors in Germany.[30]

In the last week of July 1946, Friedman traveled to Poland with Rabbi Phillip Bernstein, adviser of Jewish affairs to General Joseph McNarney, to assess the on-the-ground situation for Jews after the Kielce Pogrom on July 4, 1946. The trip proved revelatory for Friedman; he told stories about what he saw there for years after the war as a pulpit rabbi, on tour for UJA, and as a UJA executive after 1955.[31] After this trip, Friedman was transferred to Bernstein's Office for Jewish Affairs and traveled throughout Europe, meeting with survivors in Germany, Sweden, Denmark, Austria, Italy, and Poland. As Bernstein's aide, Friedman gained firsthand knowledge of all aspects of postwar Jewish activity, including daily experiences of survivors and efforts of American Jewish groups to organize and aid DP life. He navigated between these worlds with ease, communicating productively with both Jewish leaders and DPs.[32] This unique perspective made him an ideal witness to the postwar Jewish world, and his own commitment to DPs made him a passionate advocate on their behalf.[33]

Friedman's sense of moral obligation remained when he returned to America in June 1947 and began speaking on behalf of UJA. His experiences in Europe resonated with American audiences, and Friedman's insistence that American Jews could alleviate the suffering of Jews in Europe produced powerful results. Henry Morgenthau Jr., UJA chairman from 1947 to 1950, called one of Friedman's talks in New York "the most stirring appeal that has been made here in years" and recruited Friedman to tour the country with him on behalf of the organization.[34] Friedman's ability to give voice to his own experience, the postwar suffering of survivors, and the urgency of American Jewish philanthropy successfully communicated the demands of Europe. These intersections defined the Americanization of Holocaust narratives in the postwar period. And Friedman excelled at this translation process.

Friedman first narrated his trip in an August 30, 1946, letter addressed to his constituents in Denver. The letter, sent two weeks before the absent speech quoted above, was meant for publication in his synagogue bulletin, where it could be read by the large congregation and reprinted. Written two weeks after his trip, the letter expressed an immediate reaction to the chaos he had seen among Polish Jews. He wrote, "We found the Jewish community all over Poland in a state of near-hysteria. . . . Jews are leaving Poland and running, running, running." Here, as earlier, Friedman's letter is not about Jewish experience during the war but about the postwar experience of Polish Jews who continued to face violent persecution. Although he described the "haggard" faces of Jewish refugees repatriated from Russia, he evaded more explicit descriptions, declaring, "I can't begin to describe in detail all the things that we saw."

In the August letter, he described the exhaustion, fear, and frenzy of surviving Jews at the border of Czechoslovakia and Poland: "Hundreds of infiltrees streaming across the border without baggage, without papers, in a mad flight to safety. It was heartbreaking and nerve-racking to witness the indignity of this flight. Harassed and bounded, these people, the few survivors of the long terrible years under Hitler, again found themselves insecure, frightened, in danger of their lives—and once again assuming the role of the ever wandering Jew."[35] Friedman offered an eyewitness account of the postwar experience of survivors from outside the insecurity and fear. He expressed the failure of liberation to alleviate Jewish suffering and blurred the boundary between wartime and postwar. Yet he remained apart from the emotional reality of Europe's Jews; his perspective remained American. By evoking the "ever wandering Jew," Friedman provided his audience a more mythic understanding of the Jews of Europe. He defined the experience of Europe's surviving Jews as one of continuous displacement rather than as a tragedy of the DP period.

In the speech Friedman sent to Denver in September 1946, he conveyed this scene again but omitted the "ever wandering Jew." Instead, Friedman's speech rooted the postwar struggles of Jews in the immediate political context of illegal border crossings.

> They fought and clawed to get a place in the truck. A little baby started
> wailing in the pitch darkness. More and more people tried to crowd in—
> nobody wanted to be left behind. Baggage was thrown out to make room for

people. A woman cried out. Off they went, absolutely empty-handed, into the uncertain unknown future—perhaps to jail if they were caught trying to make the illegal crossing; the best they had to hope for was some DP camp in Germany, if they could get that far. But they were going anyhow, because they couldn't stay in Poland.[36]

Friedman's language here is more descriptive. The visual and auditory signals invite the audience to envision themselves at the scene. Yet both versions of the story are refracted through Friedman's own experience. He offers no quotes from survivors or entry into their lived experience. That this story, ostensibly about Jews escaping postwar Poland, became transformed into a story about Friedman's experience of witnessing is best expressed in the opening passage of his August letter to his constituents: "The Polish mission was one of the most exciting things that ever happened to me."[37] Friedman's sense of adventure thus framed his personal story and translated the tragedy and sadness of the Holocaust into American terms.

Friedman's excitement illustrates the distance between the experience of Jewish survivors and American aid workers, a distance that integrated an outsider's shock and astonishment into a story of the Holocaust. Although Friedman was there and saw, with his own eyes, the fear of Jewish survivors, he did not and could not experience the terror of Europe's Jews. The witness accounts that informed Americans about Jewish persecution were always, in this sense, secondary. In trying to depict the postwar reality for American audiences, Friedman illustrated the abyss Lawrence Langer described in 1995—the distance between the world of the Holocaust and the outside world.[38]

Friedman was not alone in expressing the pace and urgency of postwar Europe as thrilling. Many aid workers traveled to Europe looking for adventure, an impulse seemingly at odds with the emotional and physical demands of the work. Yet the desire for excitement did not diminish their commitment for the cause of aiding DPs.[39] Henry Levy, JDC director in Bulgaria in 1947, similarly expressed the particular excitement and importance of life in Berlin, the center of the demanding and urgent work of responding to Holocaust survivors. In August 1947, Levy wrote to Friedman from Sofia, Bulgaria, noting, "I miss the dramatic quality of the Berlin assignment for I know that the real and immediate problem is the early resettlement of our camp brethren." Levy thus articulated how the frenzy of aiding survivors could translate into a feeling of adventure and excitement—one deeply intertwined with a commitment to humanitarian work.

Levy also relayed the emotional toll of such jobs; correspondence between him and Friedman reveals how time spent in DP camps, even if exciting and adventurous, altered the way they saw the world. Levy wished the Friedmans an easy adjustment back in Denver because "I suspect that for some time to come your dreams will be disturbed by Jews in Camps and that Chaplain Herb Friedman will see himself wandering from Camp to Camp, talking to this committee or that committee, giving them hope and courage and feeling more enriched personally, by it."[40] Clearly, the events Friedman and Levy witnessed had a lasting psychological impact. Friedman responded, "Life in America is still somewhat strange to us. It really takes much longer than one thinks to adjust properly to the problems which are agitating people here, which seem rather petty in the face of the things we saw overseas."[41] Friedman's changed perspective, however temporary, informed the narratives he crafted for American donors. He recognized that American Jews lacked a deep identification with and understanding of problems facing Jews in Europe.

Seen in this context, Friedman's concern about the priorities of his congregants seems related to Alvin Rosenfeld's concern (five decades later) that Americans had no interest in confronting the realities of the Holocaust. Rosenfeld writes, "It is part of the American ethos to stress goodness, innocence, optimism, liberty, diversity, and equality. It is part of the same ethos to downplay or deny the dark and brutal sides of life and instead to place a preponderant emphasis on the saving power of individual moral conduct and collective deeds of redemption. Americans prefer to think affirmatively and progressively. The tragic vision, therefore, is antithetical to the American way of seeing the world."[42] Friedman sought to make his experiences understandable to an American audience by employing the kinds of optimistic narratives Rosenfeld describes. We see a similar narrative framing in radio broadcasts from CCDP that centered survivors' gratitude and optimism for life in America.

Toward that end, Friedman's 1946 letter highlights the spiritual strength and courage of survivors: "You might think . . . that the DPs themselves, homeless and without future, living on a marginal standard, would be the first to be bitter and disillusioned. . . . Dear friends, the opposite is true—the exact opposite. The Jewish DPs in Germany today have a strength of spirit, a measure of courage which I have never seen anywhere else."[43] Friedman thus complicates his depiction of ragged and harried Jewish survivors running from Poland and shoving themselves on transports by offering an uplifting narrative. To prod his constituents to look beyond their "petty" problems, he sent the following Rosh Hashanah wish: "May the year 5707 bring you strength and happiness and a deep thankfulness that you are in a position to help with all your resources."

86   SAVING OUR SURVIVORS

When Friedman returned to the US, his appeals became more explicit and his insistence that American Jewish intervention was the only answer to Jewish suffering in Europe became more acute. The transformation of his personal story into a pointed appeal was most dramatic at the June 1947 Emergency UJA Conference in Wernersburg, Pennsylvania. This "Crisis Event" brought together three hundred UJA leaders to respond to an urgent call for cash from Dr. Joseph Schwartz, chairman of the European Executive Council of the JDC. Schwartz warned that the end of UNRRA activities and the US Army feeding program for DPs on July 1, 1947, along with the inadequacy of International Relief Organization (IRO) efforts, would have disastrous results for Jewish survivors. To generate the needed response, UJA general chairman Henry Morgenthau Jr. assembled community leaders and a number of key officials who could "assure firsthand interpretation of the picture as it now exists."[44] The list of witnesses with firsthand knowledge of the situation in Europe included General Joseph McNarney, former commander of American forces in Europe; Dr. Schwartz; Eliazer Kaplan, treasurer of the Jewish Agency; and Rabbi Friedman.

Friedman passionately addressed the crowd about the situation of DPs and the immediate needs of Jewish survivors, becoming so heated that he apologized at the end of his speech.[45] Again, the central narrative he presented to the audience involved Jews escaping Poland. He echoed his earlier correspondence: "The Jews came running to us. They didn't stop, they didn't wait, they came across borders."[46] The trajectory of the story that followed was similar to that of the 1946 letter and absent speech—the frenetic pace of Jews escaping Poland remained palpable. But in speaking to the UJA leaders, Friedman added rhetorical devices that elevated the drama to engage his audience. Speaking in person, Friedman shifted the tense of his narrative from past to present and employed a second-person perspective, more effectively conveying the immediacy of the survivor experience and inserting the audience directly into the action.

Imagine being in that crowd in 1947. Imaging hearing Friedman shout out: "Take a bunch of people on a truck. Make them throw all the baggage away so you can get one or two more people on that truck, and you have saved another life or two." We hear the echoes of the 1946 absent speech, when Friedman said that the survivors "fought" to get on the truck and "baggage was thrown." The pointed "you" could refer to himself, to another UJA member who had worked in Europe, or to the UJA donors in his audience. He accentuated the role of the communal leaders in attendance in saving individual lives as he continued, "Your money—that's what helped. When they gave a kid on the border at Austria a cup of hot chocolate, it was your money." In this way, Friedman constructed a story about the desperation of Jews after the Kielce Pogrom that transformed the philanthropic work of American Jewish leaders into lives saved—a dramatic rhetorical act of transformation.

Friedman continued to speak directly to his audience, using "you" to arouse and awaken personal investment in events in Europe and, in so doing, responding to Morgenthau's call to assess the situation of Jews in Europe. The second-person "you" forced audience members to identify with Jews in DP camps as Friedman painted a detailed picture of postwar life.

> Life in a camp means getting up in the morning, trying to dress yourself with the other six or seven or eight people who are in the room. And don't talk to me about privacy. If they are lucky and they had a blanket to spare, they would spread a blanket across the room to divide one bed from another bed. One couple could live alone behind a blanket. If they didn't have a blanket to spare, which was more often the case than not, everybody slept together—a husband, wife, six, eight, nine people in a room. You get up in the morning, and you try to get yourself warm, because the buildings were wooden shacks most of the time, and the dew would seep in and the blankets would have a thin film of ice on them in the morning; and you would try to shake yourself warm.[47]

Friedman continued at length, walking the audience through a day of DP life, from the lack of sugar and milk with oatmeal for breakfast to the "tiny precious butt of a cigarette" they might enjoy to the dreary emptiness of the day ahead. He detailed the complications of everyday life: the monotony of canned food at lunch and the possibility that new supplies would not arrive from Bremerhaven in Germany.

Like his story about Polish Jews, Friedman's representation of DP life does not depict the stories of individual survivors or their experiences during the war. His stories convey a composite picture of postwar Jewish life. Speeches like his introduced American Jews to Holocaust survivors through their postwar challenges—the exact challenges funds could alleviate. American Jewish philanthropy could not minimize the loss or the trauma of the Holocaust, but it could alleviate the hunger, displacement, and overcrowding of the postwar period. It is not surprising, then, that the stories Friedman told American Jews and communal leaders focus on possible points of intervention.

Friedman's ability to express the connection between Jewish survival in Europe and American Jewish philanthropy made him a powerful and sought-after speaker on the UJA circuit, and his knack for galvanizing a crowd is evident in a fourth articulation of his story. On April 11, 1948, Friedman addressed a crowd

88 SAVING OUR SURVIVORS

of ten thousand in St. Louis.[48] His speech was part of the opening event for the 1948 UJA campaign and appeared in the middle of the program, between choral performances of "God Bless America" and "Rock of Ages," under the title "The Appeal of Our Rabbis."[49] In preparation for the event, he edited the transcript of his 1947 Emergency Appeal speech, customizing his address for an audience beyond Jewish communal leaders. In communication with event planners, Friedman noted that the speech was "pithy... direct, forthright, and not couched in particularly elegant language."[50] This was not modesty; Friedman recognized that "it does not make as good reading as it does speaking." His awareness of oral techniques informed the changes he made to the speech and the differences between the written letter from 1946 and the versions of his story meant to be spoken aloud.[51]

A direct comparison of the 1947 speech and its reworked articulation in 1948 reveals Friedman's rhetorical strategies. In the June 1947 speech, Friedman addressed the audience as "you." This dialogic approach was meant to provoke the assembled leaders—as he said, "You've got two jobs. . . . you have got to feed them . . . because no one else is going to feed them . . . and the second thing, you have got to get them out."[52] A year later, in St. Louis, Friedman changed each instance in which he said "you" to "we" to more directly address and involve the larger crowd of donors: "We've got two jobs" and "we have got to feed them." In this iteration, Friedman made himself part of the collective and reshaped the end of his address into a more forceful appeal. Rather than calling on assembled leaders to find a way out of Europe for the survivors, he begged assembled donors to give generously and rooted this request in the tragedy of the Holocaust, saying, "Six million were killed—they are dead and burned— and they now cost us nothing to support—they are cheap. The million and a half alive are expensive—we must help them, at any cost—I beg you to give."[53] Despite its continued articulation of the postwar challenges of surviving Jews of Europe, his speech also reflects how the figure of six million was already a central marker in narratives about the Holocaust.

In each of these settings, Rabbi Friedman conveyed his experience visiting Poland in the wake of the Kielce Pogrom and depicted a sense of being there as Polish Jews feverishly sought to escape to the American zone. In print, he conveyed the overlapping stories of his own engagement and excitement, the desperation of survivors in the postwar, and the role American Jews could play in postwar intervention. In person, he gave a pithy speech to the leaders of UJA and passionately invited audience members to picture themselves in DP camps and envision the fear and chaos of the postwar world. For a larger audience in St. Louis, he channeled even more passion. As the story was reshaped for each new audience and setting, Friedman strengthened his authority as an eyewitness to the aftermath of the Holocaust.

Activating a Network of Secondary Witnesses

A vast network of speakers shared similar stories about survivors with communities across the United States for JDC, UJA, and other Jewish organizations. For example, Leo Lania, author of *The Nine Lives of Europe*, who had lived in Europe as a correspondent for *United Nations World* magazine, became one of those speakers, joining the staff of JDC.[54] In the fall of 1946, he traversed the East Coast of the United States and Canada, telling stories about his experience in Europe and serving as a witness to the survivors he had met abroad. He spoke to meetings of JDC Educational and B'nai B'rith committees in Newark on September 10 and Maplewood, New Jersey, on September 12. On September 15, he spoke at a JDC campaign committee meeting in Far Rockaway, New York, and the following week visited Caldwell, New Jersey; Philadelphia; and Morristown, New Jersey.[55] In October, he ventured south, traveling from Philadelphia on October 2 to Bristol and Knoxville in Tennessee and to Norfolk, Virginia, before heading back to locations in New Jersey—Jersey City, Elizabeth, Hillside, and Kearney—by October 22. Between October 23 and 31, Lania went to Canada to speak to the Jewish communities of the Maritime Provinces.[56]

A robust network of speakers and a professional infrastructure planned tours and supported travel for speakers at large regional campaign events as well as small local committee meetings. Speakers traveled across the country from Alabama to Texas, West Virginia, New Jersey, Michigan, Colorado, and California, speaking to local Hillel groups and Hadassah groups. They were invited onto pulpits to speak directly to congregations in synagogues of all sizes.[57] This scope highlights the role of secondary witnesses in translating stories about Jewish survivors of Nazism into direct fundraising campaigns, as well as the work of Jewish communal organizations in organizing conversations about the Holocaust and its survivors through local chapters. The network of traveling speakers reveals not only the power of individual secondary witnesses but also the logistics of Jewish communal life. Stories circulated through established networks built on community engagement by organizations across the Jewish communal landscape.

UJA and other organizations so valued personalized eyewitness stories that they sent their leaders to Europe to achieve the legitimacy of having seen for themselves. Jewish leaders toured DP camps of Europe, met with survivors, and reported back to donors about the impact of their dollars. In January 1948, for example, the UJA sent forty Jewish leaders to Europe and Palestine on a trip titled the Star of Hope. The trip was as much publicity stunt as witnessing mission: a chartered flight stopped in Los Angeles en route to New York before departing for France, Germany, Italy, and Palestine. The Jewish Telegraphic Agency reported that the leaders made the "trip at their own expense," but events were organized in Los Angeles, Chicago, and New York to support the 1948 $250 million UJA campaign.[58] The trip was intended to allow Jewish leaders from around the country to "study the needs of 1,500,000 Jews left on the continent," and it was promised that "upon their return to the U.S. the leaders will report to the American public on the actual needs of the Jews of Europe."[59] Rather than listen to "messiahs" in Europe, these Jewish leaders sought to understand and communicate postwar needs—a difference that calls attention to the unique role of secondary witnesses in the immediate aftermath of the Holocaust, when many survivors did not have a way to share stories directly with American audiences.

These American Jewish communal leaders saw themselves as actors poised at a significant turning point in Jewish history. Irving Rhodes, chairman of the overseas delegation, was quoted as saying, "We are fully aware of the fact that this overseas mission comes at a time when the entire course of Jewish history for centuries to come will be determined." Rhodes highlighted the importance of witnessing in defining the historical import of the trip: "We are undertaking this arduous flying trip to study at first hand" the needs of Jewish survivors in Europe and "to see for ourselves" the challenges in Palestine that must be addressed in 1948.[60] Framing appeals through the lens of one's own eyes was part of the strategy for postwar Jewish philanthropy that generated a culture of secondary witnessing. As the Star of Hope trip showed, this culture relied on firsthand understanding for fundraising and political advocacy.

Hadassah similarly sent leaders abroad to bring back personal stories. In 1947, Tamara de Sola Poole, Gisela Wyzanski, and Martha Sharp embarked on a trip to tour the DP camps of Europe, Cyprus, and Palestine. On returning home, the three women spoke about their experiences at local committee meetings and published reports on the situation facing Jews abroad to amplify the reach of what they had seen.[61] Tamara de Sola Poole, Hadassah's representative on the Youth Management Committee of the Jewish Agency's Youth Aliyah Bureau, published numerous accounts of her experience at the Cyprus detention center. In June 1947, she wrote "a first hand story of today's Wandering Jew" titled *The Exiles on Cyprus*, and an account of her trip was published for Hadassah members in *Hadassah Headlines* in May 1947.[62] Like Friedman, de Sola Poole evoked the figure of the wandering Jew to frame the journeys of

Jewish survivors within a long history of Jewish displacement and to accentuate the need for a Jewish state. Sharp served as an important witness in representing the needs of Jews to non-Jewish Americans; she spoke across New England about the need for a Jewish state and led the advocacy and fundraising group Children for Palestine.[63]

Like the radio strategies detailed in chapter two, American aid workers and Jewish communal leaders advocated for American immigration reform and for a Jewish state. Toward these ideological ends, secondary witnesses translated survivor experiences into stories that reflected American values of democracy and industriousness. Individuals like Leo Srole shared experiences working with Jewish DPs not for fundraising purposes but to shift public opinion and understanding of DPs. A University of Chicago–trained sociologist, Srole served as a military psychologist for the US Air Force during the war and remained in Europe as UNRRA welfare director in the Landsberg DP camp through 1946. In 1947, he published "Why the DPs Can't Wait" in *Commentary*, documenting the failure of liberation to bring about freedom for Jewish survivors. He wrote, "Twenty months later [the liberated Jew] is still captive and still in jeopardy.... The victims *still* await final rescue."[64] While he noted the resilience of Jewish victims, he did not use the term "survivor" because he felt they were not yet safe from captivity and suffering. Like Friedman, Srole highlighted the failure of liberation to free surviving Jews in Europe for an American public. However, the DPs Srole depicted were not running or fleeing; they were productive and forward thinking. He described schools established, libraries organized and utilized, newspapers created and published, elections held, and work training conducted.

Srole affirmed the need for an open-door immigration policy, suggesting that 100,000 Jews and 45,000 orphans should settle in Palestine and 175,000 Jews should be absorbed by each of the occupying nations. By writing that "a million lives are at stake" and "also at stake are our own professed humane and democratic standards," he Americanized the story of the Holocaust to justify postwar intervention.[65] Unlike Friedman, who built emotional connections between American and European Jews to inspire donations, or Razovsky, who implored aid workers to recognize their unique position as listeners to survivors with stories to tell, Srole centered stories Americans told about themselves to communicate the viability of political reform. As such, his article represents productive and industrious Jews primed to become active Americans. Compare the Jews of Landsberg, democratically electing representative leadership and developing schools for orphaned children, to the Jews of Friedman's story. The image expressed by Srole of organized, politically democratic DPs argues more strongly for immigration than the desperate Jews fleeing Poland in Friedman's story. Both communicate the reality of Jewish life in Europe and the urgent need for intervention. Srole calls for political change, asking that future citizens be given an opportunity to restart their lives.

Jewish leaders reshaped stories of Jewish life in Europe for political venues as well, giving congressional testimony as part of two active domestic debates: the future of a Jewish state in Palestine and the reformation of American immigration policy.[66] Both political concerns were related to the need for Jewish survivors to get out of Europe, and Jewish leaders evoked the experiences of having seen survivors to strengthen their cases. In January 1946, Dr. Joseph J. Schwartz, European director of JDC, testified before the Anglo-American Committee of Inquiry. His testimony asserted the desire of DPs to move to Palestine. He described children, in particular, who had suffered in the concentration camps and "have seen their mothers and fathers taken from them, and in many cases where they have seen them murdered before their eyes."[67] Schwartz's authority came precisely from having seen survivors in Europe. His testimony repeated these sentences: "I have been in Poland," "I have been in Hungary and Slovakia," and "I have seen the conditions under which the remnant of Jews in those countries live today." As a witness to the postwar, to the suffering of Jews after the Holocaust, Schwartz brought the needs of survivors into the American political sphere.

Over a year later, in June 1947, Herbert Lehman spoke on behalf of the National Community Relations Advisory Council (NCRAC) and the American Jewish Conference in support of the Stratton Bill HR 2910 before the Subcommittee on Immigration and Naturalization.[68] Having served as general director of UNRRA, Lehman used his personal experience and authority to make a strong case for suspended quota regulations on American immigration policies. Like Schwartz, he repeated the phrases "I have been" and "I have seen," and like Srole, he represented Jewish survivors as primed for American citizenship, drawing on American values to justify changed political policy. Lehman said, "I have seen these displaced persons and I have had firsthand reports of their character and their activities. They know what freedom means, having been deprived of it. Their talents and loyalties would be as valuable to us today and in the future as those of the immigrants of the past. I know that they are first-rate material for citizens of a democracy and for American citizenship. The victims of totalitarianism make good defenders of democracy." The explicit connection of DPs to the fight against totalitarianism was a strong argument for more lenient immigration quotas, especially as the Cold War began. To add potency to this claim, Lehman articulated a uniquely Jewish experience under Nazism, defining Jews as the victims most worthy of American aid: "For these people, many of the countries of Europe are the graveyards of their loved ones. The six million Jewish dead who fell victims to Hitler's merciless savagery has left scattered survivors only. If they wanted to go home, for the most part there are no homes left for them to return to. They are of a people which made the costliest, percentally [sic] the greatest, sacrifices in the war of civilization against the Nazi barbarism. They have a special and unique claim on the sympathy and the charity of mankind."[69] This last point, rooted in the particular experience of Jewish survivors, was meant to inspire political action. The story Lehman told of his experience working with the DPs validated the potential for survivors to become Americans.

Curating Survivor Voices for American Audiences

Alongside this network of secondary witnesses, what role could survivors play? For them, too, having been there and having seen were powerful modes of expression. Their accounts were published in the American press and in countless memoirs.[70] In person, survivors were welcomed as honored guests at events of all sizes, from mass rallies in New York and Chicago to local chapter meetings around the country.[71] Nonetheless, American Jewish communal organizations working on behalf of survivors more often relied on secondary witness accounts than on those of survivors. The ability of secondary witnesses to translate the urgency of the crisis into an American cultural milieu most successfully fulfilled the mission of Jewish organizations to mobilize Americans and raise unprecedented amounts of money.

Yet for some, including Leo Schwarz and David Boder, the narratives constructed by survivors had significance beyond their political or philanthropic value. Both Schwarz and Boder worked to collect and publish firsthand accounts by survivors to document and preserve the experiences of Jews during the Holocaust. These efforts were not without their own layers of mediation and ideological zeal. Schwarz's collection *The Root and the Bough: The Epic of an Enduring People* (1949) highlights the optimism of survivors and accentuates the role of uprising and rebellion in the Jewish experience under Nazism. Although the collection reproduces survivor narratives, Schwarz's role as an intermediary is pronounced. The book presents heavily edited narratives that celebrate freedom and spiritual strength. We see Schwarz's intentions clearly if we compare his collection to David Boder's *I Did Not Interview the Dead* (1949), which was published in the same year but presented American audiences with starkly different narratives. Boder also collected and published the stories of survivors in their own words. As detailed in the last chapter, he collected audio interviews with over one hundred survivors of Nazism in 1946 and translated over eighty of the interviews for publication by 1956. Of these, nine were published in *I Did Not Interview the Dead*. These survivor narratives stand in contrast with those described thus far; they detail the war years in depth, reflecting loss, loneliness, desperation, and displacement. In the postwar years, such documentation was exceptional.

Leo Schwarz, born in New York in 1906, served in the US Army during the war and remained in Europe after his discharge to work for the JDC. While there, he met thousands of survivors and collected many written narratives. On returning to New York, Schwarz compiled thirty-three eyewitness accounts, including diary excerpts, memoirs, and other written testimonials (some of which had been published before), to convey "the heroic resistance and survival of indomitable men, women, and children in the face of a diabolical plan of extirpation."[72] The narratives translated and edited by Schwarz are polished and structured to focus on the triumph of good over evil, conforming to the same structure as the examples of Jewish literature he had previously published in *The Jewish Caravan* (1935) and *A Golden Treasury of Jewish Literature* (1937). These stories of triumph also aligned with the American postwar zeitgeist, in which, as Riv-Ellen Prell has claimed, a "triumphant optimism not only for American Jews, but for a great swatch of the American people, marked the uniqueness of the era."[73]

Schwarz aimed to transport the stories of survivors to America in their own words, yet his mediation determined the kinds of stories that reached American audiences. *The Root and the Bough* is organized in three parts: "The Fire's Center," "Flame of the Spirit," and "The Undying Spark." Schwarz employed uplifting titles to underscore the theme of resistance, which appear in accounts of the Warsaw Ghetto Uprising, resistance groups in the forests of Eastern Europe, and the uprising at Treblinka.

The first story in Schwarz's collection ties together the broad ambitions of his project. It is the eyewitness account of Henry Lilienheim, a young man who survived the bombing of Warsaw, the Vilna Ghetto, deportation to Riga, transfer to a camp in Dautmergen (near the Swiss border), and another transfer to Dachau. He was liberated near Munich, where Schwarz met him through his work with the JDC. Schwarz encouraged Lilienheim to write down his experiences and published an excerpt of a larger manuscript under the title "Mine Eyes Have Seen," with an epigraph from Job 13:1, "Lo mine eye hath seen all this." This title underscores the importance of eyewitnessing while elevating Lilienheim's personal testimony to biblical stature.

As the opening narrative in the collection, it introduces themes high-lighted throughout: resistance, resilience, and hope. Lilienheim details his time in the Vilna Ghetto, losing track of his wife and family at liquidation, and his deportation to Dachau. The account recalls terrors of his wartime experience, including forced labor in Riga and his presence at the execution of Avraham Chwojnik, a resistance leader who was hanged alongside three resistance members. Yet rather than dwell on details of wartime experiences, the story builds to a postwar crescendo. After the war, Lilienheim searched across Europe for his wife, and they were eventually reunited. He reflects on their reunion at the end of his story: "The pendulum of time swings rhythmi-cally. My wife has borne a child. For weeks after, I wasn't sure how I felt about my little daughter. But when she smiled for the first time, I knew that I loved her and my heart was filled with sweetness. Looking at her, I seem to see my mother, my sister, my niece, and a prolongation of my own life. She has come into this world because I survived, and belong once more to the fraternity of the living."[74] Lilienheim's story ends with a spirited optimism that brings together the loss of the war with the possibilities for the postwar. While this story, like the others in the collection, offers an eyewitness account of Nazi crimes, it also demonstrates how Schwarz Americanized the experiences of survivors. A heavy-handed mediator, he crafted an optimistic narrative that transformed the depths of human despair into the promise of the human spirit.[75]

Boder, too, approached survivors with a documented bias. He approached the project of recording eyewitness interviews with strict psychological and anthropological methodologies and intended to document the experience of trauma on individual narrative expressions.[76] His approach yielded much dif-ferent narratives than those published by Schwarz. Boder's interviews, con-ducted in over ten languages with Jewish survivors and non-Jewish refugees, do not attest to a spirit of redemption and dignity; rather, they are marked by long breaks of weeping and incoherence. For Boder, the power of survivor eyewitnessing was to create a record for future generations of the "impressions still alive in the memories of displaced persons referring to their suffering in concentration camps and during their subsequent wanderings," both "directly in their own language" and "in their own voices."[77] Survivors were not symbols of resistance, endurance, or spiritual strength. The voices Boder translated for American audiences spoke of loss and torture. Boder's project is an im-portant counterexample here—especially because his efforts to bring stories from survivors to listeners was not supported by Jewish communal groups and struggled to find an audience.

Boder was born in 1886 to a Jewish family in Libau, Latvia (under Russian rule at the time). He was educated at Jewish schools in the Russian Empire before leaving to study psychology in Leipzig, Germany, under Wilhelm Wundt. There, Boder developed a strong commitment to experimental psychology, which he maintained as a student at the Psychoneurological Institute in St. Petersburg, professor at the University of Mexico, director of psychological research for the federal Mexican prison system, and in Chicago, where he obtained an MA in psychology from the University of Chicago and a PhD from Northwestern University. By the mid-1930s, Boder was employed at Lewis Institute, later the Illinois Institute of Technology (IIT), and had founded the Psychological Museum in Chicago.[78] After a life of traversing borders and resettling around the globe, Boder became a US citizen in 1932 and settled in Chicago.[79]

His nomadic life made him uniquely qualified to act as interviewer in postwar Europe; he spoke Yiddish, Russian, Latvian, German, Spanish, and English fluently and could communicate in French, Polish, and Lithuanian. Committed to serving as the Ernie Pyle to Europe's DPs, Boder worked to secure funds and visas enabling him to travel openly in Europe, and in August 1946, he traveled there alone with only a fifty-pound wire recorder and two hundred spools of wire.[80] The recently invented wire recorder allowed Boder to conduct oral interviews across Europe, and he recorded over one hundred in two months, stopping in DP camps in France, Italy, Switzerland, and Germany. He also recorded informal musical performances by groups of DPs, religious hymns by refugee Mennonites, and speeches from DP leaders.

Thanks to the IIT's Voices of the Holocaust project, Boder's original recordings have been digitized and made available for listeners.[81] But Boder's contemporary audience was never able to hear the interviews and could only access his vast collection through interviews he translated and printed. In 1947, Boder published the first description of his project in the *Illinois Tech Engineer*, an IIT journal that did not command national attention. The title of the article suggests Boder's scientific leanings and his early intentions for the project: "The Displaced People of Europe: Preliminary Notes on a Psychological and Anthropological Study."[82] It is not surprising, given the secondary witness culture described in this chapter, that Boder's "preliminary notes" primarily tell his own story.[83] In this initial article, Boder told the story of the Holocaust through the lens of his own attempt to lug the heavy wire recorder from interview to interview in the same way that Schwarz, Razovsky, and Friedman filtered the stories of DPs through accounts of their own work. Yet even in this first iteration, the narratives conveyed by Boder are wholly different from the stories of the other secondary witnesses considered thus far. Three specific differences

Translating Postwar Europe   97

are clear even in this 1947 essay: first, Boder evokes the experience of listening; second, the survivors he cites speak directly about their experiences during the war; and third, Boder documents the interaction between himself and his interviewee, calling attention to a postwar encounter and creating something akin to contemporary survivor testimony.[84]

Boder's commitment to preserving an aural quality shows in his translation process. Rather than translate transcripts of the interviews, Boder verbally translated from one wire to another, rerecording the interview into English and then transcribing.[85] His commitment to the aurality of the recordings is also evident in his initial 1947 publication, in which he writes about his experience as a "hearer" and invites his readers to "listen to a fragment of spool 138."[86] Unlike other secondary witnesses, Boder found legitimacy not in having seen but in having heard. Let me quote at length to elucidate the second and third qualities of Boder's distinct approach. This excerpt from his article reflects his reliance on extended passages taken directly from the recorded spools to give a "literal translation" of a survivor's account to American audiences. Boder asks his reader to "listen" to Jürgen Bassfreund's description of a "typical transport," quoting:

> "The word trickled through that this transport was going to Dachau. We stepped forward, we were given a plate of soup, and, accompanied by S.S., we were sent to the station and were loaded into wagons. They were in part open, in part closed cars. We thought that the closed cars were better, but later it appeared we were worse off. When we were standing at the cars, the S.S. drove us into the cars, one hundred twenty people into each car. It was an impossibility."

> Boder: "You were in a closed car?"

> Jürgen: "Yes, in a closed car. The doors were shut. We had no food with us, and now we tried to sit down. When eighty people sat down the others had no place to stand, and there were many people who were very tired. It was not possible, otherwise one stood over the other. We stepped on other people's fingers, and these people, of course, resisted and were striking the others, and so a panic began. It was so terrible that people went crazy during the trip, and while we were traveling there appeared among us the first man dead.

> "And we did not know where to put the dead—on the floor they were taking up space—because they had to lie stretched out. And then it occurred to us—we had a blanket with us so we wrapped up the dead man into this blanket, and there were two iron bars in the car, and so we tied him on above."

Boder: "Like in a hammock?"

Jürgen: "Yes, like in a hammock. But soon we understood that that wouldn't do, because we had more and more dead, because of the heat in the car, and the bodies began to smell."[87]

Boder quoted significantly more from his interview with Bassfreund to give voice to the process of deportation. By using such long quotations, Boder replicated his own experience of learning about what life was like for Jews during the war, allowing readers to learn about the Holocaust from the words of survivors.

Both the tone and structure of this passage are noticeably different from those of the stories presented or published by other secondary witnesses. Boder invited survivors to speak specifically about their wartime experiences rather than their postwar lives or hopes for the future. He encouraged them to be as descriptive and detailed as possible. And his published work maintained his frequent interruptions to ask questions about terminology or seemingly small details.[88]

Boder's audio recordings were never available to listeners during his lifetime, and each of his publications failed to find an audience. Even in an explicitly Jewish context, Boder had a difficult time finding traction for his interviews. The Jewish Publication Society (JPS) initially expressed interest in publishing *I Did Not Interview the Dead* but ultimately rejected Boder's submission because it did not fit the society's mold. Boder's explicit attention to the tragedy of and trauma in eyewitness accounts deviated from its focus on resistance and rescue, which better aligned with American values and interests. As Alan Rosen has argued, Marie Syrkin's *Blessed Is the Match*, published in 1948, better exemplified JPS publications, which "deliberately eschewed a direct confrontation with the destruction of European Jewry."[89] Instead, Boder's manuscript was published by the University of Illinois Press, and the more complete set of transcripts in *Topical Autobiographies* was self-published. Boder worked to make the material available by personally funding the printing of the transcripts on microcards and writing letters to libraries around the country offering free copies of the work.[90]

That his work was not published by a mainstream American Jewish press is only one example of lack of support from American organizations, Jewish or not. In July 1945, before he traveled to Europe, Boder wrote to Samuel A. Goldsmith of the Jewish Charities of Chicago and declared, "I shall not hesitate to convert the investigation into what may be called a Jewish project, if under such circumstances either the Joint Distribution Committee or the American Jewish Congress should be willing to take this study under their wing."[91] At the same time, Boder wrote to a number of military offices, stating that he was "willing to modify the project to suit any requirements of the Armed Forces or of the United States Government in general."[92] As these letters show, Boder was ready to shape his project according to funding possibilities, but he nonetheless recognized the uniquely Jewish story waiting to be told by survivors in Europe. Had a Jewish organization recognized the potential of Boder's project, his interviews might have been different; he might have spent time exclusively with Jewish victims or asked a different set of questions. Instead, his trip to Europe was sponsored by his home institution, the IIT, and the Psychological Museum, of which he was the executive director, and his decade of translation work was sponsored by the National Institute of Mental Health and the US Public Health Service.[93]

The lack of support from American Jewish organizations underscores the differences between Boder's recorded testimonies and the narratives constructed by secondary witnesses at the time. Boder rejected the emotional appeals for postwar aid of people like Friedman and the heroic survival narratives of Schwarz, allowing survivors to speak directly about their experiences during the war. In this way, he preserved accounts of the Holocaust as the central event—more closely foreshadowing modern testimony collections.

Conclusion

Instead of amplifying the voices and stories of Boder's interviewees, Jewish communal organizations chose to employ people like Friedman, Razovsky, and Lania to transform the stories of survivors into fundraising and political appeals that integrated American ideals. These secondary witnesses communicated the postwar needs and lives of surviving Jews, motivating American Jewish giving according to the priorities of Jewish organizations, particularly the JDC, and providing for the immediate physical needs of survivors—food, clothing, and medicine. Rabbi Friedman documented the continued insecurity Jews faced in Poland and the pace of movement that defined their postwar escape from antisemitic violence, while Cecilia Razovsky conveyed the need survivors felt to be heard and the importance of listening. Despite having different themes, styles, and audiences, both translated and transformed stories about Holocaust survivors through their own experiences in postwar Europe and employed those stories for fundraising purposes.

These secondary witnesses, encouraged and enabled by networks of American Jewish communal organizations, brought passion, training, and commitment with them to Europe and then brought stories home, interpreting the experiences of survivors under and after Nazism through their own perspectives. As a result, their stories served to introduce American Jewish audiences to survivors of Nazi atrocities through an American lens focused on the aftermath of the Holocaust rather than wartime experiences. The ability of American aid workers and Jewish leaders to translate the urgency and crisis of the postwar period into an American vernacular and according to American ideals made them essential mediators.

Survivor voices were not as potent in activating Americans—for either fundraising purposes or political advocacy. Rather, we see only traces of the culture of witnessing would subsequently develop around survivors. Razovsky's insistence on listening and her understanding of survivors as messiahs stands out. Likewise, Boder's work to center not only survivor voices but also survivor interviews points to early ways American audiences could have engaged directly with survivor accounts.

The next chapter illuminates other ways Holocaust survivor voices fit into the postwar landscape of Jewish communal activity. Jewish communal organizations sponsored letter writing and material aid campaigns, providing opportunities for American Jews to connect directly with survivors in Europe. As we will see, these campaigns opened pathways for survivor voices to reach American Jewish homes—though still often mediated by institutional priorities. At the same time, volunteer programs engaged large numbers of American Jews and affirmed symbols of the Holocaust that continue to resonate today.

4

Sending Hope, Securing Peace

Volunteerism and Direct Aid in the Early Cold War

STORIES ABOUT JEWISH NEED in Europe inspired more than financial giving; images, narratives, and voices from DPs in Europe also activated unprecedented levels of volunteerism and direct aid among American Jews. Programs like Supplies for Overseas Survivors (SOS) reflect the work of American Jews, and American Jewish women in particular, to provide material aid in the aftermath of the war outside formal fundraising campaigns. SOS was launched in late 1945 as an initiative of several New York Jewish women's organizations to augment fundraising campaigns that could not meet all needs on the ground in 1945 and 1946.[1] As Paul Baerwald, chairman of the American Jewish Joint Distribution Committee (JDC) from 1932 through 1945, explained in October 1945, "For some time now, it has been obvious that the large monetary relief program which the JDC has been conducting will have to be supplemented by a material aid project if we are to meet the most serious needs of the Jews who have survived the last terrible years in Europe."[2]

American Jewish women especially responded to immediate calls from Europe asking for material goods. They received letters from their rabbis (now acting as chaplains) and sons or nephews (now soldiers) identifying the needs of Jewish women and children in Europe as the war ended and converted their communal efforts to meet these needs.[3] They created "Help-a-Chaplain" committees to collect materials requested by rabbis overseas; bundled items for women and shipped them directly to DP camps; formed knitting circles and crafted layettes for newborn Jewish babies; and transformed Russian War Relief work into SOS collection.[4]

SOS invited American Jews to participate directly in humanitarian relief. Like other communal activities highlighted in this book, SOS emboldened

American Jews to see themselves as the only hope for world Jewry. The initial appeal letter for SOS asserted: "You can save Jewish lives and rebuild hope from the rubble of despair. Food and knitted items, medicines and comfort goods, layette and toys are the means. . . . Through your help it will be possible to . . . provide milk for newly-born Jewish babies and children, to put toys in the hands of Jewish orphans, and to bring smiles of hope and courage back to the faces of hundreds of thousands in Poland, Rumania, France and almost every other country of the continent."[5] This idea—that the donation of material goods could save lives and build hope—was repeated in SOS campaign materials and events; posters, pamphlets, and oral appeals that promoted the project depicted American Jews as saviors alongside lists of needed goods and images of destitute survivors. In 1946, JDC assumed management of SOS and launched a network of SOS committees across the country.

The scale of participation was remarkable. Between January 1946 and December 1949, SOS collected a declared 26 million pounds of relief goods from nearly 1,000 communities across the country, sending to Europe 14 million pounds of food, 11 million pounds of clothes (including 3 million pounds of layette materials), more than 1 million medical drug items, thousands of religious items, and over 170,000 toys—enough for each surviving Jewish child to have 1.[6] This total reflected the work of hundreds of thousands of American Jews across the country. We can look to Boston, where, on May 16, 1948, 15,000 men, women, and children volunteered as door-to-door canvassers, the greatest number of volunteers for any single effort in the history of the Boston Jewish community.[7] JDC announced that nearly 35,000 families (almost every Jewish family in the Greater Boston area) had donated an average of 30 pounds of clothes each; the organization amassed nearly 1 million pounds of used clothes and other supplies.

We can see in this brochure from 1947 that even as the SOS program grew, promotion remained focused on the idea that American Jews were the lifeline for their European brethren. A rope encircles images of "ill clad" survivors eating and receiving toys and books, all supplied by SOS donations.[8] The image's caption lists challenges of the moment: "The failure of large scale emigration, the termination of UNRRA [United Nations Relief and Rehabilitation Administration], the inadequate funds of the IRO [International Relief Organization], postwar famine and inflation."[9] Nonetheless, the surviving Jews of Europe "won't give up now. . . . Their fight for life goes on." In order to win the fight, Europe's Jews needed help that could only come from America. And unlike the audacious fundraising programs described in earlier chapters, SOS provided a way for individual Jews to participate materially in the project of postwar rehabilitation.

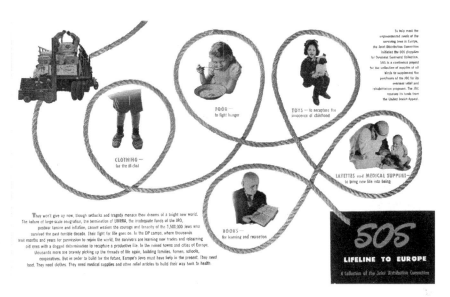

Figure 4.1. A 1947 brochure for SOS depicts a rope encircling pictures highlighting clothes, food, toys, layettes, medical supplies, and books—the primary needs of Jewish survivors in Europe. SOS: Lifeline to Europe, *They Need These Things to Live!* brochure, Item ID 646520, November 28, 1947, NY AR194554/3/5/9/1345, SOS Publicity Printed Materials, 1947–1949, JDC Archives. *Courtesy of the American Jewish Joint Distribution Committee.*

Other Jewish communal organizations similarly sought to inspire and harness the enthusiasm of American Jews to participate in postwar aid. The World Jewish Congress (WJC) Child Care Division, Vaad Hatzala's new Rescue Children initiative, Organization for Rehabilitation through Training (ORT), the National Council of Jewish Women (NCJW), the Jewish Labor Committee (JLC), B'nai B'rith, and more launched "adoption" programs that facilitated direct aid from American sponsors to Europe's surviving Jews. These campaigns took different forms, reflecting the varied priorities of their host institutions, but each allowed individual American Jews to connect with a designated child or family in Europe. As Catherine Varchaver, director of the WJC Child Care Division, wrote in 1949, "It is not enough to make impersonal financial contributions to various agencies. We must speak to people directly. . . . The warmth extended in your letters by personal words of friendship and encouragement will not only inspire the will to survive among individuals but will raise in them hope for a better world as a whole."[10]

This chapter examines SOS, WJC Child Care Division, and Rescue Children, asking how material aid programs shaped narratives about Holocaust survivors alongside the assertion that help for survivors could only come from America. Through brochures and program newsletters, these efforts echoed narrative strategies explored in the last three chapters by inviting American Jews to act as heroes to save postwar Jewish life. However, these programs functioned differently than broad communal fundraising campaigns or public advocacy initiatives; they allowed American Jews to develop pen pal and direct aid relationships with European Jewish survivors. As a result, individual American Jews could communicate directly with survivors, creating an opportunity for narratives from survivors to reach American Jewish homes.

That said, aspirations for individual relationships were often subsumed by institutional priorities, with the need for aid at scale (as opposed to between individuals) driving humanitarian activities. As the immediate urgency of liberation yielded to the prolonged postwar DP period, these programs shifted away from individual knitters, letter writers, and adopters. Organizations engaged manufacturers and wholesalers as important links in the chain of material aid and reduced initiatives to connect individual American donors with survivors. But for a short period of time, these programs activated American volunteers—many of them women—who sought ways to connect and communicate directly with Jewish survivors in Europe.

Promotion for these programs also extended the reach of Holocaust symbols, like concentration camp tattoos and cattle railcars. For example, an SOS film documenting the 1948 campaign in Rochester depicted bundles of used clothes and piles of shoes loaded onto a railcar as symbols of hope.[11] In the film, young volunteers organize large mounds of clothes, pack boxes of canned food, and load freight cars with bundles. The film then features thirty seconds of footage of a loaded train moving down the tracks with the caption, "130,000 pounds of life and hope on its way to JDC."[12] Although this film was never finished or circulated, it offers an important window into an American Jewish response that generated joyful and hopeful stories about the Holocaust and its survivors through symbols that have come to stand for the dehumanization and industrial murder of the Holocaust.

As such, this chapter weaves together three primary themes already introduced in the book: American Jews as saviors, the institutional mediation of survivor narratives, and the creation of Holocaust symbols. Efforts to sustain and promote material aid and direct sponsorship programs provide more opportunity to see these themes as central to the construction of postwar Holocaust narratives. A close examination of programmatic communications also invites us to see how American Jews engaged with narratives from and about Holocaust survivors. How did they see themselves in relation to survivors, and what did they come to understand about the Holocaust through communal activity?

To address these questions, the chapter starts with a description of the national context for collecting used clothes and explores how SOS fit into similar efforts to send material aid abroad after the war. It then returns to a close reading, this time of imagery generated through SOS and the way that piles of clothes and shoes and the packed trains that took goods to Europe predate Holocaust icons that "have been culturally absorbed and sublimated."[13] The juxtaposition between how these symbols were understood at the time and how they are understood in contemporary Holocaust memory culture illuminates about how Holocaust narratives change over time, even if they remain focused on the same set of central motifs.

The chapter then looks directly at the potential of the WJC Child Care Division programs, run by Varchaver, to facilitate direct relationships between American and European Jews. Letters sent back and forth across the Atlantic did, on occasion, communicate in-depth stories about the Holocaust, and Varchaver used the communication platforms of the WJC to amplify those voices. Finally, the chapter tells the stories of Irene Guttman (later Hizme) and Charles Karo (later Friedman) as poster children for the Vaad Hatzala project Rescue Children. Rescue Children launched as one of many adoption programs where donors could support individual children living in Vaad Hatzala Children's Homes. The leadership of Vaad Hatzala waged a broad public campaign to raise awareness of the program, resulting in a three-page spread in *Life* magazine of two young Holocaust survivors and a *New York Times* article about their visit to President Truman. Such promotion ensured that images of Holocaust survivors and their postwar plight were recognized by a broad American public but communicated little about the Holocaust. What did it mean for survivor stories and images to be represented in these ways?

Used Clothes in the Postwar Battle for Peace

Months before SOS was launched, President Truman called for a United National Clothing Collection (UNCC) to send aid and friendship abroad. The UNCC was launched by UNRRA in April 1944 and mobilized 18,000 communities across the country to collect over 150 million pounds of clothing.[14] The effort was so successful that another nationwide campaign was launched at the end of the war; the Victory Clothing Collection amassed nearly 100 million pieces of clothing in January 1946. Through these programs, used clothes became expressions of American friendship and weapons in the postwar battle for peace, as Truman announced in a radio address in August 1945: "Victory in a great war is something that must be won and kept won. It can be lost after you have won it—if you are careless or negligent or indifferent. . . . If we let Europe go cold and hungry, we may lose some of the foundation of order on which the hope for world peace must rest."[15]

UNCC publicity echoed Truman's understanding of used clothes and canned food as weapons in the postwar battle for peace. An August 1945 press release, distributed four days after Truman's address, stated, "Now that Europe's guns have cooled, food must continue the fight for freedom if starving millions are to survive and justify the price paid in freedom's name."[16] In pursuit of securing peace, American goods could be exported as signs of optimism and friendship. Truman reinforced this idea privately, writing to Henry Kaiser, chairman of the UNCC and the Victory Clothing Collection, "Without adequate clothing and other necessities of life to sustain victims of war on the long road to rehabilitation there can be no peace."[17]

By the time SOS launched in the fall of 1945, this idea had taken root among a diverse swath of Americans. UNCC worked through agencies registered with the President's War Relief Control Board, including Jewish institutions, union groups, churches, rotary clubs, scouting groups, and political associations, to collect and ship used clothing to central depots and then distribute around the world.[18] Among hundreds of the diverse groups that promoted UNCC giving were the Philharmonic-Symphony, American Retail Federation, Needlework Guild of America, American Legion, United States Department of Agriculture, National Women's Trade Union League, Camp Fire Girls, and Boy Scouts. Americans across the country had been asked to give used clothes as part of the battle for peace—and they answered the call.

The idea that used clothes could promote world peace also found traction in political spheres in relation to fears of atomic war. Hugh DeLacy, a Democratic representative from Washington State, addressed the House of Representatives about the humanitarian work of UNRRA: "Scientists say there is no defense against the awful destructiveness of the atomic bomb. No material defense. It behooves man to strengthen his spiritual defense. Surely the steadfast helpfulness and kindliness and humanity of the American spirit will generate its own energy of constructiveness."[19] DeLacy claimed that the UNCC, through the collection of household goods (an example of "kindliness" and "the American spirit"), could generate "spiritual defense" against the threat of atomic war. The Victory Clothing Collection project picked up this language in its publicity, stating in a press release that "in this atomic age, we all live on the same street" and insisting that we can "all do our part" by donating clothes, food, or other materials.[20] Asserting that the donation of material goods could fend off atomic war cemented the association of used clothes as weapons for peace, suggesting that such donations could save the world.

JDC organized the efforts of Jewish organizations for UNCC, coordinating campaigns from the Council of Jewish Federations and Welfare Funds, Women's American ORT, B'nai B'rith, and NCJW, among others.[21] Working as part of a united force for UNCC, Jewish organizations invited American Jews to act distinctly within a national campaign. Jews could participate in the effort to secure postwar peace alongside their neighbors while still addressing specifically Jewish needs abroad. Significantly, Louis Sobel, chairman of the Jewish Coordinating Committee of UNCC, negotiated for Jews in Europe and secured 2.5 million pounds of collected clothing to be distributed to the Jews of Bulgaria, Romania, and Hungary, where UNRRA did not operate.[22]

At the same time, SOS offered a particularly Jewish version of securing peace abroad, and American Jews took seriously their responsibility to provide aid for Jewish victims of Nazism. Public statements and promotion related to SOS highlighted how material aid was part of a battle not only for peace but also for Jewish lives in the wake of Jewish destruction. As Robert Dolins, national director of SOS from 1947 to 1949, stated in 1948, "every section of the American Jewish community" was engaged in SOS work, allowing volunteers "to express their faith and hope in their fellow Jews."[23] In a 1946 announcement celebrating the first 3.5 million pounds of material sent through SOS, Frieda Schiff Warburg articulated this distinctly Jewish approach to aid in the postwar world: "Their lives depend upon the help that can come only from America. Our contributions of food, warm clothing, and other relief items will help them not only physically to withstand the rigors of the coming winter, which already has set in over Central Europe, but also will serve to restore their dignity and self-respect."[24]

Blanche Gilman similarly voiced the import of SOS work, saying, "We could not restore to Europe's Jews the six million fathers and mothers, brothers and sisters slain by the Nazis. But we can be thankful that we could and did help them with the supplies they needed to begin life again."[25] Gilman recognized the limitation of American intervention in the experience of Jewish survivors, articulating how material donation from American Jews could not alleviate the losses of the Holocaust but was nonetheless more than "just" the collection of used clothes. Donating was a venue for sending friendship and love to Jews overseas in the late 1940s. The rhetoric of helping Europe's Jews "begin life again" focused Americans' attention on the challenges they could alleviate through direct aid after the war.

Participation in direct aid programs like SOS allowed donors, and women donors in particular, to feel they were contributing more than money and

108 SAVING OUR SURVIVORS

engaging directly in the postwar work of rehabilitation. SOS, founded by Jewish women's organizations, provided a pathway for communal leadership that had previously been largely denied. Women had long contributed to American Jewish communal life as leaders of women's organizations such as Hadassah and NCJW. Through SOS, women across the country became local leaders of JDC committees as well.[26]

Even for those outside organizational leadership, material aid offered a greater sense of participation in postwar rehabilitation efforts. Dolins noted, "There is a certain amount of psychological value to the giver, and in turn to a campaign, where the individual sends directly to another individual or institution. . . . Experience has shown that this value is far outweighed by the greater returns from a central campaign effort."[27] Providing "actual goods and not impersonal cash" benefited not only the campaign but also the participants, eager to develop relationships with Jewish survivors in Europe. To offer just one example from the many collected letters preserved in the JDC archive, Mrs. Alfred R. Bachrach wrote to the National Jewish Welfare Board to explain that the personalized giving of knitting circles, letter writing, and material collection was based on "relationships and correspondence that will be developed between the groups in this country and groups of women in the cities of the liberated countries."[28] For American Jewish donors, SOS offered a way to participate in postwar aid efforts by giving more than just money.

For American Jewish women, in particular, SOS allowed participation in postwar aid through traditional material and commercial activities—making, purchasing, and collecting household goods like food and clothes.[29] Religious and secular, Zionist and non-Zionist, Jewish women across the American landscape sought to help Jews in Europe through SOS.[30] Again, letters from the archive illuminate how American Jews understood their role in these programs. Mrs. Benjamin Diamond of the Bronx submitted a letter along with a layette donation, writing that she had "done a fine job for the Russian War Relief," but "while the need is great there also, I feel that I owe it to my people to direct some of my energies thusly, now."[31] Like Mrs. Diamond, many women rolled established philanthropic practices into responses to the needs of European Jewish survivors. SOS channeled these efforts into an organized program to meet the enormous scale of need after the Holocaust.

SOS promotion encouraged this kind of personal giving experience, often describing "overseas survivors" as "our survivors." The use of "our" as the central pronoun conveys the sense of common identity woven into all aspects of SOS work. At the January 1948 SOS annual dinner, Gilman drew out this idea. Her emotional speech evoked "our displaced persons," "our second remnant," "our people," "our 40,000 souls," and "our overseas survivors."[32] In this way, her speech catalogs some of the nomenclature used about survivors in this period and underscores how American Jews understood their role in aiding Jews abroad.

Of course, for many American Jews, the use of personal pronouns reflected familial relationships. The idea of "our survivors" was, for American Jewry, a personal and collective concept used in institutional materials outside the SOS context, notably in the title of Adele Levy's 1946 UJA report *Our Child Survivors*. Levy, daughter of famed philanthropist Julius Rosenwald, was a founder of UJA and became the first chairwoman of its National Women's Division. In this capacity, she toured orphanages of postwar Europe and documented the work of UJA with child survivors. Her report offers another way to understand how American Jews conceived of themselves as the saviors of European Jews.

In addition to saving Jewish lives, Levy asserted that American Jews were responsible for preserving a Jewish future. She wrote, "If we save the children, we save the Jewish people for generations to come. If we fail to help adequately, we may be faced with the tragic prospect of the disappearance of the Jews of Europe."[33] In this way, Levy suggested that the future of the Jewish people rested with American Jewish action—only American Jews could "adequately" prevent the further destruction and disappearance of European Jewry.

SOS, Materiality, and Holocaust Memory

Could used clothing collection truly protect the world from nuclear disaster? Could SOS and other Jewish philanthropic projects prevent further decimation of Jewish life? The stakes for cleaning out closets had never been so high.[34] Perhaps a more accurate way to understand the impact of SOS as a site of knowledge formation and transfer was articulated by Raphael Levy, JDC publicity director, who noted in 1945 that "it is amazing how little most of the people who are going to receive this letter know about the need overseas."[35] Levy believed that SOS could be a way of sharing knowledge about the realities of Jewish survival in Europe and the urgency around postwar aid.

Seen in this light, the ubiquitous promotion for SOS reveals how the program inserted awareness of survivors and their postwar needs into the everyday lives of American Jews. Consider that in 1946, the town of Long Beach, NY, organized four days of SOS events and solicited participation from civic organizations, churches, schools, and local merchants.[36] Summer camps and vacation resorts asked for donations, and over four hundred summer and day camps participated in the SOS Camp Program, which urged campers to make toys and layettes for DPs in Europe and resulted in the donation of one hundred thousand pounds of food and clothing.[37] SOS committees organized collection events such as theater parties, dances, and layette showers where guests were encouraged to bring clothes and canned foods as entry fees. SOS drop-off boxes with life-size cutout advertisements were placed at grocery stores.[38] SOS publicity instructions specifically encouraged the use of all possible media to "reach the people you want to contribute to SOS. This means using Anglo-Jewish, Yiddish Press, and organizational bulletins, just as much as the general press, posters and exhibits at Jewish organizations in Temples, synagogues and community centers, as well as outdoor auto, truck, window signs."[39]

How did these ubiquitous images shape an initial framework for understanding the Holocaust? We have seen images from the launch brochure for SOS—the pair of shoes falling apart, the little girls eating soup with a doll, and the older man engaged in a book (see fig 4.1). These images tell us little about survivors other than that they require aid that can only come from America. And yet these kinds of images engaged American Jews in the project of aiding survivors and activating their neighbors and communities to join them.

Let us also consider a radio ad from 1948 featuring Eddie Cantor.[40] Cantor's ad presented his experiences traveling to Europe with JDC in the summer of 1948 and seeing the delivery of SOS packages in a particularly somber tone. Like the American intermediaries from the last chapter, Cantor addressed the need for American aid through his own experience with survivors in Europe.

> Ladies and Gentlemen, going to Europe this summer has taught me the true meaning of your help to the surviving Jews of Europe. You have given more by your personal gifts of milk, fruit juices, of canned meats than one can imagine. Through your SOS sacks of canned goods, you've said to these brave people, that you want them to live and be happy. I needn't tell you that there was a time, a long time, of deliberate murder, of mass starvation, of hideous torture. Yes, their troubles are still very real. The Jews of Europe still need your help. Your cans of food, your gifts expressing trust and love. You can help this week by giving to your city SOS drive. SOS stands for Supplies for Overseas Survivors. The food line from your home to those who suffered most.[41]

Cantor's story highlights the experience of Jews in Europe under Hitler, specifically calling attention to "deliberate murder," "mass starvation," and "hideous torture." Like Levy, he called on Americans to give to "those who suffered most" as a necessary, lifesaving intervention.

These examples suggest that SOS, like many postwar campaigns for Jewish aid, referenced the suffering of Jews under Nazism with little specificity, letting

Sending Hope, Securing Peace   111

other stories, newsreels, and war reporting convey the deeper tragedies. Instead, SOS focused on postwar needs, specific gaps in international aid (namely food), and the power of American donations to fill those gaps. But what did it mean for American Jews to give material items as a sign of hope and friendship? How did they think about the used clothes, canned food, and knitted layettes sent, in vast piles, to Europe?

If we think about the SOS film recorded in Rochester in 1948, we can remember that SOS generated images of bundled clothes in trains packed and chugging down the tracks. We should also consider the May 16, 1948, SOS campaign in Boston that collected over one million pounds of used clothes and was communicated publicly as an abundant success: twenty-four railroad boxcars filled instead of the fifteen set as a goal.[42] Oren Baruch Stier has offered a framework for understanding our association of these public symbols with the Holocaust, writing that "we live in the age of the Holocaust's cultural aftermath," which includes "a sense of the meaning of the past in the present reflected in a conglomeration of artistic, literary, cinematic, museological, ritual, documentary, monumental, and other genres of cultural-memorial acts and activities."[43] In other words, from within our contemporary Holocaust culture, it is hard to see piles of shoes and clothes and trains headed toward survivors and recognize them as hopeful.

As Stier writes, "shoes, in the aggregate, are one of the most common symbols of the devastation and loss of the Holocaust."[44] The train car, too, Stier notes, "functions symbolically . . . as an icon of modern, industrialized mass murder, an artifact instrumental in the processing of human beings into commodities, whose unusable parts were tossed, literally, into ash heaps, the by-products of a kind of manufacturing process."[45] Laura Levitt similarly explores the resonance of clothes in relation to Holocaust memory in *The Objects That Remain*.[46] On seeing the mending of a concentration camp uniform at the US Holocaust Memorial Museum (USHMM), for example, Levitt notes how each piece of clothing is "also witness to the atrocities performed on those who wore them. . . . Bound to those bodies and those legacies, they offer silent testimony."[47] Stier and Levitt locate these objects and images in a context that is memorial by nature: Holocaust museums. But these symbols echo throughout multiple forms of Holocaust memory—viewed in museum exhibits, seen in books and documentary films, read about in poetry. They are central to the ways Holocaust memory has circulated over eight decades.

In trying to understand how American Jews first encountered and shaped stories about the Holocaust, we must peel back contemporary associations. We must consider how the network of volunteers in Boston and in SOS committees across the country could understand the trains and piles as "130,000 pounds of life and hope." At the same time, the same American Jews could recognize destruction and loss through similar images out of Europe.

We can glean from Avrom Sutzkever's poem "A Load of Shoes," written in 1943 in the Vilna Ghetto, that even during the war, a pile of shoes, heaped and unembodied, could offer a powerful illustration of the scale of death during the Holocaust. The shoes of Sutzkever's poem, "crushed together," are feet-less; the poet asks, "Who have these shoes left behind?"[48] Was this poem well known in the 1940s by American Jews? Were the organizers and donors of SOS haunted by the "shoes, shivering"? Perhaps not. But they had likely read a report published in *Hadassah Headlines* documenting the "820,000 pairs of shoes, shoes belonging to the victims of murder, inc. found in a warehouse in Poland."[49] Although less literary, this report similarly depicts piles of shoes as a representation of the scale of death wrought by the Nazis and their industrialized murder.

Outside of a museum context, in the immediate aftermath of the war, the relationship between a pile of shoes and the scale of death in the Holocaust was still clear. The same can be said for other objects collected through SOS that later became museum exhibits—clothes, suitcases, medical objects, and religious materials. And yet, at the time, these objects simultaneously represented hope and friendship as a balm to the Holocaust. Intended as supplies rather than remnants, they were proudly portrayed in piles to be sent to Europe for surviving Jews and quantified in celebration of American generosity. More pointedly, these piles were bundled up, packed on to train cars, and shipped to the DP camps of Europe, many of which were housed at former concentration camps. The material goods that outlived their owners remained stored in warehouses while donated goods were sent from America in much the same fashion Jews had been sent to their death: by train.

Stier reminds us, "As anyone who has ever watched a significant part of Claude Lanzmann's film *Shoah* or read the groundbreaking research of Raul Hilberg knows, trains are some of the most significant and recurring images and symbols of the Holocaust, for they represent a monumental turning point in the destruction of European Jewry: deportation via railway marked a key systemic shift from mobile murderers and stationary victims to stationary murderers and mobile victims."[50] At the USHMM in Washington, DC, an estimated 1.5 million annual visitors are invited to enter a German railcar and experience what it might have felt like to be transported to a concentration camp. As Edward Linenthal writes, the museum encourages visitors to follow the movement of Jews "from their normal lives into ghettos, out of ghettos into trains, from trains to camps"—believing that "if visitors could take that same

Sending Hope, Securing Peace 113

journey, they would understand the story because they will have experienced the story."[51] In this way, the actual railcar inspires the idea of a train moving to the camps and allows museum visitors to experience one essential element of a Holocaust experience.[52]

In the immediate aftermath of the Holocaust, images of trains similarly conveyed a sense of death and horror to American audiences while simultaneously representing progress, hope, and friendship. The 1948 short film *Placing the Displaced* serves as an example of how these multiple meanings could coexist. The film, produced by HIAS, aired on CBS in 1948 and tells the story of Sam Miller, a Jewish man from Warsaw who survived Auschwitz and was reunited with his family after the war. The film details the dispersion of Sam's family following the bombing of Warsaw in 1939: "Sam Miller was sent to Auschwitz, his wife to Dachau, their oldest son was killed resisting arrest, their babies were taken by a friendly gentile family."[53] To depict this journey, the film projects a series of images. First is an image of a group of people marching down the middle of a road with suitcases, then an image of a railcar riding down the train tracks, and finally one of the men standing behind barbed wire. Each of the objects depicted in this sequence has become symbols of the process of deportation and dehumanization that defines the Holocaust in museums around the world: piles of suitcases, packed railcars, and barbed wire. In postwar America, these images similarly expressed a Holocaust experience—and a train moving along its track was primary among them. Eventually, the film offers a happy ending for Sam, who finds his wife and two children after the war. They all find a new home in America. As Sam's family is leaving the DP camp, the film dwells on another shot of a moving train; this time, people are leaning out of the windows, waving, and the narrator reveals that the train (and Sam) are "going to freedom, to live, to hope." These competing notions of train transportation—as a symbol of death and a symbol of freedom—existed simultaneously for the surviving Jews of Europe and for American donors.

The front cover of the 1948 UJA Year of Destiny yearbook (fig. 4.2) also creates a visual relationship between trains and a Jewish future by featuring a group of young people leaning out of a train car window. They are smiling widely and joyfully, on their way to Palestine. In December 1948, the *JDC Digest* also featured a train on its cover (fig. 4.3); again, people lean out the window and wave while others standing outside the train wave back. The caption reads, "DP emigrant train leaving Munich," and the accompanying article, written by Raphael Levy, reports that "each month some 4,000 Jewish DPs leave Germany by train for France, where they board the ships that take them to Israel."[54] In describing the departure of one of these trains, Levy exclaims, "Over the entire

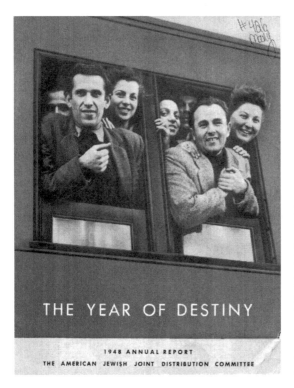

Figure 4.2. A trainload of survivors cheer their departure from Germany en route to Israel on the cover of the 1948 JDC annual report. 1948 JDC Annual Report, Box 3, Folder 2, HAFP/AJA. Courtesy of Jacob Rader Marcus Center of the American Jewish Archives, Cincinnati, Ohio, at americanjewisharchives.org.

scene hung an air of triumph." Thus, even for the Jews who had been subject to Hitler's deportations and who understood the relationship between trains and the Final Solution, trains became symbols of hope as they enabled immigration out of Germany.

In America in the late 1940s, trains were ubiquitous symbols of movement and progress, often employed as sites of patriotism. Projects such as the Friendship Train and Freedom Train exemplify a postwar zeitgeist that melded a belief in American progress with an early Cold War spirit of sending friendship abroad. The Freedom Train, a traveling exhibit of items from the National Archives, brought defining American documents, including a rough draft of the Declaration of Independence, an annotated Constitution, and the flag planted at Iwo Jima, to Americans across the country, allowing people who would never visit Washington, DC, to connect with core American ideals.[55] The train, dubbed Spirit of 1776, toured America for two years (1947–1949), welcoming fifty million Americans on board to celebrate American values and affirm citizenship as a unifying identity for all Americans.[56]

Sending Hope, Securing Peace 115

Figure 4.3. A trainload of survivors joyfully wave goodbye to Germany on the cover of the December 1948 *JDC Digest*. *JDC Digest*, December 1948, Box 3, Folder 2, HAFP/AJA. Courtesy of Jacob Rader Marcus Center of the American Jewish Archives, Cincinnati, Ohio, at americanjewisharchives.org.

Wendy Wall contends that the Freedom Train was the most ambitious example of how unity was publicly depicted as an American ideal in the postwar period, and train infrastructure was a key part of how the message was carried from town to town.[57] Cities hosted celebrations at train stations and held weeklong rallies to promote civic pride. As the vessel chosen to teach patriotism and civic unity across the country, the Freedom Train celebrated both the American past and the industrial achievements and possibilities that would define an American future.

Similarly, the Friendship Train celebrated American values and organized yet another effort to send friendship abroad. The Friendship Train was a grassroots effort that collected household goods from across the US and sent them to Western Europe. Following Drew Pearson's October 11, 1947, syndicated Merry-Go-Round column about a French celebration of gifted Soviet grain, Pearson urged America to launch a more robust publicity campaign: "This time we take steps to see that the people of Europe evaluate this campaign for exactly what it is—a genuine sacrifice from the heart of America."[58] Pearson encouraged his readers to donate food to be sent to Europe from their homes, kitchens, gardens, and fields and to "visualize" and "dramatize" the "real story" of Americans "trying to help."

Like the Freedom Train, the Friendship Train inspired celebrations at train stations across the country and ended with a ticker-tape parade in New York City.[59] The train cars were then loaded on ships and sent to Europe, where they were delivered with pomp and circumstance in France, Italy, Greece, Germany, Norway, and Austria. To assure that Europeans knew where the goods had come from, each item was labeled with the following copy: "All races and creeds make up the vast melting pot of America, and in a democratic and Christian spirit of goodwill toward men, we, the American people, have worked together to bring this food to your doorsteps, hoping that it will tide you over until your own fields are again rich and abundant with crops."[60] From within this symbolic space of the early Cold War, American Jews could see trains filled with used clothes and donated canned foods as symbols of hope. Their enthusiasm for participating in programs like SOS points to the expansiveness of an undefined set of Holocaust symbols. The spirit of humanitarian aid, of sending friendship abroad, securing postwar peace, and, for American Jews, securing a Jewish future, could all fit within these representations.

Pen Pals and Survivor Narratives in American Jewish Homes

Catherine Varchaver, director of the WJC Child Care Division, similarly believed that inspiring American Jews to send material goods abroad could foster love and trust while contributing to postwar rehabilitation. Toward this end, she launched the Chanukah Campaign for European Jewish Children in September 1945. In only two months, the small division collected 7,400 packages, 6,000 pounds of used clothing, and approximately $7,000 in donations, delivering 10,000 presents to individual children.[61] Varchaver declared that the Chanukah Gift Campaign "awakened the sympathies of large segments of American Jewry to the needs of our European brethren."[62] Such sympathies inspired three subsequent projects: the Correspondent's Service for European Jewish Children, which paired American volunteers with designated European pen pals; the Adopt-a-Family Plan, which paired American volunteers with families they could support through direct care packages; and the Foster Parents Plan, which asked sponsors to donate $300 per year to support maintenance and education for one "foster child."

These programs enacted Varchaver's belief in "Rehabilitation for European Jewish Children through Personal Contact," as she titled her 1948 article about this model of humanitarian work.[63] The Correspondent's Service allowed her to demonstrate how correspondence and personal relationship building were primary needs for Jewish children in Europe. While her commitment to the practice of correspondence and direct aid appears to have been more fervent than that of other organizational leaders at the time, the Child Care Division was not alone in creating adoption-like programs that paired individual (or groups of) Americans with individual Jewish children, families, or adults. ORT created a guardianship plan that allowed supporters to sponsor individual survivors to enroll in the organization's classes; the nonsectarian Foster Parents Plan for War Children, led by Edna Blue, asked for $180 annually to support one child; and NCJW sponsored children's homes across Europe, supporting the education and living expenses of children in them.[64] These projects were not unique in their appropriation of adoption terminology: the JLC established a Child Adoption Program and the Synagogue Council of America created an Adopt-a-Synagogue program.[65] B'nai B'rith initiated an Adopt-a-Family Abroad program in response to interest from members eager to open correspondence with distant B'nai B'rith members.[66] In this way, American Jews found ways to participate more directly in the rehabilitation of Jewish life in postwar Europe through established institutional affiliations. As Mrs. C. L. of Kansas City, Nebraska, wrote in to the WJC Child Care Division office, all were "anxious to do our bit, and though we all contribute to the various drives there is a satisfaction in doing something for someone personally."[67]

From 1945 through 1948, Varchaver led the Child Care Division and sustained the Correspondent's Service of WJC. During that time, the program facilitated hundreds of pen pal and "foster" relationships. In 1948, JDC took over the homes run by the WJC, and the correspondence program was ended. But Varchaver remained committed to the idea of "rehabilitation through personal contact" and founded a new organization in June 1949 to continue the work: the Friendship Service for Jewish Children, Inc.[68]

Varchaver's letter-writing programs provided opportunities for individual Jewish survivors to communicate with American Jews and brought narratives from Jewish survivors into Jewish homes across America. On occasion, her dream of creating lasting relationships across the boundaries of Jewish life was realized. For example, a group of fourteen-year-old girls in Chicago formed the Club Cher Ami and communicated regularly with young Jews in Europe from 1946 through 1948; the Joycrafter Group from Snyder, NY, was delighted by its correspondence with Fiorina Di Veroli; and Janet S. of New Hope, PA, met her pen pal, Madeleine, in Paris during a summer vacation in 1948.[69]

118   SAVING OUR SURVIVORS

Each of these examples suggests that individuals and letter-writing groups across America maintained connection with matched pen pals and that, to some extent, Varchaver's intention succeeded. But what did these American letter writers glean about the Holocaust? How did they understand their encounter with survivors? Barbara S. wrote to the Child Care Division office about her pen pal, George: "His parents were taken away in 1944 to Germany. He was left alone. He said that he suddenly turned from a fourteen-year-old child into a grown-up man. He said that he sometimes had to defend himself with a gun from German and Hungarian Nazis. He said that he would write me about his many adventures."[70] The Joycrafter group wrote that letters from Fiorina were "heartbreaking, and yet in spite of the horrors she and her family have endured, there is no discernable bitterness in the letter."[71] Both of these notes offer insight into the American reception of letters from Europe. Americans focused on stories of the Holocaust as adventures and showed a preference for a positive tone over a bitter one.

Hilda Herschaft of Newark, NJ, was more explicit. In a survey response from September 6, 1946, she wrote that she had been in correspondence with Minnie Chochema but "asked her nothing of what happened to her during the war for I feel that if she had any hard times she would rather forget them. My letters are very cheerful and full of news about things that are going on over here."[72] Beth Cohen's assessment of Jewish social workers in postwar America is relevant here.[73] In *Case Closed*, Cohen argues that Jewish social workers tasked with helping newly immigrated Jewish survivors start their lives in America were more concerned with assimilating survivors than with listening to their needs, concerns, and traumas. She highlights how aid organizations overlooked the trauma of these New Americans and how survivors felt silenced through efforts to move forward. In some ways, pen pals who did not want to confront the "hard times" echoed this stance, hoping to look past more difficult realities. Nonetheless, Herschaft Doris Lesik of the Joycrafters, Barbara, and other pen pals continued their correspondence. They believed "cheerful" letters could bring relief or support to Jewish survivors. Were they not, after all, responding exactly to the kind of promotional aspirations of programs like SOS—sending out lifelines, acting as heroes?

Often, the WJC Child Care Division acted as mediator, translating letters and crafting a monthly newsletter that shared voices of young survivors eager to make connections with American Jews.[74] Varchaver used multiple communications platforms, including a regular bulletin for the Correspondents' Service for European Jewish Children, promotional materials, conference papers, and written work published in the *Jewish Social Service Quarterly*, to amplify letters exchanged through the Correspondents' Service and share the impact the program was having on survivors and volunteers alike. As a result, narratives formed through the WJC Child Care Division programs reached beyond the homes of individual pen pals.

Letters shared publicly were vague about individual experiences and focused instead on children's desire to communicate with a pen pal. For example, the first bulletin of the Correspondents' Service for European Jewish Children, sent out in January 1946, includes a letter from Robert S. in France, who writes, "I am a Jewish boy, 16 years old; my parents have been unfortunately deported by the Nazis, and I am living now in a children's home."[75] This reproduction reveals no additional details about the war years, noting only that Robert was now an orphan. The except from his letter continues, "As I have no family anymore, I would like very much to start a correspondence with a Jewish family who would understand what I suffered during these horrible years, and I will show myself grateful for the affection that they will give me."[76] Such letters affirm the central work of the Correspondents' Service and speak to Varchaver's belief that letter writing could offer hope and love to European Jewish children, but they do not reveal what we might now call a Holocaust story.

Less commonly shared were letters offering a deeper look into survivor experiences and postwar lives. A letter by Rose D., a twenty-year-old Jewish woman in Budapest, exemplifies how Holocaust narratives could be constructed through a program like the Correspondents' Service. Varchaver quoted Rose's letter in an article in the May 28, 1947, organizational bulletin, titled "Let Us Help Jewish Boys and Girls Who Want to Study!"

> What I lived through under the German occupation and in the concentration camps is to other people an ordinary and perhaps dull story—for me it is an ineffaceable memory. . . . During one year, '44–45, I grew old—10 years. The effect of physical suffering passed quickly—the bald head, the skeleton-thinness are past. But psychological effects have not lost their intensity.
>
> I often remember my relatives who burnt in Auschwitz—the dear old men and women, the children; young men and young mothers with babies. I was in two camps, in Ravensbruck and in Penig. . . . My number was 93,317. It was and still is readable on my left arm. A man was only a number—nothing more. . . . If you or your acquaintances can do something for me, I shall be very happy. But I shall be happiest if you will answer me a few words.[77]

Rose's request for financial aid to facilitate her continued studies in chemistry is representative of the kinds of letters highlighted by programs of the WJC Child Care Division. The details about her own experiences and the lingering memories of her family members foreshadow richer, more personal witness accounts later included in survivor testimony collections. Then, as now, Rose's number tattoo was a meaningful symbol, representing the dehumanizing process of Nazi oppression.

Over a year later, in October 1948, Varchaver published another letter from Rose. This one more explicitly identifies the connection between writing about her Holocaust story and asking for financial aid. The Correspondents' Service bulletin included the following letter: "When I began to write to you I made it first to become material support [sic]. Therefore, I gave you an account of the events of my deportation. I wrote about the sufferings of European Jews, etc. I made it, because I remembered the kindness of American Jews, whom I met in Germany, and who were so kind to us liberated Jews, as if they were our relatives. . . . I was not disappointed, when I wrote to you. I received the support, packages, books, letters. You send them, as if you were my relative."[78] This letter frames Rose's storytelling as a successful means of achieving her goal of financial support. We can be more assured that this letter reflected a success for Varchaver—that is, it represented proof that correspondence programs could succeed in sending hope and friendship.

The story of Oskar L.'s letter further exemplifies the power survivor narratives had to motivate and the way organizations shaped survivor accounts to best address constituents. Varchaver received a letter dated September 8, 1946, from Mrs. R. of Brisbane, Australia, which included a copy of a letter from thirteen-year-old Oskar from Budapest.[79] Mrs. R. described Oskar's letter as "a pathetic and, at the same time, deeply tragic story. This letter created a miracle here. I don't know how to say anymore. The letter speaks for itself. It has the power to break through the hard shell of human egoism and goes straight to the heart. You, too, might use this boy's letter to support and facilitate the noble purpose of your work."[80] Mrs. R.'s letter is a reminder of the seriousness with which donors took up the work of humanitarian aid in the aftermath of the war. Mrs. R., her network of volunteers, Varchaver, and others who created and sustained pen pal relationships through the Correspondents' Service were moved by the stories they heard; they participated in the "noble work" of communicating directly with young Holocaust survivors and believed that such efforts could bring relief and aid to those in need.

That these stories were also used in the promotion of the Correspondents' Service does not undermine the sincerity and authenticity of the exchanges. Rather, the use of Oskar's story in promotion speaks to the way Holocaust narratives circulated at the time and to the global reach of Jewish communal initiatives. Varchaver distributed full copies of the letter, along with Mrs. R.'s introduction, throughout the WJC offices and included an excerpt of his letter in her presentation to the 1947 National Conference of Jewish Social Welfare and in a subsequent paper published in the *Jewish Social Service Quarterly*. In the paper, she quoted Oskar as writing, "My dearest father and beloved brother of 12 were deported and we never heard from them again. I have not seen my mother's face otherwise but sad. However, when reading your letter, I saw my mother's face change, even smiling. She said, 'Tell me, my child, is this a dream or is it reality? Is there someone in the world who is willing to take an interest in us?'"[81] In this excerpt, Varchaver communicated only one small part of Oskar's Holocaust story, the story of his father's deportation; she mainly chose to transmit his and his mother's joy and gratitude for the friendship and support offered through correspondence.

Oskar's full letter details his trials during the war. Oskar wrote to Mrs. R. about how his mother smuggled him out of the Budapest Ghetto and into a Christian Red Cross Institute just before the bridges in the city were bombed. When he heard that Budapest had been liberated, he found his way back to the city but could not find his mother. He wrote that he had tried to find any relative, but all of their homes were empty and destroyed. He continued: "By coincidence, I was passing a big yard and there I saw a heap of 150 dead Jewish women. Somebody told me that this was a part of the Jewish victims. I stopped there almost frozen to the marrow and I began to sob. Dear Lord, is it possible that my mother is here? Terrible, terrible! What am I to do in this world? No father, no brother! All relatives dead! I must put an end to my sufferings. And I decided to commit suicide."[82] As Oskar turned away, a woman approached him who knew his mother and told him that she was alive in a camp just outside Budapest. He was reunited with her, and a few days later they returned to their bombed-out home, where they continued to live.[83] The complete letter conveys a personal Holocaust story with deep emotion and unique details.

Varchaver distributed the longer story, but her presentation to social workers—people trained to work with survivors like Oskar—filtered out the despair of his experiences, focused on the successful results of forging personal connections, and aimed to inspire other social workers to carry out projects based on emotional rehabilitation. We hear echoes here of Razovsky's call to social workers to give their time to listen to Holocaust survivors. Yet Varchaver's advice is different from Razovsky's. Where Razovsky urged social workers to listen to each individual story—to stop and really listen—Varchaver suggests that the power of survivor stories is not in their individual details but in their collective representation. In fact, in reference to the Holocaust narratives of European Jewish children, Varchaver noted, "In different ways, they all tell the same story."[84]

For Varchaver, the recovery from pain and loss illuminated the value of programs like the Correspondent's Service. Her process of excerpting letters for published papers and the Child Care Division newsletters favored expressions of gratitude and joy that communicated that the children found "an atmosphere of warm friendship" through pen pal relationships without revealing the emotional and physical challenges they lived through.[85] In this way, Varchaver's mediation is less like Razovsky's and more like the narratives disseminated by the CCDP or Hadassah, highlighting an urge to look forward and forget the past. Varchaver's redactions are a reminder that at the time, Holocaust survivors were often represented not through their experiences under Nazism but through the success of communal projects aimed to aid them in their postwar struggles. This was true even of programs focused particularly on individual rehabilitation.

By prioritizing hope over despair, the excerpts fit the ethos of postwar America and echoed fundraising campaigns that "looked to the future to blot out the past." Rose's letters once again serve as a particularly articulate example. In her 1947 paper, Varchaver excerpted from Rose's May 12, 1947, letter:

> You American Jews send us, Europeans, presents and support, to unknown persons, living in the other half of the globe, as if it would be the most natural thing in the world. If it is unprecedented in history—what the Nazis did to European Jewry, so it is unprecedented, too, what the Americans did along economic lines after the war for the 'shoerit hapleta' for the rest of Jewry. We see in you the Jewish solidarity, the acceptance of the common Jewish fate. Knowing this, it is easier for us to accept your support and we hope that very soon, we shall not need it any more.[86]

Rose expresses gratitude for the economic support of American Jews and apparently took to heart the sense of Jewish community the WJC intended to spread.[87] She also succinctly articulates the American response to the desperation of the "shoerit hapleta" as a heroic feat.[88]

Rescue Children and Mass Appeal for the Future of Jewish Life

Herbert Tenzer, chairman of Rescue Children, quickly moved away from facilitating direct relationships, seeking mainstream advertisements and celebrity endorsements to solicit financial donations in support of kosher children's homes. Vaad Hatzala, an emergency committee created by the Union of Orthodox Rabbis of the United States and Canada, launched its Rescue Children campaign in 1946 to support child survivors in religious children's homes across

Europe.[89] It called for "foster parents" to donate $365/year ($1/day) to support a child. Initially, Rescue Children called on donors to write letters and send small packages because the Jewish children in Europe, Tenzer noted, "need the love and affection which we, in America, can bring to them even though it is only through our support and by means of correspondence, occasional remembrance, and birthday gifts."[90]

Yet the organization quickly abandoned the work of facilitating relationships. It shifted focus to mass publicity and succeeded in elevating the work of Rescue Children through public relations. In 1946, the organization sponsored an "adoption" by Mayor William O'Dwyer of New York, pairing him with eight-year-old Gaston Maurice Friedman of Poland, who lived at a Rescue Children home in Belgium. The *Herald-Tribune* ran a large picture of Mayor O'Dwyer receiving his adoption certificate from a committee of Polish rabbis. The image is striking: the mayor in a suit surrounded by three orthodox rabbis with beards and hats solemnly exchanging the certificate. The caption explains, "The committee of rabbis will pay for the care of the boy for one year in the mayor's name."

The publicity investment continued to pay off. In April 1947, Rescue Children distributed a press release with a photo of Gaston wearing a beret and holding a pen set sent to him by Mayor O'Dwyer.[91] At the 1947 fundraising dinner for Rescue Children, Mayor O'Dwyer presented a bicycle for Herbert Tenzer to take overseas and hand deliver to Gaston. The master of ceremonies for the dinner later said, "This is the first time we have ever seen a bike with a throbbing heart and I think it is really a symbol. It is not just a bike. And I am sure it won't be just the mayor's kid that will ride that bike, but lots of kids are going to get a chance to develop their limbs on that bicycle."[92] Photos of Gaston on the bike circulated around the New York press following Tenzer's trip to Europe and appeared in the *New York Times* on July 4, 1947.[93] This kind of publicity succeeded in perpetuating public interest in the problem of war orphans and robust American response without communicating anything about the Holocaust.

In October 1947, Rescue Children brought two young survivors from France to New York for a ten-day publicity blitz. The trip was covered by *Life* magazine, and the November 17, 1947, edition featured three pages of images of young Irene Guttman and Charles Karo under the title "Orphans Clothed."[94] Irene and Charles were photographed around New York City in a variety of posed scenarios: trying on new clothes (fig. 4.4), carrying stuffed animals while gazing up at skyscrapers, and grabbing, wide-eyed, at a magnificent pile of sandwiches (fig. 4.5).[95]

Figures 4.4 and 4.5. Images of Irene Guttman and Charles Karo in and around New York City celebrating the efforts of American Jewish sponsors who raised money to support Jewish orphans. These images depict the amazement and abundance of America in contrast to the destruction of war and scarcity in postwar Europe. "Orphans Clothed," *Life* magazine, November 17, 1947, 57, 58.

Sending Hope, Securing Peace

The trip continued. On October 20, 1947, Irene and Charles were the guests of honor at the annual gala luncheon and fashion show of Busy Buddies, a New Jersey–based women's group that sponsored the Flublaines Children's home under Rescue Children Care.[96] Three days later, Irene and Charles visited the White House and met President Truman. These events were covered by national and local press.[97] Like the mayor's sponsorship, this kind of publicity sparked attention for Rescue Children and Busy Buddies but brought little awareness to the experiences of either Charles or Irene during or even after the war. The images in *Life* were posed to focus on the joys of American life and celebrate those who had sponsored the trip for these two young children. The accompanying article included no detail about their wartime experiences, noting only that "both of Irene's parents were exterminated in a concentration camp. Charles' father was killed and his mother died of starvation."[98]

Rather than tell a story about the Holocaust, *Life* magazine told an American story about abundance and consumerism.[99] Irene and Charles were poster children who signified the desperation of postwar Europe, not embodied survivors who could speak about their own experiences. The publicity worked for Rescue Children and Busy Buddies. As *Life* reported, "The sight of Irene and Charles at daily luncheons and parties has already touched so many hearts that donations to Busy Buddies, Inc. have jumped 30%."[100] That the presence of Irene and Charles in America sparked participation in the adoption program speaks to the importance of children as symbols of the Holocaust and the resonance of America as part of a Holocaust story.

The article, the luncheon, and other publicity surrounding Irene and Charles were joyous and celebratory, drawing optimism and hope from the despair of the children's lives. For the ten-day trip, this American spirit prevailed. But Rescue Children's involvement with Irene and Charles did not end after the publicity tour. The two children were intended to return to their children's home in France after their visit to tell other survivors "about the Busy Buddies and the United States of America."[101] However, both Irene and Charles remained in the United States when Rescue Children leadership decided they could not send the children back to the depravation in Europe after having shown them the comforts of America.[102] Charles lived for some time with the Gut family on Long Island before being placed with Helen and Ernst Friedman in 1950.[103] By September 1951, Charles was enjoying a fully American Jewish life with the Friedmans, preparing for his Bar Mitzvah, making the JV basketball team, and opening a checking account.[104] On March 4, 1952, the Friedmans legally adopted Charles, and he took their name. They were eager to bring Charles's

126 SAVING OUR SURVIVORS

sister, Helene, to America; she was living with them by 1952, although her adoption was not legalized until 1956.[105]

Efforts by Tenzer and William Novick of Rescue Children also resulted in Irene Guttman's adoption by the Slotkyn family of Lawrence, NY. Like the Friedmans, the Slotkyns committed to reuniting Irene with her twin brother, Rene, and pursued his immigration for over two years. In 1950, Irene was finally reunited with Rene, who was also eventually adopted by the Slotkyn family.

Irene and Charles represented, in one sense, great successes for Rescue Children and all adoption-like programs. They were both legally adopted in the US and reunited with family members through Rescue Children's efforts. Their actual adoptions were exceptional, but their travel to the US resulted in extensive symbolic adoptions of children who had survived the Holocaust—adoptions in which "parents" and "children" would never meet. Their stories illustrate how representations of Holocaust survivors were manufactured by these kinds of programs to keep them going. As poster children for Rescue Children, Irene and Charles toured the US not as part of a healing process but to appeal to American donors and spread awareness of the Rescue Children's program. Extant public narratives from *Life* magazine and multiple newspapers suggest that Americans were moved to help orphans like Irene and Charles—not by the details of wartime experiences but by the aid and joy they could bring to survivors of Europe.

Conclusion

I want to share two stories by way of conclusion. First, despite the celebrations and public displays of success, SOS struggled to provide clothes that were of value to DPs in Europe. Memos from Europe suggest that the old items given by American Jewish donors were useless and did not meet the gap left by international aid efforts.[106] Donated clothes—cleaned out of closets—were ratty and often had holes. JDC established workshops in DP camps, providing sewing machines where "skilled workers repaired and remodeled garments."[107] But JDC workers in Europe offered sharp criticism that high-heeled shoes, gowns, and fur coats donated through SOS were unsuitable. Adele Levy, chairman of the UJA National Women's Division, reported that on visiting a JDC-sponsored children's home in Paris, she saw "long rows of tiny fur coats."[108] She wrote, "They were coats which the furriers guild of Paris had contributed . . . it was somewhat incongruous to see these tiny tots running around in fur coats and shoes that were full of holes."

UNCC faced the same challenge in reference to inappropriate clothing donations—especially fur coats. Anticipating such problems, it included a note in some advertisements that "evening dresses, tuxedos, and dress suits cannot be used."[109] Nonetheless, a fur dealer donated twelve coats to UNCC; while the organization publicly celebrated the generosity of the gift, internal memos detail a debate about how to deal with the coats that resulted in their discreet sale for additional aid money.[110]

Reports from JDC staff in Europe suggest that such donations worked against the SOS intention of sending hope to survivors. As Yehuda Bauer has found, "Some complaints spoke of the self-esteem of Jewish survivors being undermined by such gifts. One must, however, understand that that was not the spirit in which these things were sent. People in Ohio, Brooklyn, or Seattle had no clear picture of the life of Jews in Europe or Shanghai, and sent what they could spare, and felt proud doing so."[111] The dissonance between survivor needs and material donations raises questions about how much American Jews really understood what Jewish survivors had lived through. As seen from SOS promotion, it may have been very little.

But let us imagine these children, Holocaust survivors who had been hidden and forced to live in attics or under assumed identities, children who had just been liberated from concentration camps and work camps, who had lost their families, walking around in fur coats. Or let us imagine war victims anywhere around the world wearing tuxedos because that was what they were given at an aid depot, that was all that fit, all that was left.

Let us hold on to that image as I offer a second closing story. In a 1995 oral history recorded by Irene (Guttman) Hizme at the USHMM, she remembers the following story:

> One day a shipment came and there were these beautiful red sandals and I had been wearing brown shoes and this plain dress. We wore the same cloth- ing every single day except for Shabbat, and I really wanted those red shoes desperately. So, when we got to trying them on the shoes were really tight on me but I said, "They feel great. They're perfect. I love them." I got them. The next day we were on an outing near Paris and we went on this long walk and I'm walking in my red sandals and before very long I can barely walk because I've got blisters and sores and my feet are bleeding. The shoes don't fit me. The shoes don't fit and the counselor who was with us noticed and looked at my feet and said "Why did you say that they fit?" "I wanted red shoes and they were the only red shoes." I hated my brown shoes. The upshot of the story was they took the red shoes away from me, but they had to buy me shoes and I got white, white sandals.[112]

This is near the end of the recorded interview, as Hizme is showing a set of memorabilia to the interviewer. She pulls out a folder of letters and tells this story. She laughs, recognizing her own vanity. But she also looks proud, triumphant even, as though the white sandals were the prize and worth all the blistered, sore feet. The memory is lovely, not the kind of memory at the center of a Holocaust testimony. It speaks to the importance of the postwar in Holocaust narratives and to what is lost when survivor testimonies jump from liberation to new life.

We should think about these stories together. Maybe some of those donations were inappropriate. Maybe they do suggest that the promotional campaign for SOS needed more information about the Holocaust and less celebration of American prosperity. But maybe there was something valuable in Catherine Varchaver's approach to children in postwar Europe who were sitting in group homes, traumatized and uncertain about their future. Maybe what they needed at the time was some kindness from America, a gift just for them, some red shoes that fit horribly and made their feet hurt.

Irene has recorded many testimonies over the years, including three with her brother Rene for the USHMM.[113] She also spoke at schools about her experiences during the Holocaust and was featured in a documentary titled *Rene and I*.[114] As a regular speaker about her experiences, Irene gave a range of interviews, and each of these expressions of her testimony is fundamentally different from the images of her at nine years old in *Life* magazine. Between then and now, Holocaust testimony has been formalized. We have expectations about how a Holocaust story should sound or look. We have a sense of the progression of the story from one of fear and persecution to ghettoization to deportation. Most importantly, Irene became empowered to tell her own story. She controls what she says and how and when she shares parts of her experiences.

In 1947 and throughout the second half of the 1940s, survivors did not have this kind of agency. Instead, the work of American Jews and Jewish organizations to provide material aid shaped their stories. But that does not mean the stories were without power. The stories crafted, promoted, shared, and publicized through programs like SOS, the Correspondents' Service, and Rescue Children invited American Jews to act as saviors in response to material and emotional needs of survivors. And they did. They gave old clothes, canned food, layettes, and small Chanukah gifts. They wrote letters and sent money. In so doing, they saw themselves in the stories of Holocaust survivors and became the lifelines that kept Jews and a Jewish future alive.

Conclusion

Toward a Longer History of American Holocaust Memory

BY 1953, SURVIVORS WERE, for the most part, no longer DPs or refugees, resolving the multiplicity of survivor identities that proliferated during the postwar period. US administration of DP camps had ended, and the majority of Jewish survivors had been resettled.[1] Survivors who immigrated to America had started to adapt to American life, and a new story of survivors emerged—one that portrayed a neat ending in new homes, a tidy conclusion to the messiness of the DP period. It is this narrative that entered into American pop culture on May 27, 1953, when Hanna Bloch Kohner became the first Holocaust survivor to appear on TV as the featured guest on *This Is Your Life*.[2] Just as broadcast radio had allowed survivor voices to reach a broad American audience, network television depicted survivors as embodied individuals for millions of viewers, and Kohner became the first survivor to tell her story in this medium.

Kohner was young, pretty, and, according to host Ralph Edwards, "looked more like an American college co-ed than a survivor of Nazi death camps."[3] She spoke excellent, almost accentless English, and her husband, a Czechoslovakian Jew by birth, had served in the US Army during the war. These details made Kohner an ideal but atypical representative of Jewish Holocaust survivors for American TV. Hanna's story is depicted like all other stories on *This Is Your Life*: significant people in her life wait offstage and surprise her as Edwards narrates each turn in her journey. He describes Hanna's refuge in Amsterdam after Czechoslovakia was invaded by Nazi Germany, followed by her deportation to a series of transport, concentration, and extermination camps: first, Westerbork, then Theresienstadt, Auschwitz, and Mauthausen.[4] Throughout the show, Hanna is reunited with other survivors, including her friend Eva and her brother, whom she had not seen in a decade.

Through the show's format, Hanna's story is transformed, as Jeffrey Shandler suggests, from one "of rupture, loss and displacement . . . into a cohesive narrative of triumph over adversity."[5] And yet, Hanna's interactions with Edwards and the surprise guests complicate the composed nature of the show's template. Verbally, Hanna responds to each new reunion with joy, repeatedly exclaiming, "Oh, isn't this wonderful." Her brother is also delighted and, on being reunited with Hanna, exclaims, "This is the happiest day in all my life." The juxtaposition between the joy of the reunions and the tragedy of the story narrated by Edwards is jarring to watch, and Hanna's facial expressions betray her sense of loss. She repeatedly covers her face with her hands to shield tears and discomfort.[6] When her brother appears on stage, she hugs him so tightly and for so long that he has to coax her to sit back down and rejoin the show. At the end of the episode, Edwards summarizes Hanna's experience, declaring, "The never to be forgotten tragic experiences of your life, Hanna, have been tempered by the happiness you've found here in America."[7] Then, Edwards announces that viewers should donate to UJA to help other people like Hanna and that the show's sponsor, makeup company Hazel Bishop, will be the first to donate, sending $1,000 to UJA in her name.[8]

That Hanna's Holocaust story was told as one of haven in America was not unusual for the postwar period and echoes many of the stories detailed in this book. In fact, Hanna's episode reflects many of the themes explored here, including the centrality of immigration in telling Holocaust narratives, the role of fundraising in depicting survivors for American audiences, and the spirit of optimism and triumph that marked so many postwar stories. Each of these narrative strategies defined how American Jews first encountered stories about the experiences of Holocaust survivors, and the transformation of Hanna's story into the *This Is Your Life* model did not deviate from accepted norms at the time. That her story should be told on national television, however, was unusual, offering a significant challenge to scholars who assert that America did not confront the Holocaust in the postwar period and to a broader audience that has accepted this received knowledge about postwar silence.

But Hanna's story offers more than another example of how stories about the Holocaust circulated in postwar America. It provides an opportunity to consider how contemporary expectations about Holocaust survivor narratives impact our understanding of Holocaust memory and the history of Holocaust representation in America. On March 4, 2011, the popular radio show *This American Life* aired an episode titled "Oh, You Shouldn't Have," which features four stories about problematic gifts. In the show's first act, reporter Allison Silverman analyzes Kohner's episode of *This Is Your Life*.[9] Silverman's assessment is unsympathetic. She starts by condemning Edwards's narration that

Conclusion

recounts dangerous showers of liquid gas alongside a celebration of Hanna's life in America. However, Silverman also sums up what she sees as the gift of Kohner's episode: "Calling anyone a patriot in front of 40 million Americans is nice. Calling a Jewish immigrant from Czechoslovakia, a Communist country, a patriot is more than nice." Silverman's point is that in May 1953, a month before the execution of the Rosenbergs, being identified as American was a powerful statement of acceptance, especially for a Jewish immigrant. In this way, Silverman recognizes the overlapping narratives of the Holocaust and the Cold War, an important historical marker that identified Jewish survivors as warriors for peace in battles for immigration reform and humanitarian aid. But Silverman wields sarcasm to mock the material gifts Kohner received as a participant on the show, including a copy of the episode, a projector, a mirrored lipstick case, and a fourteen-karat gold charm bracelet, about which Silverman jokes, "It's the kind of Holocaust charm bracelet you pass down to your kids."[10] But how would viewers in 1953 have understood those gifts? Silverman acknowledges that Edwards used the show to help people and that at the time, "there were just no rules for how" to tell the story of a Holocaust survivor.

In many ways, Silverman is right: in the immediate postwar period, there were no rules for how to tell the story of a Holocaust survivor, and there were equally no rules for describing the Holocaust. She is also right when she asserts that the term "Holocaust" was years away from standardized use. Overall, Silverman's critique reflects an enormous shift in cultural norms regarding Holocaust narratives between 1953 and 2011 and exposes contemporary assumptions about how Holocaust survivor narratives should be told. Silverman cannot disguise her disapproval for the celebratory way Edwards chooses to tell Hanna's story. Her report takes for granted that a 2011 audience would hear the "wholesome all-American spirit" and "game show tactics" of *This Is Your Life* as inappropriate for talking about the Holocaust.[11] Silverman's indignation serves as a reminder to recognize the specific context of postwar memory while inviting questions about a longer history of Holocaust memory construction.

***

Kohner's episode of *This Is Your Life* marks a significant transition for Holocaust survivor representation in America. The episode depicts a survivor not as a helpless figure wrapped in rags; instead, a survivor like Hanna is a beautiful, vivacious young woman with a comfortable American life. The UJA had referred to survivors as "New Americans" from the beginning of the postwar period, consciously depicting the resilience and strength of DPs who could one day become citizens. By 1953, Hanna's story aptly fit this cohesive narrative arc. The desperate needs of the postwar period no longer defined the content of survivors' narratives because their futures seemed assured. It was as though the promise of liberation, a promise failed in so many postwar narratives, was resolved by 1953, and the survivors who were "working towards the future to blot out the past" had found that future.[12]

Hanna's episode marks the end of the immediate postwar moment for this study, even as the appeal for UJA serves as a reminder that American Jewish humanitarian intervention abroad did not end. American Jewish communal activity continued to generate representations of Holocaust survivors. Nonetheless, the end of the DP crisis, alleviated by the creation of the state of Israel and subsequent reduction in immigration pressure, changed the nature of American Jewish fundraising efforts. As survivors found new homelands and adjusted to life in Israel, America, or elsewhere, the uncertainty and indeterminacy of postwar survivor narratives ended, and the liminality of the postwar period lost its potency in fundraising appeals. Narratives about the Holocaust could conclude with happy endings, as Hanna's joy in America demonstrates, and as a result, liberation could become a definitive marker signaling the end of Jewish persecution. The resolution of these narratives highlights how Jewish organizations, having seen to the physical welfare of survivors, depicted the success of their postwar response.

During the first few postwar years, it was exactly the spaces and struggles of the DP experience that most powerfully motivated American Jewish action. Communal organizations became driving mediators in this period, translating the reality of postwar Europe for American Jews to tug at their heartstrings and purse strings. This was not an empty goal; Jews in Europe faced unprecedented challenges as they emerged from concentration camps or came out of hiding, searched for family members, and tried to rebuild their lives. Narratives constructed for fundraising appeals thus defined early Holocaust narratives as DP stories, depicting life in DP camps and the continued violence and insecurity of Jewish life in Eastern Europe. American Jews responded to these stories in extraordinary ways, raising ever more money, advocating for immigration possibilities in Palestine and America, and engaging in volunteer efforts like clothing collection and letter writing.

Nonetheless, competing visions for a Jewish future complicated a cohesive representation of survivors for American audiences as Jewish organizations across the political, cultural, and religious landscape defined opposing priorities for postwar aid. Zionist organizations like Hadassah and the United Palestine Appeal (UPA) / United Israel Appeal (UIA) focused on the need for a Jewish state as the only way to secure a Jewish future. The Jewish Joint Distribution Committee (JDC), World Jewish Congress (WJC), and National Council of Jewish Women (NCJW) provided aid in Europe and sought to rehabilitate Jewish life around the world. The United Service for New Americans (USNA), Hebrew Immigrant Aid Society (HIAS), and Citizen's Committee on Displaced Persons (CCDP) worked with Jewish immigrants in the US and fought for more lenient immigration quotas to America. The diversity of these philanthropic and political ambitions, in addition to power struggles within and between organizations, complicated a unified American Jewish response to the Holocaust and refracted survivor representations. As a result, survivors were not only depicted as DPs and refugees but also transformed into pilgrims, pioneers, and New Americans, identities that reflected a range of postwar possibilities and competing ideological priorities.

Despite these differences, narratives about the Holocaust constructed by American Jewish communal organizations employed American themes and motifs to translate the stories of survivors for American audiences. Like Hanna Kohner's story, survivor narratives from the time tended to emphasize joy and resettlement, turning away from the dark toward the light. Specific postwar values, like the centrality of children in nuclear families, the celebration of diversity, and a return to consumerism, were also integrated into Holocaust narratives. The transformation of DPs into Delayed Pilgrims most explicitly established American motifs as central components of early Holocaust narratives and conveyed the political underpinnings of such narrative construction. By referring to Jewish survivors as pilgrims, organizations concerned with immigration reform in America inserted DPs into a long history of American immigration and evoked America's founding myth as a haven from religious oppression to influence postwar debate. The spirit of Thanksgiving thus defined survivors through American myths and represented America as a symbol of hope, site of opportunity, and bearer of freedom.

In each of these narrative frames and for each possible Jewish future, American Jews defined themselves as saviors, responsible for not only saving Jewish lives but also preserving a Jewish future. As a result, early Holocaust narratives constructed to motivate American Jewish aid told stories about American Jewry that highlighted its new position in the postwar Jewish world. In the aftermath of the Holocaust, American Jewish communal organizations told stories that connected American Jews with European Jews and, in so doing, crafted Holocaust narratives that reflected, demanded, and celebrated American Jewish action abroad.

***

So how can we understand the transformation of survivor narratives and our expectations about those narratives from the immediate postwar period to today? This close examination of early postwar survivor narratives offers a starting point for the development of Holocaust memory in America. However, this study also suggests that the burst of expression in the immediate postwar period does not form a continuous history with later models of Holocaust memory. We can see that while they anticipate many themes that have come to define Holocaust testimony, these early narratives were largely forgotten as time passed. New technologies emerged for capture, preservation, and dissemination; new crises arose around the Jewish world; new generations of Jewish leaders sought to tell the stories of their organizations in different ways; and Holocaust survivors became empowered to tell their own stories. As Hasia Diner has argued, early efforts at Holocaust commemoration may be overlooked because they do not look like later attempts.[13] The ephemeral narratives explored in this book have been presumed missing because they do not fit the mold of survivor memory that has come to be revered.

David Boder's work is a prime example of how early memory has been overlooked. Boder's work, poorly received in his own time, was stored in archives and libraries around the country. In 1998, at a time of expansive Holocaust testimony creation in America, Donald Niewyk published a heavily edited collection of Boder's testimonies.[14] Niewyk's edits reposition Boder's work to better fit into contemporary expectations of survivor narratives, removing inconsistencies, lapses in chronology, and Boder's own voice. In the same year, a librarian at the Illinois Institute of Technology discovered wire recordings from Boder's collection and began digitizing his early oral histories. In 2000, the Voices of the Holocaust website was first launched, and by 2009, 118 interviews had been translated, transcribed, digitized, and made available online.[15]

Digitization has inserted Boder's recordings into the history of Holocaust memory. Boder's testimonies have been not only reexamined by scholars but also preserved and made openly accessible online for a wide audience now committed to survivor memory as a privileged source of Holocaust knowledge—in some ways, fulfilling Boder's initial hopes for the project. But what would he have made of an open online repository of his oral history interviews?

We can look to the USC Shoah Foundation to see how some of the ethical issues at stake in making survivor testimonies available online have unfolded. Thus far, the foundation has made a small subset of full-length Holocaust survivor testimonies openly available online through YouTube.[16] Users can search the catalog of the full collection, over fifty-five thousand Holocaust testimonies, by registering on the Visual History Archive website.[17] Making a subset of the archive available online represents a middle ground in terms of public access and points to a tension between the responsibility of protecting survivor

Conclusion

memories and the cultivation of a public culture of Holocaust engagement. When testimonies are openly accessible online, they become available for comments as well as reuse beyond the Shoah Foundation's control. Testimonies can be edited, remixed, or recontextualized in ways that challenge their authenticity. At the same time, online access to survivor testimony furthers the goal of providing eyewitness accounts of the Holocaust for educational and historical purposes. How this new space changes the way American and international audiences hear, see, and understand survivor accounts is still an open question.

Recognizing the similarities and differences between survivor accounts from the 1940s and '50s and the 1980s and '90s also helps us confront the ways new technologies and listening practices will again reshape Holocaust memory in the digital age. To start, the agency of survivors to tell their own stories drastically altered the way testimony was collected, preserved, and disseminated. By the 1970s and '80s, survivors were no longer DPs, refugees, or even New Americans; they were citizens of America, Israel, Australia, or wherever they had settled. They knew the language and could communicate their stories in their own words to their intended audiences. Nonetheless, institutional limits and priorities continued to shape how survivor voices were captured and how their stories were heard.[18] By the 1980s, such framing and mediation was at least done with the survivor's consent and in their own words. In the immediate postwar period, Jewish organizations constructed narratives without the input (or knowledge, in many cases) of survivors in Europe.

Unlike in the 1990s, when institutions could limit access to the memory they had created and construct specific points of entry, the digital world expands access for individual listeners and viewers. Anyone with access to the internet can now view available testimonies; they can start and stop videos at any point and link to them from any site on the internet. While the USC Shoah Foundation has limited the number of testimonies openly available on YouTube, it has embraced the idea of online curation in other ways, including the creation of platforms that invite interactive engagement with survivor testimony. For example, iWitness invites students to edit testimonies to create short films.[19] Unlike the testimonies available on YouTube, using iWitness requires registration and log in, and the site provides guidance on how students can benefit from remixing different Holocaust survivor testimonies.

The Dimensions in Testimony (DiT) initiative of the USC Shoah Foundation pushes this idea even further. The DiT project "enables people to ask questions that prompt real-time responses from pre-recorded video interviews with Holocaust survivors."[20] The team has used computation to render 360-degree footage of Holocaust survivors into digital representations that can respond to user-defined questions.[21] The goal is to preserve the discursive element of Holocaust testimony between interviewer and interviewee even after survivors have died. But the project also reimagines the nature of testimony from a structured interview to an open experience that is oriented to user questions and audience interests. While the ambitious DiT project feels far from the fundraising narratives, radio dramas, and short films that documented survivors' experiences in the wake of World War II, we can connect the dots between these different moments. In both, audience interest and institutional priorities shape the narratives and infrastructures that allow stories to be recorded, shared, and received.

As we continue to respond to the humanitarian challenges the world faces today and employ narratives that fulfill diverse political and philanthropic ambitions, we must contemplate how we craft the stories that will come to define American engagement with these global events. We must confront the ways fundraising for humanitarian aid shapes the stories we encounter and recognize that narrative strategies meant to pull at our purse strings are also inviting us to see ourselves as part of a meaningful and effective response. I return to Allison Silverman's indignation on watching Hanna Bloch Kohner on *This Is Your Life* and wonder how our own constructions of memory will be judged by scholars and journalists in the next generation. By expanding our understanding of what it means to know the Holocaust and our consideration of multiple forms of Holocaust survivor accounts, perhaps we can increase our awareness of the messy, diffuse, and contested nature of narrative construction in the immediate aftermath of each new tragedy we confront.

NOTES

Introduction

1. "Delayed Pilgrims Dinner," produced by the USNA, WMCA, November 27, 1947, YIVO Sound Archive.

2. Ibid. For a detailed exploration of the War Refugee Board, see Rebecca Erbelding, *Rescue Board: The Untold Story of America's Efforts to Save the Jews of Europe* (New York: Doubleday, 2018).

3. "Delayed Pilgrims Dinner."

4. For more about the CCDP, see Leonard Dinnerstein, *America and the Survivors of the Holocaust* (New York: Columbia University Press, 1982), especially chapter 5, "The Formation of the Citizens Committee," 117–136.

5. "An American with a Mission," produced by the CCDP, 1948, Marr Sound Archive.

6. Ibid. Sudduth introduced Peter as a young boy found in a German hospital in the wake of the war. No one knew who he was, so Sudduth took him home and brought him to America, where he was adopted by the Forshee family of Washington, DC. (We are told that Peter was renamed Peter *Sudduth* Forshee.) When Sudduth asked Peter, "What do you think of America?" Peter responded by launching into the song.

7. "An American with a Mission."

8. This phrase is part of Sudduth's description of the young refugees featured on the broadcast. "An American with a Mission."

9. There are two scholarly threads to this argument: first, that American Jews manipulated memory of the Holocaust over the decades following the war to match communal priorities, and second, that America and American Jews in particular turned their backs on European Jews, failing to aid them during and immediately after the war. The first of these arguments is explored in the chapter text.

For the second, see, among others, David S. Wyman and Charles H. Rosenzveig, ed., *The World Reacts to the Holocaust* (Baltimore: Johns Hopkins University Press, 1996) and Rafael Medoff, *The Deafening Silence: American Jewish Leaders and the Holocaust* (New York: Carol, 1986).

10. Hasia R. Diner, "Origins and Meanings of the Myth of Silence," in *After the Holocaust: Challenging the Myth of Silence*, ed. David Cesarani and Eric J. Sundquist (London: Routledge, 2012), 192–201, 194–195.

11. Leon Jick, "The Holocaust: Its Uses and Abuses in the American Public," *Yad Vashem Studies* 14 (1981): 301–318.

12. For more about the development of the Fortunoff Video Archive for Holocaust Testimonies at Yale, see Geoffrey H. Hartman, *The Longest Shadow: In the Aftermath of the Holocaust* (Bloomington: Indiana University Press, 1996), particularly 133–150, and Geoffrey H. Hartman, *Holocaust Remembrance: The Shapes of Memory* (Oxford: Blackwell, 1994).

13. The Historian's Debate is a particularly public example of how concerns about writing Holocaust history intersected with ethical debates taking place in Europe around the same time. Saul Friedländer and Martin Broszat, "A Controversy about the Historicization of National Socialism," *Yad Vashem Studies* 19 (1988): 1–47. See also Dominick LaCapra, "Revisiting the Historians' Debate: Mourning and Genocide," *History & Memory* 9, no. 1/2 (October 1, 1997): 80–112 and Peter Baldwin, *Reworking the Past: Hitler, the Holocaust, and the Historians' Debate* (Boston: Beacon Press, 1990).

14. Peter Novick, *The Holocaust in American Life* (Boston: Houghton Mifflin, 1999); Norman G. Finkelstein, *The Holocaust Industry: Reflections on the Exploitation of Jewish Suffering* (London: Verso, 2000); Alan L. Mintz, *Popular Culture and the Shaping of Holocaust Memory in America* (Seattle: University of Washington Press, 2001).

15. Mintz, *Popular Culture*, 3.

16. David Cesarani, "Introduction," in *After the Holocaust: Challenging the Myth of Silence*, ed. David Cesarani and Eric J. Sundquist (London: Routledge, 2012), 3. For a more complete assessment of the Myth of Silence, see Hasia R. Diner, *We Remember with Reverence and Love: American Jews and the Myth of Silence after the Holocaust, 1945–1962* (New York: New York University Press, 2009), 4–9.

17. Cesarani, "Introduction," 2.

18. See, among others, Diner, *We Remember with Reverence and Love*; Jeffrey Shandler, *While America Watches: Televising the Holocaust* (New York: Oxford University Press, 2000); Kirsten Lise Fermaglich, *American Dreams and Nazi Nightmares: Early Holocaust Consciousness and Liberal America, 1957–1965* (Waltham, MA: Brandeis University Press, 2006); Laura Jockusch, *Collect and Record! Jewish Holocaust Documentation in Early Postwar Europe* (New York: Oxford University Press, 2012); Alan Rosen, *The Wonder of Their Voices: The 1946 Holocaust Interviews of David Boder* (New York: Oxford University Press, 2010); Jürgen Matthäus, ed.,

Approaching an Auschwitz Survivor: Holocaust Testimony and Its Transformations (Oxford: Oxford University Press, 2009); Beth B. Cohen, *Case Closed: Holocaust Survivors in Postwar America* (New Brunswick, NJ: Rutgers University Press, 2007); Lawrence Baron, "The First Wave of American 'Holocaust' Films, 1945–1959," *American Historical Review* 115, no. 1 (February 2010): 90–114; and Elisabeth Gallas and Laura Jockusch, "Anything but Silent: Jewish Responses to the Holocaust in the Aftermath of World War II," in *A Companion to the Holocaust*, ed. Simone Gigliotti and Hilary Earl (Chichester: John Wiley & Sons, 2020), chapter 17.

19. The conference "The Myth of Silence: Who Spoke about the Holocaust When?" was held in October 2009 at UCLA. The resulting collected edition expands the conversation. David Cesarani and Eric J. Sundquist, ed., *After the Holocaust: Challenging the Myth of Silence* (London: Routledge, 2012). Cesarani, "Introduction," 10.

20. Eric Sundquist, "Silence Reconsidered," in Cesarani and Sundquist, eds., *After the Holocaust*, 202–216, 213–214.

21. Cohen, *Case Closed*.

22. "An American with a Mission."

23. Annette Wieviorka, *The Era of the Witness* (Ithaca, NY: Cornell University Press, 2006), xii.

24. Dominick LaCapra, *History and Memory after Auschwitz* (Ithaca, NY: Cornell University Press, 1998), 11. Scholarship on Holocaust testimony is vast and bridges many fields and methodologies. For a summary of different approaches to considering survivors as eyewitnesses, see Henry Greenspan et al., "Engaging Survivors: Assessing 'Testimony' and 'Trauma' as Foundational Concepts," *Dapim: Studies on the Holocaust* 28, no. 3 (2024): 190–226, https://doi.org/10.1080/23256249.2014.951909. For earlier approaches and understanding of survivors as witnesses, see, among others, Shoshana Felman and Dori Laub, eds., *Testimony: Crises of Witnessing in Literature, Psychoanalysis, and History* (New York: Routledge, 1992).

25. This idea is repeated throughout the narratives detailed in the chapters ahead. To cite one particularly resonant example, see Frieda Schiff Warburg quoted in, Press Release, "More Than 3,500,000 Pounds of Contributed Relief Supplies Shipped Overseas by JDC's SOS Collection," November 8, 1946, USHMM Archives, JDC-J.

26. "Ephemera," Library of Congress Collections Policy Statements, https://www.loc.gov/acq/devpol/ephemera.pdf.

27. For an analysis of these different testimony collections, see Noah Shenker, *Reframing Holocaust Testimony* (Bloomington: Indiana University Press, 2015).

28. See Samuel D. Kassow, *Who Will Write Our History? Emanuel Ringelblum, the Warsaw Ghetto, and the Oyneg Shabes Archive* (Bloomington: Indiana University Press, 2007). For online access to the collection, see https://www.yadvashem.org/yv/en/exhibitions/ringelblum/index.asp.

29. See Yad Vashem archival collection M.1: Documentation of the Central Historical Commission (CHC) of the Central Committee of Liberated Jews in the American Occupied Zone, Munich.

30. For more about eyewitness diaries written by Jewish victims, see Alexandra Garbarini, *Numbered Days: Diaries and the Holocaust* (New Haven, CT: Yale University Press, 2006). For more about the testimonial efforts captured after the war and historical commissions in particular, see Jockusch, *Collect and Record!*

31. Jason Lustig, *A Time to Gather: Archives and the Control of Jewish Culture* (New York: Oxford University Press, 2022), 1.

32. Mark L. Smith, "No Silence in Yiddish: Popular and Scholarly Writing about the Holocaust in the Early Postwar Years," in Cesarani and Sundquist, eds., *After the Holocaust*, 55–66; Anita Norich, *Discovering Exile: Yiddish and Jewish American Culture during the Holocaust* (Stanford, CA: Stanford University Press, 2007); Ari Kelman, *Station Identification: A Cultural History of Yiddish Radio in the United States* (Berkeley: University of California Press, 2009). For records of circulating books, see "Telling the World," chapter 2 in Diner, *We Remember with Reverence and Love.*

33. For more about the history of *Anne Frank's Diary*, see Barbara Kirshenblatt-Gimblett and Jeffrey Shandler, eds., *Anne Frank Unbound: Media, Imagination, Memory* (Bloomington: Indiana University Press, 2012) and Cynthia Ozick, "Who Owns Anne Frank?," *New Yorker* 73, no. 30 (October 6, 1997): 76.

34. This book looks at the immediate postwar period to consider how shifting technologies shaped Holocaust narratives and the forms in which they were heard, seen, and read by American Jews. But we can also look ahead to consider the use of artificial intelligence and computation analysis to generate, share, and preserve Holocaust testimony currently under development by leading organizations like the USC Shoah Foundation. Some of these connections are explored in the conclusion to *Saving Our Survivors.* See, among other texts, Todd Presner, *Ethics of the Algorithm: Digital Humanities and Holocaust Memory* (Princeton, NJ: Princeton University Press, 2024).

35. The DP camps of Europe did not close entirely until 1957. A group of Jews known as the "Hard Core" remained in DP camps for a variety of reasons. Some Jews even chose to return to DP camps after immigrating to Israel. Nonetheless, by 1953, the majority of DP camps were closed, and most Jewish survivors had resettled. See Avinoam J. Patt and Kierra Crago-Schneider, "Years of Survival: JDC in Postwar Germany, 1945–1957," in *The JDC at 100: A Century of Humanitarianism,* ed. Avinoam J. Patt et al. (Detroit: Wayne State University Press, 2019), 361–420, and Kierra Mikaila Crago-Schneider, "A Community of Will: The Resettlement of Orthodox Jewish DPs from Föhrenwald," *Holocaust and Genocide Studies* 32, no. 1 (spring 2018): 93–110, https://doi.org/10.1093/hgs/dcy007.

36. Shenker, *Reframing Holocaust Testimony.*

NOTES TO PAGES 10–11

37. Dinnerstein, *America and the Survivors of the Holocaust*, 273. Dinnerstein notes that the exact number of DPs was never accurately assessed, with estimates ranging from five to ten million in Germany and up to thirty million around the world. He notes that *Life* magazine quoted a total of nine-and-a-half million DPs in an issue published May 14, 1945.

38. Zeev W. Mankowitz, *Life between Memory and Hope: The Survivors of the Holocaust in Occupied Germany* (New York: Cambridge University Press, 2002), 11–12. For a detailed description of the interaction between DPs, occupying armies, and UNRRA, see Dinnerstein, *America and the Survivors of the Holocaust*, in particular 9–38. For detailed figures and statistics related to displaced persons, 281 and table A.5.

39. Hagit Lavsky, *New Beginnings: Holocaust Survivors in Bergen-Belsen and the British Zone in Germany, 1945–1950* (Detroit: Wayne State University Press, 2002), and Irving Heymont, *Among the Survivors of the Holocaust, 1945: The Landsberg DP Camp Letters of Major Irving Heymont, United States Army* (Cincinnati, OH: American Jewish Archives, 1982).

40. Atina Grossmann, *Jews, Germans, and Allies: Close Encounters in Occupied Germany* (Princeton, NJ: Princeton University Press, 2007).

41. For more about the Harrison Report and life in DP camps, see Dinnerstein, *America and the Survivors of the Holocaust*, 39–71; Arieh J. Kochavi, *Post-Holocaust Politics: Britain, the United States & Jewish Refugees, 1945–1948* (Chapel Hill: University of North Carolina Press, 2001), 89–97; and Ben Shephard, *The Long Road Home: The Aftermath of the Second World War* (New York: Alfred A. Knopf, 2011).

42. Earl G. Harrison, *The Plight of the Displaced Jews in Europe: A Report to President Truman* (New York: Reprinted by United Jewish Appeal for Refugees, Overseas Needs and Palestine on behalf of Joint Distribution Committee, United Palestine Appeal, National Refugee Service, 1945), 12.

43. Images of Jewish DPs protesting and advocating for opportunities to immigrate to Palestine in particular can be found in multiple archives. See, for example, "November 1947, A Zionist Demonstration Being Held in a DP Camp in Landsberg, Germany," Yad Vashem Photo Archives 1486/612, https://www.yadvashem.org/holocaust/this-month/november/1947-2.html.

44. For more about the White Papers and postwar immigration politics, particularly about Israel, see (among many others) Kochavi, *Post-Holocaust Politics* and Michael J. Cohen, *Truman and Israel* (Berkeley: University of California Press, 1990). For a deep dive into US immigration options at the time, see Libby Garland, *After They Closed the Gates: Jewish Illegal Immigration to the United States, 1921–1965* (Chicago: University of Chicago Press, 2014) and Dinnerstein, *America and the Survivors of the Holocaust*.

45. The illegal immigration route, known as *Brichah*, is detailed in Yehuda Bauer, *Flight and Rescue: Brichah*, 1st ed., Contemporary Jewish Civilization Series (New York: Random House, 1970). See also Sarah A. Cramsey, *Uprooting the*

Diaspora: Jewish Belonging and the "Ethnic Revolution" in Poland and Czechoslovakia, 1936–1946 (Bloomington: Indiana University Press, 2023).

46. See Garland, *After They Closed the Gates*, 189–192; Dinnerstein, *America and the Survivors of the Holocaust*, 174–287; Kochavi, *Post-Holocaust Politics*, 98–153; and Shephard, *The Long Road Home*, 344–345.

47. Dinnerstein, *America and the Survivors of the Holocaust*, 287.

48. Shephard cites Hanna Yablonka's *Survivors of the Holocaust: Israel after the War* (New York: New York University Press, 1999), 18–42 for these figures but explicitly notes that Yablonka does not define "Holocaust survivors." This is to say these figures provide only a rough estimate of the emigration route from DP camps in Europe to Israel in 1948 and 1949. *Long Road Home*, 365.

49. Garland, *After They Closed the Gates*, 190.

50. For details about Jewish "infiltrators" coming to occupation zones from the east and the change in policy that allowed Jews entry into the American zone, see Kochavi, *Post-Holocaust Politics*, chapter 6, "American Occupation Zones Offer Asylum," 134–153.

51. See Jan T. Gross, *Neighbors: The Destruction of the Jewish Community in Jedwabne, Poland* (Princeton, NJ: Princeton University Press, 2012).

52. For example, when Jews seeking to enter Palestine illegally were sent to Cyprus, communal campaigns highlighted the conditions of Jews held in internment camps on the island. From 1946 until the establishment of the State of Israel, roughly five hundred thousand Jews were detained on Cyprus.

53. For more about OWI and its efforts during the war, see Gerd Horten, *Radio Goes to War: The Cultural Politics of Propaganda during World War II* (Berkeley: University of California Press, 2002) and Allan M. Winkler, *The Politics of Propaganda: The Office of War Information, 1942–1945* (New Haven, CT: Yale University Press, 1978).

54. "World Relief Is America's Job," *Saturday Evening Post* 218, no. 25 (December 22, 1945): 112.

55. For more about Vaad Hatzala, see Efraim Zuroff, *The Response of Orthodox Jewry in the United States to the Holocaust: The Activities of the Vaad Ha-Hatzala Rescue Committee, 1939–1945* (Brooklyn, NY: Ktav Publishing House, 2000).

56. The USNA was founded in 1946 through the merger of the NRS and the Service to Foreign Born Department of the National Council of Jewish Women. The NRS was the successor to the National Coordinating Committee for Aid to Refugees and Emigrants Coming from Germany. Each of these organizations worked to aid Jewish immigration to the United States and supported Jews through the resettlement process.

57. See Sarah Kavanaugh, *ORT, the Second World War and the Rehabilitation of Holocaust Survivors* (London: Vallentine Mitchell, 2008).

58. Shulamit Reinharz and Mark Raider have collected works that examine women's roles in Zionism in *American Jewish Women and the Zionist Enterprise* (Waltham, MA: Brandeis University Press, 2005). For more about women's organizations and women's participation in communal organizations, see Melissa R. Klapper, *Ballots, Babies, and Banners of Peace: American Jewish Women's Activism, 1890–1940* (New York: New York University Press, 2012) and Kathleen D. McCarthy, ed., *Lady Bountiful Revisited: Women, Philanthropy, and Power* (New Brunswick, NJ: Rutgers University Press, 1990).

59. Postcard Appeal, Box D78, Folder 9: Publicity, World Jewish Congress (WJC) Papers, AJA.

60. The postwar period has been called a golden age for American Jews, an idea challenged by renewed awareness of antisemitism in America and a more nuanced understanding of the postwar period. For more about the American Jewish experience in the postwar period and the debate about whether it constitutes a golden age, see (among others), Arthur Goren, "A 'Golden Decade' for American Jews: 1945–1955," in *The American Jewish Experience*, ed. Jonathan D. Sarna (New York: Holmes & Meier, 1986), 294–313; Deborah Dash Moore, *To the Golden Cities: Pursuing the American Jewish Dream in Miami and L.A.* (New York: Free Press, 1994); Hasia Diner, *The Jews of the United States, 1654 to 2000* (Berkeley: University of California Press, 2004), 259–304; Edward S. Shapiro, *A Time for Healing: American Jewry since World War II* (Baltimore: Johns Hopkins University Press, 1992); and Riv-Ellen Prell, "Triumph, Accommodation, and Resistance: American Jewish Life from the End of WWII to the Six-Day War," in *The Columbia History of Jews and Judaism in America*, ed. Marc Lee Raphael (New York: Columbia University Press, 2008), 114–141.

61. For more about the relationship between suburbanization, "becoming white," and "silence" after the Holocaust, see Karen Brodkin, *How Jews Became White Folks and What That Says About Race in America* (New Brunswick, NJ: Rutgers University Press, 1998) and Eric L. Goldstein, *The Price of Whiteness: Jews, Race, and American Identity* (Princeton, NJ: Princeton University Press, 2006).

62. Lila Corwin Berman, *Metropolitan Jews: Politics, Race, and Religion in Postwar Detroit* (Chicago: University of Chicago Press, 2015).

63. Berman writes that "Jews' increasing urban power in economic, political, and cultural terms offered them privileges reserved for white Americans but did not align their interests neatly with the generalized whiteness that historians often describe as characterizing the postwar years." *Metropolitan Jews*, 6.

64. Barry Trachtenberg, *The United States and the Nazi Holocaust: Race, Refuge, and Remembrance* (London: Bloomsbury Academic, 2018), 8. Trachtenberg highlights, in particular, how race impacted immigration policy during and after the war: "The antisemitism that was influential in shaping the US response to the

refugee crisis occurred within a much larger and more complicated racial context that included, but was not exclusive to Jews. Although ... in comparison to other ethnic groups such as Asian Americans, Latinos and African Americans, American Jews held significantly more power to respond to ethnic hatred ... Jewish refugees were widely considered to be one of many unwanted racial minorities looking to enter the United States against the wishes of the majority of the population" (59).

65. Dori Laub, "Bearing Witness or the Vicissitudes of Listening," in Felman and Laub, *Testimony*, 57–74.

66. Greenspan et al., "Engaging Survivors."

67. Marc Nichanian, "Catastrophic Mourning," in *Loss: The Politics of Mourning*, ed. David L. Eng and David Kazanjian (Berkeley: University of California Press, 2003), 99–124. Alexandra Garbarini offers important analysis for thinking about how eyewitness testimony from the Armenian Genocide can be seen alongside Holocaust survivor testimony and other forms of victim testimony. Alexandra Garbarini, "Document Volumes and the Status of Victim Testimony in the Era of the First World War and Its Aftermath," *Études arméniennes contemporaines* 5 (June 2015): 113–138.

68. Kenneth Waltzer writes: "We use the term 'testimony' elastically, I think, because it implies a general affirmation of truth, as in court proceedings or religious attestations. The term connotes truth value or sincerity of belief about truth." Greenspan et al., "Engaging Survivors."

69. "Historic U.P.A. Drive on for '45: Statement by Dr. Heller," *UPA Reports*, February 1945, 1, Nearprint UJA/AJA.

70. Mintz, *Popular Culture*, 3.

71. Diner, *We Remember with Reverence and Love*, 21.

72. Hagit Lavsky uses the term to mean Jewish survivors who were forced to stay at DP camps and refused to be repatriated to their home countries. Meanwhile, Zeev Mankowitz believes the term best applies to DPs in Germany, Italy, and Austria who created a self-conscious community. He considers this identity to be uniquely part of the experience of DPs in the American zone. For more information about the term *She'erit Hapletah* and the DP experience in postwar Europe, see Michael Brenner, *After the Holocaust: Rebuilding Jewish Lives in Postwar Germany* (Princeton, NJ: Princeton University Press, 1997); Grossmann, *Jews, Germans and Allies*; Lavsky, *New Beginnings*; and Mankowitz, *Life between Memory and Hope*.

73. Gary Weissman, *Fantasies of Witnessing: Postwar Efforts to Experience the Holocaust* (Ithaca, NY: Cornell University Press, 2004), 26.

74. Yehuda Bauer, *Out of the Ashes: The Impact of American Jews on Post-Holocaust European Jewry* (Oxford: Pergamon Press, 1989), xviii. Shapiro also points to guilt to explain the increased amounts of giving in the postwar period. *Time for Healing*, 63.

NOTES TO PAGES 18–24

75. Letter from Mrs. Charles E. Wyzanski Jr. and Mrs. Siegfried Kramarsky, cochairmen of the National Youth Aliyah Committee, to Youth Aliyah coworkers, July 27, 1945, Box 17, Folder 118, YAP/Hadassah.

Heartstrings and Purse Strings

1. Koppel Pinson, "The Jewish Spirit in Nazi Germany," *Menorah Journal* 24, no. 3 (autumn 1936): 235. The *Menorah Journal* was launched in 1915 by the Menorah Society at Harvard University as a space for Jewish intellectual writing in English. The magazine published many well-known Jewish writers during its run, including I. L. Peretz, Isaac Bashevitz Singer, Salo Baron, and Simon Dubnow, serving as a platform for "new models of historiography, criticism and fiction" until 1962, when it ceased publication. Daniel Greene, *The Jewish Origins of Cultural Pluralism: The Menorah Association and American Diversity* (Bloomington: Indiana University Press, 2011), 13.

2. Letter signed by R. Cohen, October 27, 1936, from 854 West 181 Street, Box 1, Folder: Lectures, letters read, Koppel Pinson Collection, New York Public Library.

3. Marc Lee Raphael, *A History of the United Jewish Appeal, 1939–1982* (Chico, CA: Scholars Press, 1982), 1.

4. Raphael cites the figure of $124 million as the amount *pledged* between 1939 and 1945 in *United Jewish Appeal*, 13.

5. Hilene Flanzbaum, *The Americanization of the Holocaust* (Baltimore: Johns Hopkins University Press, 1999), 1–17.

6. Ibid., 8.

7. "Statement by Jonah Wise," *JDC Digest*, March 1945 (4:1), 1, YIVO Library.

8. "Historic U.P.A. Drive on for '45: Statement by Dr. Heller," *UPA Reports*, February 1945, 1, Nearprint UJA/AJA.

9. See Bauer, *American Jewry and the Holocaust*, and Raphael, *United Jewish Appeal*.

10. Raphael, *United Jewish Appeal*.

11. *UPA Reports*, June 1945, Nearprint UPA/AJA. The June 1945 agreement yielded one fundraising concession to each side: the Jewish National Fund (JNF, a constituent group of UPA) was allowed to conduct traditional collections up to $1.5 million, and JDC could collect earmarked funds for *landsmanschaften* up to $800,000. JNF "traditional" collections referred to fundraising efforts conducted directly by the JNF, which existed outside the UJA appeal. "The Dissolution of the National United Jewish Appeal," 1945, 6, Box 2, Nearprint JDC/AJA. *Landsmanshaftn* were groups formed by Jewish immigrants from the same villages, towns, and cities in central and eastern Europe. They formed in the late 1800s and served as social organizations, providing religious and cultural services for members through the nineteenth century. Throughout the war and postwar period, they raised money to send directly to the towns they represented. *Landsmanshaftn*

activities were administered through the JDC. For more about *landsmanshaftn*, see Hannah Kliger, ed., *Jewish Hometown Associations and Family Circles in New York: The WPA Yiddish Writers' Group Study* (Bloomington: Indiana University Press, 1992) and Daniel Soyer, *Jewish Immigrant Associations and American Identity in New York, 1880–1939* (Cambridge, MA: Harvard University Press, 1997).

12. See David S. Wyman, *The Abandonment of the Jews: America and the Holocaust* and *Paper Walls, 1941–1945* (New York: Pantheon Books, 1984); Medoff, *The Deafening Silence: American Jewish Leaders and the Holocaust* and *The Jews Should Keep Quiet: Franklin D. Roosevelt, Rabbi Stephen S. Wise, and the Holocaust* (Lincoln: Jewish Publication Society, 2019); and Segev, "Rethinking the Dilemma of Bombing Auschwitz."

13. "Rabbi Heller Is Back," *New York Times*, August 18, 1945, 11.

14. Bauer, *Out of the Ashes*, xvii.

15. Raphael, *United Jewish Appeal*, 37.

16. Berman highlights the wartime campaigns of the NY Jewish Federation, noting that in the 1940s, "NY Federation year after year exceeded yield" in Lila Corwin Berman, *The American Jewish Philanthropic Complex: The History of a Multibillion-Dollar Institution* (Princeton, NJ: Princeton University Press, 2020), 56–57.

17. Raphael, *United Jewish Appeal*, 21.

18. Foster R. Dulles, *The American Red Cross: A History* (New York: Harper & Brothers, 1950), 509. For more about the December 1945 meeting and debate about the $100 million goal, see Abraham J. Karp, *To Give Life: The UJA in the Shaping of the American Jewish Community* (New York: Schocken Books, 1981), 87–89.

19. The figure of $103 million comes from Raphael, *United Jewish Appeal*, 136, table 4:1. The total collection for 1946 is cited as $105 million in Hasia R. Diner, *We Remember with Reverence and Love: American Jews and the Myth of Silence after the Holocaust, 1945–1962* (New York: New York University Press, 2009). While the goal amounts were made public in nearly every press release, appeal letter, and publicity document, the total collected amounts were not publicized. The figures remain unspecific throughout this period.

20. The total collection from 1948 has been cited as high as $200 million. Edward S. Shapiro, *A Time for Healing: American Jewry since World War II* (Baltimore: Johns Hopkins University Press, 1992). But a *Jewish Telegraphic Agency* article from January 3, 1949, cites $150 million raised from more than one million Jewish contributors. The article also calls the 1948 UJA campaign the "greatest campaign in the history of private philanthropy" ("United Jewish Appeal Raised Total of $150,000,000 in 1948").

21. Harold J. Seymour, *Design for Giving: The Story of the National War Fund, Inc., 1943–1947* (New York: Harper, 1947), 123.

22. Robert H. Bremner, *American Philanthropy* (Chicago: University of Chicago Press, 1960), 172–173.

NOTES TO PAGES 27–29   147

23. Bauer, *Out of the Ashes*, xviii.

24. Shapiro also points to guilt to explain the increased amounts of giving in the postwar period. *Time for Healing*, 63.

25. Berman notes that the idea of a "battle for Jewish survival" was central to UJA wartime fundraising campaigns. New York Federation campaign chair Norman Goetz "described American Jews' dollars as their weapons in a 'battle for survival.'" Berman, *American Jewish Philanthropic Complex*, 57.

26. 1946. UJA Speaker's Manual, Box 10, Nearprint UJA/AJA.

27. "New Standards of Giving," *A Report to Members of the National Campaign Council*, Vol. 1: No. 1, February 28, 1946, 1, Box 38, HAFP/AJA.

28. The tradition of publicly declaring gifts continues for UJA events and other Jewish organizations. See, for example, figure 7.1 in Berman, *American Jewish Philanthropic Complex*, 142. In this 1977 family photograph from Cedarhurst, Long Island, all three children wear shirts that declare, "My dad upped his pledge." Milton Goldin identifies this practice as unique to the Jewish community and cites it as one of several aggressive strategies used by American Jewish communal organizations but not by nonsectarian groups: "Where else does one find 'card calling' luncheons, published lists of donors (with gifts carefully noted) and meetings, meetings, meetings?" Milton Goldin, *Why They Give: American Jews and Their Philanthropies* (New York: Macmillan, 1976), ix.

29. Berman, *American Jewish Philanthropic Complex*, 61.

30. "Warburg on One-Time Giving," *A Report to Members of the National Campaign Council*, special issue, October 16, 1946, 4, Box 39, Folder: UJA Report 1946, HAFP/AJA.

31. Undated note, Folder 6, ORT/YIVO, ORT documentary footage, USHMM Video Archive. ORT was founded in 1880 to train Russian Jews in industrial skills. Following the war, ORT opened over seven thousand schools in DP camps and across Europe to retrain Jewish survivors in preparation for emigration. ORT materials maintain that over fifty thousand survivors were trained by ORT schools and programs. For more about the organization, see Sarah Kavanaugh, *ORT: The Second World War and the Rehabilitation of Holocaust Survivors* (London: Vallentine Mitchell, 2008).

32. Hadassah employed a full-time film supervisor, Hazel Greenwald, and JDC relied on Raphael Levy, Marc Siegel, and Paul Falkenberg in its publicity department to write, supervise, and direct films. JDC also regularly received guidance from Al Paul Lefton, a well-known ad man. Many UJA films were produced by RKO or March of Time.

33. For example, the National Education Department for the Zionist Organization of America advertised lists of films to its chapter education chairs. In 1946, this list included the JDC films *The Will to Live, Shadow of Hate, Children of Destiny*, the UJA films *Battle for Survival, They Live Again, Forgotten Children*,

148   NOTES TO PAGES 29–32

and Mayer Levin's *Voyage of the Unafraid* about a Haganah immigration ship. The film brochure noted that because of the popularity of *Voyage of the Unafraid*, it had a rental cost of fifteen dollars. List of Films from National Education Department, Folder 182, LZOA/YIVO. JDC, on the other hand, offered free borrowing of films for educational events hosted by chapters across the country. "Firsthand Reports on Jewish Life Abroad Offered to Lodges, Clubs, Sisterhoods," JDC Release through Community Service Department, undated, JDC NYC, Box: Films, Folder: "Report on the Living (1946)."

34. A letter from Hadassah states that it felt a film could "help raise millions of dollars." Letter, April 1, 1946, Box 76, Folder 2, YAP/Hadassah.

35. "First hand reports on Jewish Life Abroad Offered to Lodges, Clubs, Sisterhoods," JDC Release through Community Service Department, undated, JDC NYC, Box Films, Folder "Report on the Living (1946)."

36. Junior Hadassah brochure, 1944–1945, Box 15, Folder 11, OFPA/Hadassah. The film was also referred to as *They Live Again*, but the two titles seem to refer to the same Hadassah-produced film.

37. Letter from Mrs. Siegfried Kramarsky to Mrs. Eva Michaelis, July 30, 1947, Box 17, Folder 118, Letter 1070, YAP/Hadassah. The letter asserts that the film was shown at Lugano, but it must have been shown at the Locarno Film Festival, since the Lugano Film Festival was only held in 1944 and 1945. Starting in 1946, Locarno took over the responsibilities. Hadassah seems to have established a relationship with the organizers as the full-length feature, under its Israeli name, *Adamah*, premiered at the Locarno Film Festival in 1948.

38. *Placing the Displaced*, YIVO Film Archive.

39. The rumor appears in the Wikipedia entry for *Seeds of Destiny* and in the USHMM Video Archive catalog entry for the film. *Seeds of Destiny*, Steven Spielberg Film and Video Archive of the United States Holocaust Memorial Museum. I have not found additional archival evidence or details about which organizations collected or distributed these funds. See https://en.wikipedia.org/wiki/Seeds _of_Destiny, especially "Reception."

40. *Seeds of Destiny*, USHMM.

41. *Battle for Survival*, RKO Pathe Inc., 1946, Steven Spielberg Film and Video Archive of the United States Holocaust Memorial Museum.

42. The meeting in Atlantic City took place only a few weeks after the publication and wide circulation of the Harrison Report. Harrison, *The Plight of the Displaced Jews in Europe*.

43. Rosensaft was the chairman of the Central Committee of Liberated Jews in 1946. The committee was organized in the Bergen-Belsen DP camp in 1945 and served as a voice for Jewish survivors in DP camps in the British zone until 1950.

44. *Battle for Survival*, USHMM.

45. Ibid.

NOTES TO PAGES 32–35

46. Primo Levi, *Survival in Auschwitz: The Nazi Assault on Humanity*, trans. Stuart Woolf (New York: Touchstone, 1996), 11.

47. Elie Wiesel, "Why I Write: Making No Become a Yes," *New York Times*, April 14, 1985, section 7, page 13.

48. Lawrence L. Langer, *Admitting the Holocaust: Collected Essays* (New York: Oxford University Press, 1995), 68.

49. *Battle for Survival*, USHMM. This exact phrasing is used repeatedly in UJA materials and other organizational appeals. In a radio broadcast detailed in chapter 2, Paul Muni uses the same construction to urge American action around immigration reform.

50. Ibid.

51. Other groups also sent their films to chapters around the world. The Hadassah film *They May Live Again* sold out its run through South Africa in 1947 and played across Europe for propaganda purposes. Interestingly, when European staff members asked for more copies, Kramarsky, cochairperson of Youth Aliyah, remarked that the "purposes of use of our material is really limited to the United States." Letter dated December 15, 1947, Box 17, Folder 118, YAP/Hadassah.

52. The film archive at the USHMM has two copies of *Battle for Survival*. Tape 2296 includes this extra appeal that so clearly states the power and possibility of film.

53. "Look at Their Faces," Box 23, Folder 172: Publicity Stories, YAP/Hadassah.

54. For more about how children became symbols of postwar struggles and Jewish persecution in this period, see Tara Zahra, *The Lost Children: Reconstructing Europe's Families after World War II* (Cambridge, MA: Harvard University Press, 2011) and Mark M. Anderson, "The Child Victim as Witness to the Holocaust," *Jewish Social Studies* 14, no. 1 (fall 2007): 1–22. For more about children as symbols of renewal in postwar Europe, see also Daniella Doron, *Jewish Youth and Identity in Postwar France: Rebuilding Family and Nation* (Bloomington: Indiana University Press, 2015).

55. Narrative for Slides, Vaad Hatzala Dinner, December 17, 1945, Box 6, Folder 49, Vaad Hatzala Papers (VHP), Yeshiva University Manuscripts Collection.

56. Ibid.

57. *Here Are the Facts about the 1947 Campaign*, United Jewish Appeal of Greater New York, Box 206, Folder 2, USTC/YIVO.

58. Los Angeles United Jewish Welfare Fund, *1947 Year Book* (Los Angeles: Los Angeles Jewish Community Council, 1947).

59. *What Are the Facts? The Basis for the $170,000,000 United Jewish Appeal in 1947*, United Jewish Appeal, YIVO Library.

60. For more about the realities of life in postwar Europe, see Grossmann, *Jews, Germans, and Allies* and Lavsky, *New Beginnings*.

61. A report given at that National Conference of the UJA in Atlantic City on December 12, 1947, by Isidor Coons and Henry Montor notes that although the

150 NOTES TO PAGES 35–37

"greatest hope" for "the suffering Jews of Europe" was the partition vote in the United Nations, because of changing conditions in Europe and around the world, the need was increasing, and the $170 million goal was not enough. The report also notes that even the $170 million was not going to be met. It does not give a total, stating that some campaigns were ongoing, but estimates that the campaign would raise about $125 million even though only $92,700,000 had yet been recorded in pledges and only about $70 million had been collected in cash. *Report to the National Conference of the United Jewish Appeal in Atlantic City*, Box 27A, Folder 12, USTC/YIVO.

62. *Dollars for Destiny*, Steven Spielberg Film and Video Archive of the United States Holocaust Memorial Museum. *Maps of Destiny*, YIVO. Examples of the use of the term "destiny" include, among countless others, a filmstrip by the National Educational Department of the Zionist Organization of America called *Children of Destiny*, described as "the human story of the children who come to Israel-homeless, orphaned, despairing—and of their training for healthy, useful citizenship." "Filmstrips on Israel," Box 8, Folder 5, USTC/YIVO.

63. Shapiro, *Time for Healing*, 63–64.

64. The negotiations resulted in a tiered dispersal: UPA received 45 percent of the first $50 million collected and 55 percent of the next $75 million. UPA was also allotted 75 percent of monies up to the goal of $250 million, and if more had been collected, UPA would have received 100 percent. Raphael, *United Jewish Appeal*, 136, table 4:1. See also Goldin, *Why They Give*, 196.

65. Raphael, *United Jewish Appeal*, 137, table 5:1. See also Berman, *American Jewish Philanthropic Complex*, 93–94.

66. A May 25, 1948, report to UJA campaign leaders includes the slogan: "Pledges are a promise of life—cash is life itself." These bimonthly reports reiterate the urgent need for cash, not pledges, throughout 1948. By the summer of 1949, appeals were successful enough for the Los Angeles Federation to take out a loan of $1 million as a donation to UJA, according to a report of September 26, 1949. Box 38, HAFP/AJA.

67. *The Future Can Be Theirs*, JDC, Steven Spielberg Film and Video Archive of the United States Holocaust Memorial Museum. The executive minutes of June 15, 1948, indicate that sixty copies of the film were sent to "key communities" in the "U.S., Canada, Latin America, South Africa, and Australia," with more copies to be distributed soon. 45/54, #1332, JDC-NY.

68. Warburg was the JDC chairman, Lehman was a vice-chairman of JDC and former director general of UNRRA, Linder was also vice-chair of JDC, and Leavitt was JDC's executive vice president. The men were all well-established figures, yet they look awkward and uncomfortable on screen. They narrate the film in a stiff manner that contrasts with Welles's smooth and dramatic narration of *Battle for Survival*.

69. *The Future Can Be Theirs*.

NOTES TO PAGES 37–45

70. Ibid.

71. Cited in Diner, *We Remember with Reverence and Love*, 18.

72. *The Future Can Be Theirs*.

73. For more about the Labor Zionist movement in America, see Mark A. Raider, "From Immigrant Party to American Movement: American Labor Zionism in the Pre-state Period," *American Jewish History* 82, no. 1/4 (1994): 159–194.

74. Pioneer Women, From the Old to the New, April program calendar, Page 5, Folder 252, LZOA/YIVO. Diner notes that one of the primary reasons Passover became a time for commemoration was because it was the anniversary of the Warsaw Ghetto Uprising. Diner, *We Remember with Reverence and Love*, 62.

75. Another From the Old to the New program was a silhouetted show called "Return to Life," the "story of two girls who passed through the tragedy of Europe" and ended up at the Maotzat Hapoalot, a training farm for girls. Connecting the struggle of the two girls directly to the celebration of Passover, the story ends, "This Peasach called also the Festival of Freedom, should be a source of courage for Jews the world over. We gave the world the meaning of liberation from slavery. Too large a part of the world has as yet not been freed from the bondage of tyranny, injustice, inhumanity. In our struggle in Palestine we can but muster hope and strength that through our joint redoubled efforts we will yet enjoy a true . . . era of our liberation." Pioneer Women, 6.

76. Los Angeles United Jewish Welfare Fund, *1948 Yearbook* (Los Angeles: Los Angeles Jewish Community Council, 1948), 167.

77. "Memorandum from the 1948 Campaign Chairman, United Jewish Appeal of Greater New York" (attached to contract for 1948 Campaign of United Jewish Appeal of Greater New York), Box 206, Folder 2, United States Territorial Collection (USTC), YIVO Archive.

78. *4 Tasks, 1 Answer*, pamphlet, Box 206, Folder 2, USTC/YIVO.

79. In 1946, the National Refugee Service merged with the Service to Foreign Born Department of the National Council of Jewish Women to create USNA. USNA became a constituent organization of UJA, participating in joint annual campaigns but receiving a significantly smaller percentage of collected funds than UPA or JDC.

80. The brochure further identifies the DPs as twenty-four thousand orphaned children whose "care and training are most costly." *4 Tasks, 1 Answer*.

81. ORT, *You Saved Them from Dying, Now Train Them for Living*, Box 50, ORT/YIVO.

82. Shandler, *While America Watches*, 37.

83. See also Diner, *We Remember with Reverence and Love*, 162–163.

84. Exhibit brochure, Folder 66, ORT/YIVO.

85. ORT also collected survivor narratives to use in publicity materials. Handwritten accounts from young survivors are preserved in the YIVO collection and

echo the narrative of "through the darkness to a brighter future." The narrative of Rose Zlota is particularly illuminating. She was born in Poland in 1930 and in September 1942 was sent from the ghetto to a concentration camp with her family. Her brother soon died of starvation, and her father was killed at Mathausen. Rose was liberated with her mother in 1945 and wrote, "Then we went to Ebelsburg where I joined ORT's dressmaking class. I trust I shall manage well to learn this trade and so accomplish something in my life." Life story by Rose Zlota, February 23, 1948, translation from Polish, Folder 66, ORT/YIVO.

86. Not all survivors were out of Europe by 1950. A group of survivors known as the "Hard Core" remained under the care of JDC in Europe into the 1950s. It consisted largely of survivors who could not gain access to the US or who were too ill to move to Israel. JDC told the stories of the Hard Core in films and appeals into the early 1950s. Crago-Schneider, "A Community of Will."

87. All figures reported in organizational publications. *JDC Digest*, February and April 1949, March 1950, YIVO Library; Dr. George Stefansky, "For 100,000 Souls, A New Lease on Life," *UPA Reports*, March 1950, 7, Box 5, Folder 15, HAFP/AJA; "Guide to Overseas Operations," summer/fall 1951, 31, Box 3, Folder 2, HAFP/AJA.

88. "Suggested Content for High Holy Day Synagogue Appeal on Behalf of the Emergency Campaign for Jewish Children of the United Jewish Appeal of Greater New York, 1951 Campaign," Folder 328, LZOA/YIVO.

89. *UJA Report from Israel*, 1950, Steven Spielberg Film and Video Archive of the United States Holocaust Memorial Museum.

90. Ibid.

91. New scholarship about the Holocaust in North Africa highlights the way these two histories intersect more than discussed here. Jews in Morocco, Libya, Tunisia, Algeria, and beyond suffered under Nazi laws, and many were placed in internment and labor camps. My concern is with the ways established representations and symbols of the European Jewish experience under Nazism served as a throughline even as the focus of fundraising efforts moved into North Africa. For more about North Africa and the Holocaust, see Aomar Boum and Sarah Abrevaya Stein, eds., *The Holocaust and North Africa* (Stanford, CA: Stanford University Press, 2019). See also Sarah Abrevaya Stein and Aomar Boum, eds., *Wartime North Africa: A Documentary History, 1934–1950* (Stanford, CA: Stanford University Press, 2022).

Voicing Survivor Narratives

1. Multiple copies of memoranda sent from Boder to various funding agencies reiterate this goal. Memorandum of project proposal, July 9, 1945, Box 1, Folder "Additional Notes," David P. Boder Papers (DPB), UCLA Special Collections. The wire recorder had only recently been invented by Marvin Camras, a colleague of Boder's at the Illinois Institute of Technology. Camras became a pioneer in the

NOTES TO PAGES 49–52

field of magnetic recording, developing not only the wire-based system but also multitrack tape recording, stereophonic sound reproduction, and magnetic sound for motion pictures. He held over five hundred patents. For more about Camras's contribution to the history of sound recording in America, see David Morton, *Off the Record: The Technology and Culture of Sound Recording in America* (New Brunswick, NJ: Rutgers University Press, 2000), 61–66.

2. For more about Boder's life and work, see Rosen, *The Wonder of Their Voices*.

3. David P. Boder, *I Did Not Interview the Dead* (Urbana: University of Illinois Press, 1949) and *Topical Autobiographies of Displaced People: Recorded Verbatim in Displaced Persons Camps with a Psychological and Anthropological Analysis* (Chicago: n.p., 1950).

4. In an attempt to preserve the orality of his interviews, Boder translated each interview by rerecording a voiced translation on a separate wire spool and only then transcribing the English version. Rosen, *The Wonder of their Voices*, viii. This translation system was intended to maintain the patterns of natural speech, but it was not always successful. See Matthäus, *Approaching an Auschwitz Survivor*.

5. For more about the history of the Voices of the Holocaust project, see https://voices.library.iit.edu/voices_project and Carl Marziali, "Uncovering Lost Voices: 1946 David Boder Tapes Revived," *American Libraries* 34, no. 2 (2003): 45–46.

6. James Edward Young, *Writing and Rewriting the Holocaust: Narrative and the Consequences of Interpretation* (Bloomington: Indiana University Press, 1988), 22.

7. In his 1950 study of the radio industry, Gilbert Seldes states, "Broadcasting is a medium of fact. Our myths are fabricated in Hollywood; radio is the modern oracle." Gilbert Seldes, *The Great Audience* (New York: Viking Press, 1950), 107.

8. Robert L. Mott, *Radio Sound Effects: Who Did It, and How, in the Era of Live Broadcasting* (Jefferson, NC: McFarland, 1993), 1.

9. For the history of Yiddish radio in America, see Kelman, *Station Identification*.

10. Morton Wishengrad, "Forward," in *The Eternal Light* (New York: Crown, 1947), ix. For more about *The Eternal Light* as a Jewish show and Judaism on the radio, see the chapter "Turning on *The Eternal Light*," 56–94, in Jeffrey Shandler, *Jews, God, and Videotape: Religion and Media in America* (New York: NYU Press, 2009) and Jeffrey Shandler and Elihu Katz, "Broadcasting American Judaism: The Radio and Television Department of JTS," in *Tradition Renewed: A History of JTS*, edited by Jack Wertheimer, volume 2: Beyond the Academy (New York: Jewish Theological Seminary, 1997), 363–402.

11. Markus Krah asserts that 20–21 percent of episodes between 1944 and 1950 featured stories about "the Holocaust, the fate of displaced persons, and the Jewish community in Palestine/Israel." Markus Krah, "Role Models or Foils for American Jews? *The Eternal Light*, Displaced Persons, and the Construction of Jewishness in Mid-Twentieth-Century America," *American Jewish History* 96, no.

4 (2010): 265–286. For lists of all *Eternal Light* broadcasts, see Eli Segal, *The Eternal Light: An Unauthorized Guide* (Newtown, CT: Yesteryear Press, 2005).

12. Krah, "Role Models or Foils," 267.

13. Beatrice Klein Tolleris, *Radio: How, When and Why to Use It* (New York: National Publicity Council for Health and Welfare Services, 1946).

14. Seldes notes that the public service programs in particular were somewhere in between "pure entertainment and radio as transmitter of news and opinions." Seldes, *Great Audience*, 139.

15. National Council of Jewish Women, *Radio Manual*, 1944, 2, Box 131, Folder: Public Relations Manuals, 1943–1944, NCJW/LOC.

16. Hadassah, *Radio Starter Kit*, 1947, Box 12, Folder: Radio Starter Kits, 1947, OFPA/Hadassah.

17. Krah, "Role Models or Foils," 269.

18. Shandler and Katz quote letters from non-Jewish listeners who "express their gratitude to the Seminary for its broadcasts," including one letter sent from South Carolina that thanks the show for teaching the listener all she knows about Jewish people and helping her understand Jews. In 1946, figures suggest *The Eternal Light* had a listenership of five million, and in 1947, a ratings brochure quotes listenership at six million. Shandler and Katz, "Broadcasting American Judaism," 389, 372–373.

19. *Sadie Sender for JDC in Frankfort*, aired June 6, 1946, YIVO Sound Archive. Another of this type of radio broadcast is "JDC Interview with a Czech Refugee," aired June 27, 1950, YIVO Sound Archive.

20. In this double reading, I rely on Krah's idea of *The Eternal Light*'s dual audience, where Jewish listeners heard one lesson and non-Jewish listeners heard another. "Role Models or Foils," 267.

21. Some examples of this type of radio broadcast include "Delayed Pilgrims Dinner," aired November 27, 1947, YIVO Sound Archive; "Out of the Wilderness," aired April 6, 1947, YIVO Sound Archive; "While Burns Roams," aired June 4, 1947, YIVO Sound Archive; "Freedom Train: Delayed Pilgrims," NCJW, aired January 16, 1949, YIVO Sound Archive. Survivors were also discussed in an American context through interviews, roundtables, and debates about immigration policy, but these programs did not feature survivors or speak to their experiences.

22. "Out of the Wilderness."

23. For more about Passover and Holocaust commemoration in postwar America, see Diner, *We Remember with Reverence and Love*, 62.

24. "Out of the Wilderness."

25. Some examples of radio dramas concerned with survivors include "Displaced," Marr Sound Archive; *The Golden Door*, "I Am a Displaced Person," Marr Sound Archive; *The Golden Door*, "A Parable for Easter," Marr Sound Archive; *The Golden Door*, "Joseph in America," YIVO Sound Archive; *The Golden Door*, "Case

History," aired June 8, 1947, YIVO Sound Archive; "Escape from a Dream," USNA, aired May 18, 1947, YIVO Sound Archive.

26. Shandler and Katz, "Broadcasting American Judaism," 367.

27. Seldes argues that *March of Time* had a great sense of the radio medium: "Particularly the sense of the present, that whatever you heard was happening at that moment, was energetically exploited by *The March of Time* and the mixed sense of adventure and doom, the crackling of cellophane mingled with the sound of the last trump in the portentous voice of the announcer, made this program exciting. It was one of the small number of inventions that gave listeners the experience of radio as a thing in itself, not merely a new way of transmitting the old." Seldes, *Great Audience*, 119.

28. Details about "Delayed Pilgrims Dinner" are included in the introduction. "Delayed Pilgrims Dinner," YIVO Sound Archive.

29. See Garland, *After They Closed the Gates*, 189–192 for more about the political debates regarding DPs, Jewish quotas, and US immigration more broadly in the 1940s.

30. The integration of American myths into American Jewish narratives was not new to the postwar period. As Jonathan Sarna asserts, American Jews regularly applied American themes like Thanksgiving into Jewish stories in conscious and subconscious efforts to show that American and Jewish values were not only compatible but also mutually enhancing. Jonathan D. Sarna, "The Cult of Synthesis in American Jewish Culture," *Jewish Social Studies*, n.s., 5, no. 1/2 (October 1, 1998): 52–79, 52.

31. "Delayed Pilgrims Dinner."

32. *The Eternal Light*, "The Late Comers," aired November 23, 1947, WOR NY, YIVO Sound Archive; "The Arrival of Delayed Pilgrims," WNYC, YIVO Sound Archive.

33. Dinnerstein, *America and the Survivors of the Holocaust*, 174–287.

34. Dinnerstein, *America and the Survivors of the Holocaust*, chapter 5: "The Formation of the Citizens Committee."

35. *Citizen's Committee on Displaced Persons: A Brief Statement of Aims*, pamphlet, 1947, Historical Society Library Pamphlet Collection, 54–1522, Wisconsin Historical Society Archives.

36. *The Golden Door*, "A Parable for Easter."

37. Ibid.

38. "Out of the Wilderness."

39. Daniel Lang, "Displaced," *New Yorker*, September 13, 1947, 100–111.

40. "Displaced," sponsored by the CCDP, sound recording, YIVO Sound Archive and Marr Sound Archives.

41. Lang, "Displaced," 100.

NOTES TO PAGES 59–62

42. The *Marine Perch* left Bremen on July 18, 1946. Maier is listed on the manifest of the *Marine Perch*, Document Number 81649948#1, International Tracing Service, accessed at US Holocaust Memorial Museum (USHMM), summer 2012.

43. Lang, "Displaced," 100.

44. "Displaced," sound recording.

45. In her MA thesis about USNA radio programs, Roberta Newman suggests that the USNA featured the "best of" refugees in order to portray the most positive idea of DPs. As such, in the 1944 National Refugee Service film *The New Americans*, Albert Einstein and Thomas Mann are featured. She asserts that the USNA also intentionally represented refugees who had successfully adjusted to American life. Roberta Newman, "Delayed Pilgrims: The Radio Programs of the United Service for New Americans, 1947–48," MA thesis, New York University, 1996, 20. Copy of thesis obtained through the author.

46. The basic narrative given here is expressed by Lang and in the radio drama. From documents acquired at the USHMM, I can add that Maier was born in Karlovy Vary on February 17, 1911, and moved to Prague in 1938. He was deported to Terezin on December 4, 1941, and to Auschwitz on October 1, 1944. He was then deported to Ohrdruf in December of 1944, to Sachsenhausen in February 1945, and to Buchenwald in March 1945. He was finally liberated from Buchenwald on April 11, 1945. Deportation to Terezin and Auschwitz documented on Ústřední Kartotéka—Transporty, Document Number 5012316#1, International Tracing Service, accessed at USHMM, summer 2012. Additional deportation information from Document Number 40717701#1, International Tracing Service, accessed at USHMM, summer 2012.

47. Lang, "Displaced," 108.

48. "Displaced," sound recording.

49. For the history of commemoration of the Warsaw Ghetto Uprising, see James Edward Young, "The Biography of a Memorial Icon: Nathan Rapoport's Warsaw Ghetto Monument," *Representations* 26 (1989): 69–106.

50. Christopher Browning, *Remembering Survival: Inside a Nazi Slave-Labor Camp* (New York: W.W. Norton, 2010), 11.

51. Naomi Seidman, "Elie Wiesel and the Scandal of Jewish Rage," *Jewish Social Studies*, n.s., 3, no. 1 (autumn 1996): 1–19, 8; Henry Greenspan, "The Awakening of Memory: Survivor Testimony in the First Years after the Holocaust, and Today," USHMM, Monna and Otto Weinmann Lecture Series, May 17, 2000, 19, http://www.ushmm.org/m/pdfs/Publication_OP_2001-02.pdf. See also my chapter "Holocaust Memory in Displaced Persons Camps: David P. Boder" in David Cesarani and Eric J. Sundquist, eds., *After the Holocaust: Challenging the Myth of Silence* (London: Routledge, 2012), 115–126.

52. Alan Rosen writes that Boder "had trouble following the account [of Marko Moskovitz] because Moskovitz's description of people 'often alive' being burned in

NOTES TO PAGES 62–65

pits goes against the grain of what is usual, even in times of war." Alan Rosen, *The Wonder of Their Voices: The 1946 Holocaust Interviews of David Boder* (New York: Oxford University Press, 2010), 5.

53. Lawrence L. Langer, *Holocaust Testimonies: The Ruins of Memory* (New Haven, CT: Yale University Press, 1991), 33.

54. Ibid.

55. Throughout his career, Muni was best known for his ability to become anyone through expert makeup, but he began performing on radio, on Lux Radio Theater, to rave reviews in 1935. Throughout the 1940s, he became a vocal advocate for Jewish causes—particularly Zionist efforts to support a Jewish State after 1946. Jerome Lawrence, *Actor, the Life and Times of Paul Muni* (New York: Putnam, 1974), 207, 291.

56. Shandler and Katz, "Broadcasting American Judaism," 372. Paul Muni also narrated the UJA short film *The Will to Live*, which documented DPs who had found homes in Israel. List of "Israel Resources," Box 36, Folder 25, AJC/AJHS.

57. My understanding of giving testimony is informed by (among others) Langer, *Holocaust Testimonies*; Felman and Laub, *Testimony*; Hartman, *Longest Shadow*; Henry Greenspan, *On Listening to Holocaust Survivors: Recounting and Life History* (Westport, CT: Praeger, 1998).

58. In the last three decades, scholars have extensively explored concerns about the limits of representation and the ethics of performance and re-creation of the Holocaust. Scholars are skeptical of re-creating events of the Holocaust, particularly in a performative and fictionalized way. This kind of theoretical discussion was not present in the late 1940s, and the practice of reenacting historical events was very popular on the radio. For more, see Saul Friedländer, ed., *Probing the Limits of Representation: Nazism and the "Final Solution"* (Cambridge, MA: Harvard University Press, 1992). This scholarly conversation continues, as evidenced at a 2012 follow-up conference at UCLA, "History Unlimited: Probing the Ethics of Holocaust Culture," April 21–23, 2012 and the resulting book Claudio Fogu, Wulf Kansteiner, and Todd Samuel Presner, eds., *Probing the Ethics of Holocaust Culture* (Cambridge, MA: Harvard University Press, 2016).

59. Langer emphasizes, "The witness does not *tell* the story; he reenacts it." Langer, *Holocaust Testimonies*, 27.

60. Lang, "Displaced," 104.

61. Ibid., 100.

62. "Displaced," sound recording.

63. Recordings of these broadcasts are available from the Marr Sound Archives and YIVO Sound Archives. "I Am a Displaced Person," audio recording, Marr Sound Archives; "Parable for Easter," audio recording, Marr Sound Archives; "Joseph in America," audio recording, YIVO Sound Archives.

64. Silva Maldist was a native of Estonia able to enter the US to study languages in America at Bennington College in Vermont. Her story details her time

158   NOTES TO PAGES 66–68

performing slave labor in Germany. In the dramatization, the actress portraying her has an American accent, but the Nazis in the story have sinister foreign accents. At the end of the program, Silva speaks for herself with a slight European accent. *The Golden Door*, "I Am a Displaced Person."

65. "Joseph in America" narrates the story of Joseph Marshok, a watchmaker who survived a concentration camp because he could fix clocks. He is not explicitly referred to as Jewish, and the story is focused on him as part of the new labor force in the US. On arriving in America, he joined the CIO and was elected to his local Patriots' Day Committee because he knew what it was like "to live under tyranny and under freedom." The broadcast features a speech by the president of the CIO, who says that there is no basis for fear that admitting immigrants will "jeopardize American jobs"—"they know tyranny and its destruction, here they will work for democracy and its freedom." This production was specifically designed to combat the fear that DPs would take away American jobs, a strong part of the argument against opening immigration quotas. *The Golden Door*, "Joseph in America."

66. "Case History #20,000" Script, 1, Box 12, Folder: Radio Starter Kits, 1947, OFPA/Hadassah.

67. *Ask . . . Hannah*, brochure, Box 12, Folder: Presidents and Chairmen Circulates, 1946, Oct–Dec, OFPA/Hadassah.

68. Marian G. Greenberg, *There Is Hope for Your Children: Youth Aliyah, Henrietta Szold, and Hadassah* (New York: Hadassah, the Women's Zionist Organization of America, 1986) and Sandra Berliant Kadosh, "Ideology vs. Reality: Youth Aliyah and the Rescue of Jewish Children during the Holocaust, 1933–1945," PhD diss., Columbia University, 1995.

69. Greenberg, *There Is Hope for Your Children*, 92.

70. Radio Manual, 1944, Box 131, Folder: Public Relations Manuals 1943–1944, NCJW/LOC. Similar manuals are held in Box 131, Folder: Public Relations Manuals, 1947–1957, NCJW/LOC.

71. Folders of case histories are abundant in the Hadassah papers of the archives of Youth Aliyah. For one example, Publicity Stories 1946–1947, Box 23, Folder 172, YAP/Hadassah. Also, each monthly Hadassah bulletin, *Headlines*, contained a Youth Aliyah story, generally featuring one young person's experience of getting to and thriving in Palestine/Israel.

72. *Escape to Life*, brochure, Box 21, Folder 155: Hadassah Fundraising Materials—1945, YAP/Hadassah.

73. A cover letter dated January 1947 introduces the new brochure: "*Ask . . . Hannah* is your new Youth Aliyah case-history folder. It takes the place of *Diary by Joseph*, which you used so successfully last year, and like the previous case history is a true story of the sufferings endured by a Jewish child who has been rescued and given a new lease on life by Youth Aliyah." Letter and Brochure, January 1947

NOTES TO PAGES 70–76

Publicity Kit, Box 12, Folder: Presidents and Chairmen Circulates, 1946, Oct–Dec, OFPA/Hadassah.

74. Letter from Mrs. Siegfried Kramarsky to Mrs. Eva Michaelis, August 29, 1946, Box 17, Folder 118, YAP/Hadassah.

75. The brochure and adopted radio script both were distributed to local chapters, although local groups were asked to purchase as many copies as needed for local campaigns. The brochures were thirty-five cents for one hundred copies and "designed to fit any ordinary business envelope, so there should be no problem mailing them." Cover Letter Attached to *Ask . . . Hannah*, Box 12, Folder: Presidents and Chairmen Circulates, 1946, Oct–Dec, OFPA/Hadassah.

76. The cover letter with the script explains that the radio program should be tied to all possible media, including "newspapers, membership mailings, contacts, bulletin boards, telephone squads, and more." "Case History #20,000" Script, 1, Box 12, Folder: Radio Starter Kits, 1947, OFPA/Hadassah.

77. Cover Letter, "Case History #20,000" Script, Box 12, Folder: Radio Starter Kits, 1947, OFPA/Hadassah.

78. The cover letter for the "starter" radio manual for Hadassah radio chairmen instructed, "Try, too, to work in our scripts, cutting them if necessary, into the programs of regular broadcasters who run daily or weekly shows." "Hadassah on the Air," March 5, 1947, Box 12, Folder: Radio Starter Kits, 1947, OFPA/Hadassah. Monthly bulletins included program ideas, but the annual manual was sent with instructions and lists of responsibilities when new chairwomen assumed local roles. "Presidents and Chairmen Circulates, 1946, June–Sept," "Presidents and Chairmen Circulates, 1946, Oct–Dec," "Radio Starter Kits, 1947," and "Presidents and Chairmen Circulated Press Kits, 1948," Box 12, Folders: Presidents and Chairmen Press Kits, 1946–1947, OFPA/Hadassah.

79. "Case History #20,000" Script.

80. Langer, *Holocaust Testimonies*, 19–21.

81. Hartman, *Longest Shadow*, 144.

82. Young, *Writing and Rewriting the Holocaust,* 169.

83. Amit Pinchevski, "The Audiovisual Unconscious: Media and Trauma in the Video Archive for Holocaust Testimonies," *Critical Inquiry* 39, no. 1 (autumn 2012). See also Shenker, *Reframing Holocaust Testimony.*

84. Rosen, *Wonder of Their Voices*, 150.

85. Letter to National Defense Research Committee, June 19, 1945, Box 1, Section 1, DPB/UCLA.

86. Quoted in Rosen, *Wonder of Their Voices*, 150.

Translating Postwar Europe

1. Letter from Charles Rosenbaum to Rabbi Herbert Friedman, June 20, 1946, Box 1, Folder 4, HAFP/AJA.

2. Wieviorka, *Era of the Witness*, 96–144, and Greenspan et al., "Engaging Survivors."

3. Shoshanah Felman, "The Return of the Voice: Claude Lanzmann's Shoah," in *Testimony: Crises of Witnessing in Literature, Psychoanalysis, and History*, ed. Shoshana Felman and Dori Laub (New York: Routledge, 1992), 204–283.

4. I also grapple with debates about the relationship between survivor and "listener," which defines the process of testimony for Dominik LaCapra, Dori Laub, and Henry Greenspan. See LaCapra, *History and Memory*, 11; Laub, "Bearing Witness or the Vicissitudes of Listening"; Greenspan, *On Listening*, xvii.

5. For the development of witness culture around Holocaust survivors, see Wieviorka, *Era of the Witness*.

6. Friedman's letter was read aloud to "some 1100 present" congregation members at Rosh Hashanah services and excerpted in several local newspapers. "Friedman Praised for Work," *Intermountain Jewish News*, and "Rabbi Friedman Is Lauded for German Morale Work," *Rocky Mountain News*, September 29, 1946, Clippings, Box 1, Folder 5, HAFP/AJA.

7. Remarks to Denver Campaign Dinner, September 15, 1946, Box 1, Folder 4, HAFP/AJA.

8. The strength of his language is conveyed even more boldly in the broken syntax of a telegram that reads, "Returned from Poland few weeks ago. Jews there in panic. Average of three killed daily . . . have seen with my own eyes tired sick hungry Jews shoving across border . . . American Jews must absolutely give as never before. Events here are beyond imagination." Telegram from Chaplain Friedman to Charles Rosenbaum, September 11, 1946, Box 1, Folder 4, HAFP/AJA.

9. The debate about Americanization of the Holocaust sets particularity against universalization in framing Holocaust narratives. See Alvin Rosenfeld, "The Americanization of the Holocaust," in *Thinking about the Holocaust: After Half a Century*, ed. Alvin Rosenfeld (Bloomington: Indiana University Press, 1997), 119–150. See also Michael Berenbaum, *After Tragedy and Triumph: Essays in Modern Jewish Thought and the American Experience* (Cambridge: Cambridge University Press, 1990).

10. Greenspan et al., "Engaging Survivors."

11. For more about Razovsky, see Bat-Ami Zucker, *Cecilia Razovsky and the American Jewish Women's Rescue Operations in the Second World War* (London: Vallentine Mitchell, 2008).

12. See, in particular, Rebecca Kobrin, "American Jewish Internationalism, Laura Margolis and the Power of Female Diplomacy, 1941–1943," *Journal of Modern Jewish Studies* 21, no. 2 (2022): 234–252. This special edition of *Journal of Modern Jewish Studies*, edited by Jaclyn Granick and Abigail Green, treats the role of women in international Jewish aid work across the twentieth century. See also Zhava Litvac Glaser, "Laura Margolis and JDC Efforts in Cuba and

NOTES TO PAGES 78–80

Shanghai: Sustaining Refugees in a Time of Catastrophe," in *The JDC at 100: A Century of Humanitarianism*, ed. Avinoam Patt et al. (Detroit: Wayne State University Press, 2019).

13. Kobrin, "American Jewish Internationalism," 235.

14. Letter from Cecilia Razovsky to Dr. Morris Davidson (her husband), June 12, 1945, Box 1, Folder 4, Cecilia Razovsky Papers (CRP)/AJHS. Other aid workers similarly understood the relationship between their experiences and fundraising at home.

15. Ibid.

16. For example, she wrote to Morris, "Tonight a young doctor came to see me; he has just arrived from a camp where he took care of the brother-in-law of a very important person in the USA and I am cabling details to the office first thing in the morning. You will recognize the story when you see it in the press." Ibid.

17. Letter from Olive L. Sawyer, assistant chief of groups liaison, Office of Public Information, UNRRA, October 8, 1945, Box 6, Folder 1, CRP/AJHS.

18. Dori Laub has defined the essential role of listeners in testimony creation as "party to the creation of knowledge." Laub, "Bearing Witness."

19. Sylvia Milrod, "Collected Notes on Lecture Cecilia Razovsky Davidson," July 25, 1945, Box 6, Folder 1, CRP/AJHS. These notes include long direct quotes from Razovsky and mark the most complete account of her approach to speaking engagements. For more about private agencies and the development of private aid work after the Holocaust, see Laura Hobson Faure and Veerle Vanden Daelen, "Imported from the United States? The Centralization of Private Jewish Welfare after the Holocaust: The Cases of Belgium and France," in Avinoam Patt et al., *The JDC at 100: A Century of Humanitarianism*.

20. Bela Fabian was a founder of the Hungarian Liberal Party and former head of the opposition in the Hungarian Parliament under the pro-Nazi regime of Admiral Horthy. He immigrated to the US in 1948 and became a vocal anti-Communist. Fabian died in December 1996.

21. Milrod, "Collected Notes."

22. Terrence T. Des Pres, *The Survivor: An Anatomy of Life in the Death Camps* (New York: Oxford University Press, 1976), 32. See also Garbarini, *Numbered Days* and Zoë Waxman, *Writing the Holocaust: Identity, Testimony, Representation* (Oxford: Oxford University Press, 2006).

23. Milrod, "Collected Notes." Razovsky's call for aid workers to listen as a means of helping survivors is a reminder that many social workers at the time were not focused on listening. As Beth Cohen describes in *Case Closed: Holocaust Survivors in Postwar America*, many social workers who aided Jewish survivors upon their arrival in the United States rushed survivors through services, pushing them to find jobs and permanent housing without attention to their particular experiences under Nazism or their psychological and emotional needs.

162   NOTES TO PAGES 80–83

24. Greenspan, *On Listening*, 6.

25. Milrod, "Collected Notes."

26. Des Pres, "Introduction," in *The Survivor*, xiii.

27. Between 1946 and 1950, Razovsky spoke on behalf of JDC to groups of all sizes, addressing meetings and events sponsored by NCJW, Hadassah, B'nai B'rith, and local synagogues. She traveled the entire East Coast and the American South. JDC Weekly Review, Vol II: 41–42 (October 16, 1946), Reel 112, IS 6/3, JDC Archives-Jerusalem, Istanbul Office (JDC-J), USHMM Collection Division. Letter to Cecilia Razovsky, June 22, 1946, Reports on Meetings Held on Behalf of UJA Campaign, Addressed by Cecilia Razovsky, and Field Report from Mobile, AL, November 9, 1950, Box 6, Folder 9, CRP/AJHS.

28. A significant part of the Rabbi Herbert A. Friedman Collection at the American Jewish Archives has been digitized and is available for online access at https://fa.americanjewisharchives.org/friedman.

29. Contemporary testimony collections, like that of the USC Shoah Foundation, mark liberation as a definitive transition from Jewish persecution to freedom by structuring survivor stories into a prewar, wartime, and postwar three-act structure. Shenker, *Reframing Holocaust Testimony*, 119.

30. Transfer Order, March 16, 1946, Box 1, Folder 3, HAFP/AJA.

31. Friedman served UJA as executive director and then executive vice-chairman from 1955 to 1982, when he left to help launch the Wexner Heritage Foundation with Les Wexner.

32. I. L. Kenen, executive secretary of American Jewish Conference, wrote of Friedman's "love for his work, his affection for the people whose lives he is helping to rebuild." Kenen described a visit to Ziegheim DP camp during which he felt unable to talk to the "unfortunate" DPs. He found that the survivors were not interested in American civilians, but "they were swarming about Rabbi Friedman; he became the center of a huge crowd which followed him as he walked. . . . He had an answer and a sympathetic word for them all." Letter from I. L. Kenen to Henry Winter, September 16, 1946, Box 1, Folder 4, HAFP/AJA.

33. In a letter from July 5, 1946, Friedman rejected attempts by his congregation at home to appeal for an early discharge from the army. Friedman made clear that "morally and according to the dictates of my conscience," he could not seek an early discharge. He stated that "knowing the present DP situation as I do . . . it is simply not right for me" to leave. Letter from Friedman to Louis Isaacson, July 5, 1946, Box 1, Folder 4, HAFP/AJA.

34. Telegram from Henry Morgenthau Jr. to Louis C. Isaacson, President of Congregation Emanuel, June 9, 1947, and letter from Louis C. Isaacson to Congregants, June 11, 1947, Box 1, Folder 4, HAFP/AJA.

35. Letter from Friedman to "Dear Friends," August 30, 1946, Box 1, Folder 4, HAFP/AJA.

NOTES TO PAGES 84–89

36. Remarks to Campaign Dinner, Denver, September 15, 1946, Box 1, Folder 4, HAFP/AJA.

37. Letter from Friedman to "Dear Friends."

38. Langer, *Admitting the Holocaust*, 8. A longer discussion of this gap is in chapter 1, in considering the fundraising film *Battle for Survival*.

39. Bauer notes that Jews devoted to working in Europe, the Middle East, and Shanghai "agreed to go abroad out of idealism, or adventure-seeking, or both." Bauer, *Out of the Ashes*, xx.

40. Letter from Henry Levy to Herbert Friedman, August 17, 1947, Box 1, Folder 4, HAFP/AJA.

41. Letter from Friedman to Levy, October 21, 1947, Box 23, Folder 7, HAFP/AJA.

42. Rosenfeld, "Americanization of the Holocaust," 123.

43. Letter from Friedman to "Dear Friends."

44. The IRO was the successor organization to UNRRA, founded in 1947. The organization was responsible for the relief and rehabilitation of refugees after the end of World War II. "'Crisis Meeting' Called by Mr. Morgenthau on June 7–8," *UJA Campaigner*, Vol II: 21 (June 2, 1947) 1, Box 39, HAFP/AJA.

45. Friedman said, "I am sorry about what I said to Mr. Firestein from Los Angeles. I was really pretty emotional, and you could tell it from my voice before. I was pretty burned up, so I apologize to him and to everybody now for having blown my top. But I have lived with these people for a year and a half." Transcript of Friedman's Speech, June 8, 1947, 100, Box 23, Folder 1, HAFP/AJA.

46. Ibid., 81.

47. Ibid., 83.

48. Letter from Bernard Schramm to Friedman, March 24, 1948, Box 23, Folder 3, HAFP/AJA.

49. Event Program, April 11, 1948, Box 23, Folder 3, HAFP/AJA.

50. Letter from Friedman to Schramm, April 5, 1948, Box 23, Folder 3, HAFP/AJA.

51. There is evidence that Friedman recorded what I am calling the "absent speech" in September 1946, but no conclusion about whether the speech was played at the campaign dinner or read by someone else from Friedman's transcript. Telegram text from Chaplain Friedman to Charles Rosenbaum, September 11, 1946, Box 1, Folder 4, HAFP/AJA.

52. Transcript of Friedman's Speech, June 8, 1947, Box 23, Folder 1, HAFP/AJA.

53. Inserted Hand-Written Note in Transcript of Friedman's Speech, June 8, 1947, Box 23, Folder 1, HAFP/AJA.

54. Leo Lania, *The Nine Lives of Europe* (New York: Funk & Wagnalls in association with United Nations World, 1950).

55. JDC Weekly Review II, no. 37 (September 13, 1946) and II, no. 41–42 (October 16, 1946), Reel 112, IS 6/3, JDC-J/USHMM.

164 NOTES TO PAGES 89–93

56. JDC Weekly Review, Vol II: 43 (October 25, 1946), Reel 112, IS 6/3, JDC-J/USHMM.

57. JDC Weekly Reviews (1946–1950), Reel 112, IS 6/3, JDC-J/USHMM. The next chapter explores the SOS program and the work of sending material aid to Europe in depth.

58. "Forty Jewish Leaders Leave by Plane for Europe and Palestine on U.J.A. Mission," *Jewish Telegraphic Agency*, January 28, 1948, http://www.jta .org/1948/01/28/archive/forty-jewish-leaders-leave-by-plane-for-europe-and -palestine-on-u-j-a-mission.

59. Press Release, January 16, 1948, Box 23, Folder 3, HAFP/AJA.

60. "Forty Jewish Leaders Leave by Plane."

61. Meeting Announcement, Box 18, Folder 119, YAP/Hadassah.

62. Tamara de Sola Poole, *The Exiles on Cyprus* (Survey Associates, 1947). Correspondence and Copies of Publications, Box 25, Folder 181, YAP/Hadassah.

63. Board minutes from the November 26, 1946, meeting document the negotiated arrangement with Martha Sharp, Box 18, Folder 119, YAP/Hadassah. Sharp was an important witness for Hadassah, converting the urgency of postwar Jewish emigration for non-Jewish audiences through her organization. For more about Sharp, see Susan Elisabeth Subak, *Rescue & Flight: American Relief Workers Who Defied the Nazis* (Lincoln: University of Nebraska Press, 2010). In 2005, Sharp was posthumously recognized with her husband as a Righteous Among the Gentiles by Yad Vashem for her work saving Lion Feuchtwanger from the Nazis and helping Jews from France and Czechoslovakia avoid deportation. Learn more at the Yad Vashem Righteous Among the Nations Database at https://collections.yadvashem .org/en/righteous.

64. Leo Srole, "Why the DPs Can't Wait: Proposing an International Plan of Rescue," *Commentary* 3 (1947): 13–47.

65. Ibid., 24.

66. The role of Jewish communal organizations in each of these political battles deserves concerted attention, which it will not receive here. I raise these examples only to address how the role of secondary witnesses and the authority of being there were employed not only to raise funds but also to advocate for political solutions to the postwar DP crisis.

67. Joseph J. Schwartz, *Testimony before the Anglo-American Committee of Inquiry* (New York: American Jewish Joint Distribution Committee, 1946).

68. NCRAC was made up of six constituent organizations: the American Jewish Committee (AJC), the American Jewish Congress, B'nai B'rith, the Jewish Labor Committee, Jewish War Veterans of the United States, and the Union of American Hebrew Congregations.

69. Statement of Hon. Herbert H. Lehman, June 1947, Box 131, Folder 4, AJC/YIVO.

NOTES TO PAGES 93–95

70. Firsthand survivor accounts were published in both the English and Yiddish press, as were survivor accounts in memoirs and *Yizkor* books. Diner, *We Remember with Reverence and Love*, 188, 430n101.

71. A mass meeting was held at Madison Square Garden on June 11, 1946, with an estimated eighteen thousand people in attendance to hear Dr. Emil Sommerstein, president of the Jewish Central Committee of Poland. The meeting was sponsored by AJC, the Federation of Polish Jews, the Jewish Fraternal People's Order, the Labor Zionist Committee for Relief & Rehabilitation, the United Galician Jews, and the American Council of Warsaw Jews, a diverse group of organizations that reflected the reach of survivor witnessing in the New York area. At a mass rally the next day in Chicago, Sommerstein was quoted as saying, "Hitler, the enemy of mankind, the most terrible criminal in the whole of history, had for his purpose the extermination of the Jewish people. This goal he attained, to gruesome extent, on Polish soil in the death factories of Oswiecim, Treblinka, Maidenek, Belzec, Sobibor, Chelmno, Travaiki, where three million, two hundred thousand Polish Jews were murdered in addition to three million Jews of other countries of Europe." Sommerstein's act of witnessing was tied to American Jewish fundraising, including the statement that the delegation had come to their "brethren in the United States with an appeal for immediate help." Dr. Sommerstein was a member of the Polish Parliament before the war and a member of the first postwar Polish government. He survived the war in the Soviet Union, enduring imprisonment by the Soviet authorities and deportation to a gulag. He remained in the United States after this sponsored trip and died there in 1957. Flyer for Mass Meeting, June 11, 1946, Box 23a, Folder 9, United States Territorial Collection (USTC), YIVO Archive, and "An End to the Darkness," *Chicago Sentinel* 143, no. 11 (June 13, 1946). On March 12, 1947, Etty Hassid of Salonica, a recipient of an NCJW scholarship for social work, "told her story" at the NCJW New York headquarters. An introductory pamphlet instructed the women to become acquainted with local members "by making yourself available to attend major meetings and speaking to the Section when they request it. . . . You will no doubt be asked to speak to other civic, church, and synagogue groups." What these young women were expected to talk about is unclear. Did they tell their stories? Or did they offer thanks for the support of NCJW? Press Release, March 12, 1947, and "Information for Scholarship Students," November 1948, Box 125, Folder: Overseas, Scholarships, 1946–1956, National Council of Jewish Women Papers (NCJW)/LOC.

72. Leo W. Schwarz, *The Root and the Bough: The Epic of an Enduring People* (New York: Rinehart, 1949), preface.

73. Prell, "Triumph, Accommodation, and Resistance," 115.

74. Henry Lilienheim, "Mine Eyes Have Seen," in Schwarz, *Root and the Bough*, 3–12.

166   NOTES TO PAGES 95–97

75. As Schwarz wrote of these stories: "They bear witness that hatred is human but its works are short-lived; that one can bear the yellow patch with pride, knowing that it is a badge of human dignity; that even in darkness, the heart and the mind contain the seed of all that is gracious and radiant." *Root and the Bough*, xvi.

76. For more about Boder's methodology and scientific ambitions, see Todd Presner, *Ethics of the Algorithm*, 79–122.

77. Memoranda, May 3, 1946, Box 1, Folder 3, DPBP/UCLA.

78. Boder founded the Psychological Museum in 1937 in Chicago. The museum had failed by 1957. For more about Boder's Psychological Museum project, see Ludy T. Benjamin, "David Boder's Psychological Museum and the Exposition of 1938," *Psychological Record* 29 (1979): 559–565, https://doi.org/10.1007/BF03394644.

79. He moved to Los Angeles for health reasons in 1952. He remained connected to his family and friends in Europe even after settling in America and was able to balance these different worlds. For a critical look at Boder's biography, see Rosen, *Wonder of Their Voices*, 25–43.

80. In nearly every project proposal, Boder described the need for wire-recorded interviews with survivors: "These people are entitled to their own Ernie Pyle, and since that appears practically impossible, the exact recording of their tale seems the nearest and most feasible alternative." Project Proposal, May 3, 1946, Box 1, Folder 3, DPBP/UCLA.

81. Voices of the Holocaust is available online at http://voices.iit.edu/.

82. David P. Boder, "The Displaced People of Europe: Preliminary Notes on a Psychological and Anthropological Study," *Illinois Tech Engineer*, March 1947, 18–34.

83. The article details his initial interest in interviewing DPs, his trip to Europe, and the difficulties of carrying recording equipment across Europe. As Boder wrote, "Considering that the recorder, a one-day supply of spools, and necessary accessories amounted to a load of about sixty pounds, my urgent dependence upon transportation by automobile becomes obvious." Ibid., 19.

84. In using the term "testimony" here, I mean to define Boder's interviews as distinct from other narratives at the time. Boder's materials were designed to have historical, psychological, and scientific relevance and, as such, gave survivors a chance to give testimony—to speak directly and at length about their own experiences alongside an active and intentional listener.

85. Boder described his translation process as follows: "The original stories were not transcribed on paper and then translated in the silence of the study. By the use of two Peirce Wire Recorders with stop and start controls I listened on one machine to the original, sentence by sentence, and then dictated the English translations on the other machine. Typists then transcribed the material from the translated recordings." Boder, *I Did Not Interview the Dead*, xiii.

NOTES TO PAGES 97–101

86. Boder, "Displaced People of Europe," 19–20. Rosen highlights Boder's commitment to sound even as he converted the project to print, citing Boder's 1948 article "Spool 169" as a reference to the auditory nature of the article content. Rosen, *Wonder in Their Voices*, 121. This attention to the recorded interviews and desire to recreate an auditory experience for the audience evokes Laub and Greenspan's use of the term "listener." Laub, "Bearing Witness," and Greenspan, *On Listening*.

87. Boder, "Displaced People of Europe," 20.

88. By including his own role as interviewer in the passage, Boder followed psychological and anthropological methodologies at the time. See the introduction to *The D.P. Story* (an early title for *I Did Not Interview the Dead*), unpublished manuscript, 29, Box 3, DPBP/UCLA.

89. Rosen, *Wonder in Their Voices*, 122–127. Marie Syrkin, *Blessed Is the Match: The Story of Jewish Resistance* (Philadelphia: Jewish Publication Society of America, 1976).

90. Series of Letters, Including One to Dr. Lawrence C. Powell, UCLA Librarian, December 19, 1955, Box 2, Folder "Copyright and Library of Congress," DPBP/UCLA.

91. Letter from Boder to Goldsmith, July 17, 1945, and Letter to B'nai B'rith, July 21, 1945, Box 1, Folder 1, DPBP/UCLA.

92. Letter from Boder to Lieutenant Carl Devoe, USNR, Office of Strategic Services, July 17, 1945, Box 1, Folder 1, DPBP/UCLA.

93. Boder, *Topical Autobiographies*, Addenda, 4 (3163), DPBP/UCLA.

Sending Hope, Securing Peace

1. A JDC press release from November 25, 1945, cites eight women's groups that led the charge, including Hadassah (the women's Zionist organization of America), the Council of Jewish Federations and Welfare Funds, Mizrachi Women's Organization of America, Women's Division of the Union of Orthodox Jewish Congregation of America, National Women's League of the United Synagogue of America, National Federation of Temple Sisterhoods, National Council of Jewish Women (NCJW), National Jewish Welfare Board, Federation of Jewish Women's Organizations, Women's Supreme Council of B'nai B'rith, and the Ladies Auxiliary of the Jewish War Veterans of the United States. "JDC Calls for Contributions from National Groups," press release, November 25, 1945, 45/54, #1268, JDC-NY. By November 1946, seventeen women's groups had joined the effort to launch SOS, according to a press release from November 8, 1946. "Three Years of Achievement" repeats the praise of seventeen women's organizations. "Three Years of Achievement," *SOS Bulletin* 8:1, April 1949, AR 45/54, File 1345, JDC-NY.

2. Letter from Paul Baerwald to Mrs. Anna Rosenberg, October 31, 1945, 45/54, #1268, JDC-NY.

3. For more about Jewish chaplains in World War II, see Ronit Y. Stahl, *Enlisting Faith: How the Military Chaplaincy Shaped Religion and State in Modern America* (Cambridge, MA: Harvard University Press, 2017).

168 NOTES TO PAGES 101–105

4. Many letters document the influence of chaplains in activating women's networks of philanthropy: Letter from Mrs. Alfred R. Bachrach, National Jewish Welfare Board, to Louis H. Sobel, November 7, 1945, 45/54, #1270, JDC-NY. Mrs. Bachrach noted, "Women's Division has been asked by Jewish chaplains and by our workers in Europe to try to provide small items . . . for women in the civilian communities of the liberated countries." Mrs. Anne Cohen, chairman of Help-a-Chaplain committee of the Cleveland Jewish Center Sisterhood, wrote to Mr. Goldhamer of the Jewish Welfare Federation of Cleveland, "A group of women from our Sisterhood of the Cleveland Jewish Center recently undertook to send used clothing and food to Italy and Germany in response to repeated urgent pleas from army chaplains in Europe." Letter from Mrs. Anne Cohen to Mr. Goldhamer, November 1, 1945, 45/54, #1268, JDC-NY.

5. Preliminary Announcement Letter, November 15, 1945, 45/54, #1268, JDC-NY.

6. "Three Years of Achievement" and "SOS Collected over 26,300,000 Pounds of Relief Supplies during Past Three Years," April 11, 1949, JTA Online Archive, https://www.jta.org/archive/sos-collected-over-26300-pounds-of-relief-supplies-during-past-three-years.

7. SOS Executive Meeting Minutes, June 15, 1948, 45/54, #1332, JDC-NY. Letter from Sidney S. Cohen to Mr. Robert Dolins, May 27, 1948, 45/54, #1332, JDC-NY. Yehuda Bauer also notes the success of Boston's SOS campaign in 1948. Bauer, *Out of the Ashes.*

8. *They Need These Things to Live!* brochure, Item ID 646520, November 28, 1947, NY AR194554/3/5/9/1345, SOS Publicity Printed Materials, 1947–1949, JDC Archives.

9. The challenges in 1945, when SOS was launched, had been similar. Raphael Levy, publicity director at JDC, had underscored the urgent need, noting in an internal memo that "in 1945 the JDC appropriated $28,000,000 but that this was insufficient." Memo from Raphael Levy to Louis H. Sobel, November 14, 1945, 45/54, #1268, JDC-NY.

10. "Friendship for Jewish Children, Inc.," November 1, 1949, Box D75, File 7, WJC/AJA.

11. The film was shot in color and edited to be used educationally, to "graphically" portray "the most approved methods for carrying through a drive," but it was never finished or distributed. Untitled Rochester SOS Film, YIVO Film Archive. The planning and filming are discussed in Executive Committee Meeting Minutes, May 6, 1948, 45/54, #1332, JDC-NY.

12. Untitled Rochester SOS Film, YIVO Film Archive.

13. Oren Baruch Stier, *Holocaust Icons: Symbolizing the Shoah in History and Memory* (New Brunswick, NJ: Rutgers University Press, 2015), 2.

14. Announcement from Dan West, June 19, 1945, Box 1, Folder: Correspondence, Collection of Coordinating Committee of National Jewish Organizations

NOTES TO PAGES 106–107

for the United National Clothing Collection for War Relief (CC-UNCC), AJHS; "News for Chairmen," February 11, 1946, Microfilm Reel PI/1, Side 1, Folder: Victory Clothing Collection, Press Releases, UNRRA Records, Columbia University Rare Books and Manuscript Division.

15. "Harry S Truman, Radio Report to the American People on the Potsdam Conference," August 9, 1945, American Presidency Project, UC Santa Barbara, https://www.presidency.ucsb.edu/node/230985. This quote was used by the UNCC in a press release on August 14, 1945, about a canning drive run through its administration. Americans were urged to can food they had grown in victory gardens but could not eat and donate it to a local canning center to be sent to Europe.

16. Press Release, August 13, 1945, Reel PI/1, Side 1, Folder: United National Clothing Collection Press Releases, UNRRA/Columbia.

17. "Harry S Truman, Letter to Henry J. Kaiser Calling upon Him to Head the Second United National Clothing Collection Campaign," (September 23, 1945). American Presidency Project, UC Santa Barbara, https://www.presidency.ucsb.edu/node/230475.

18. The President's War Relief Control Board had been established in 1942 to regulate wartime fundraising and monitor overseas aid. Jewish organizations working to aid Jews in Nazi Europe were all registered under the War Relief Control Board.

19. Transcript of Remarks by Hon. Hugh DeLacy in the House of Representatives, October 18, 1945, vol. 1, part 1, UNCC/LOC.

20. Special Release #117, Suggested Editorial for the Victory Drive, January 1946, Reel PI/1, Side 1, Folder: Victory Clothing Collection, Press Releases, UNRRA/Columbia.

21. The full list of participating Jewish organizations included the American Association for Jewish Education, American Committee of OSE, American Jewish Congress Women's Division, Women's American ORT, B'nai B'rith, Council of Jewish Federations and Welfare Funds, Hadassah, Junior Hadassah, Hebrew Immigrant Aid Society (HIAS), JLC, Jewish War Veterans of the United States and Women's Auxiliary, JDC Junior Division, NCJW, National Jewish Welfare Board, Synagogue Council of America, and Mizrachi Women's Organization of America. JDC Announcement from Chairman, Louis H. Sobel, Box 1, Folder 1: "Special Information for Local Communities," CC-UNCC/AJHS.

22. Letter from Louis H. Sobel, August 30, 1945, Box 1, Folder: Correspondence, CC-UNCC/AJHS.

23. "Three Years of Achievement." Yehuda Bauer argues that SOS was designed for just this purpose, "to recruit new forces in the community," an idea Hasia Diner supports by writing that SOS "bound American Jews together as they engaged in a massive rescue effort." Bauer, *Out of the Ashes*, xxi. Diner, *We Remember with Reverence and Love*, 160.

24. "More Than 3,500,000 Pounds of Contributed Relief Supplies Shipped Overseas by JDC's SOS Collection," press release, November 8, 1946, Reel 110, IS 4/2, JDC-J/USHMM.

25. Speech by Mrs. Blanche Gilman given at April 1949 luncheon in honor of SOS, JDC Archive, 45/54 #1330 [45/64 #4369], Subjects: Relief Supplies: S.O.S., 1949.

26. For more about the history of women in Jewish philanthropy, see Beth S. Wenger, "Jewish Women and Voluntarism: Beyond the Myth of Enablers," *American Jewish History* 79, no. 1 (1989): 16–36, and McCarthy, "Parallel Power Structures." For insight into the continued exclusion of women in communal leadership roles, see Amy Stone, "The Locked Cabinet," *Lilith Magazine*, December 4, 1976, https://lilith.org/articles/the-locked-cabinet/.

27. Draft Statement by Robert Dolins, March 5, 1948, 45/54, #1335, JDC-NY.

28. Letter from Mrs. Alfred R. Bachrach, National Jewish Welfare Board, to Louis H. Sobel, November 7, 1945, 45/54, #1270, JDC-NY.

29. Rendering humanitarian aid through material and consumerist terms reflects a broader trend in American Jewish philanthropy. According to Jeffrey Shandler, Jewish consumerism in the early twentieth century took on philanthropic possibilities when buying Jewish products became a way to support the *Yishuv*. He notes that Jewish women in particular invested in Zionism by buying wine, almonds, and cigarettes. Jeffrey Shandler, "Di Toyre Fun Skhoyre, or, I Shop Therefore I Am: The Consumer Cultures of American Jews," in *Longing, Belonging, and the Making of Jewish Consumer Culture*, ed. Gideon Reuveni and Nils Roemer (Leiden: Brill, 2010), 188–189.

30. The final *SOS Bulletin* stated that SOS had allowed new Jewish leaders to emerge, "especially among the women and youth." This final bulletin also repeated thanks to the women's groups that had led the SOS effort. "Three Years of Achievement."

31. Letter from Mrs. Benjamin Diamond, October 18, 1945, 45/54, #1270, JDC-NY.

32. Letter from Mrs. Louis H. Dreier, Read by Mrs. Blanche Gilman at January 3, 1948, SOS Dinner, Transcript of Dinner Proceedings, JDC Archive, AR 45/54, File 1343.

33. Adele Levy, *Our Child Survivors* (New York: United Jewish Appeal, 1946), YIVO library.

34. UNCC depicted the donation of used clothing as a way to boost the economy in a series of "Clean out Your Closet" ads and weeks, urging women to end their wartime "hoarding" and go shopping again. One particular ad in the *Chicago Times* includes three photographs of a woman in front of an open closet, dusting off items. She notes how her effort not only serves the problems of "war-stricken families overseas" but also "makes us weed out the items we've been hoarding . . . for too long a period." *Chicago Times*, April 8, 1945, clipping in vol. 2, part 3, UNCC/LOC.

NOTES TO PAGES 109–112

35. Memo from Raphael Levy to Louis Sobel, November 14, 1945, 45/54, #1268, JDC-NY.

36. "Three Years of Achievement."

37. "Summer Resort Residents Mobilize City to Aid JDC's SOS Collection," Press Release, June 21, 1946, Reel 110, IS 4/2, JDC-J/USHMM.

38. "Three Years of Achievement." These events are detailed in numerous press releases and publicity memos. One of Eddie Cantor's recorded announcements publicizes marked grocery bags that people were asked to fill with canned foods and give to SOS volunteers on their city-wide SOS collection day. "Eddie Cantor #1" Radio Spot, with memo from Robert Dolins to SOS chairmen and contributing communities conducting fall drives, September 8, 1948, 45/54, #1344, JDC-NY.

39. "SOS Goes to the People: A Campaign Manual for Leaders," September 1948, AR 45/54, File 1344, JDC-NY. The campaign manual includes press releases, suggested feature articles, radio show scripts, poster drafts, and other publicity materials like images, buttons, stickers, and cards. Memo from Robert Dolins to SOS Committee Chairmen and Contributing Communities, September 10, 1948, 45/54, #1331, JDC-NY.

40. SOS Radio Ads, YIVO Sound Archive. The publicity memo from 1948 included transcripts of a "radio platter of nine one minute transcribed appeals by Eddie Cantor, Henry Fonda, and Dick Powell, for use in house-to-house canvasses and other concentrated campaign periods." Memo from Robert Dolins to SOS Committee Chairmen and Contributing Communities. Publicity images of Cantor, Powell, and Fonda recording the radio spots were distributed under the headlines "Henry Fonda Voices Appeal to Aid SOS Fall Campaign"; "Eddie Cantor Answers SOS"; and "Dick Powell Broadcasts to Aid Local SOS Drives." "Campaign Pictures," 45/54, #1345, JDC-NY. For more about Eddie Cantor and his dedicated political advocacy, see David Weinstein, *The Eddie Cantor Story: A Jewish Life in Performance and Politics* (Waltham, MA: Brandeis University Press, 2018).

41. Three of Cantor's five short ads mention his trip to Europe.

42. Goal of fifteen boxcars: "The Campaigner," Boston, MA, April 9, 1948, 45/54, #1334, JDC-NY; total of twenty-four boxcars: SOS Executive Meeting Minutes, June 15, 1948, 45/54, #1332, JDC-NY.

43. Stier, *Holocaust Icons*, 4.

44. Ibid., 15.

45. Ibid., 37.

46. Laura Levitt, *The Objects That Remain* (University Park: Pennsylvania State University Press, 2020).

47. Ibid., 3.

48. Avrom Sutzkever, "A Load of Shoes," in *The Literature of Destruction: Jewish Responses to Catastrophe*, ed. David G. Roskies (Philadelphia: Jewish Publication Society, 1989), 493.

172   NOTES TO PAGES 112–117

49. *Hadassah Headlines*, October 1944, HN/Hadassah.

50. Stier, *Holocaust Icons*, 40.

51. Linenthal, *Preserving Memory*, 170.

52. For a discussion on the value of experiential approaches to representing the Holocaust, see Weissman, *Fantasies of Witnessing*, 95–96.

53. *Placing the Displaced*, HIAS, 1948, YIVO Film Archive.

54. Raphael Levy, "The Emigrant Train," *JDC Digest*, December 1948, Box 3, Folder 2, HAFP/AJA.

55. Wendy Wall, *Inventing the "American Way": The Politics of Consensus from the New Deal to the Civil Rights Movement* (Oxford: Oxford University Press, 2008), 202.

56. Stuart J. Little, "The Freedom Train: Citizenship and Postwar Political Culture 1946–1949," *American Studies* 34, no. 1 (April 1, 1993): 35–67.

57. Wall, *American Way*, 201, 220.

58. Drew Pearson, "The Washington Merry-Go-Round (October 11, 1947)," available at American University online archive of Drew Pearson's Washington Merry-Go-Round: http://hdl.handle.net/1961/2041-21899 (Local Identifier: bo8fo5-19471011-z).

59. "$10,000 Food Goal for Friendship Train," *Ames Daily Tribune*, November 4, 1947, https://ameshistory.org/sites/default/files/1947.11.04_friendship_train_map_article.jpg.

60. http://www.thefriendshiptrain1947.org/. The website notes that each item also included a label with a person's name and address, individualizing the donor.

61. Relief and Rescue Department Report, August–November 1945, 18–19, Box D3, Folder 3, WJC/AJA.

62. Correspondent's Service for Jewish Children Report, April 1946, Box D74, File 10, WJC/AJA.

63. Catherine Varchaver, "Rehabilitation for European Jewish Children through Personal Contact," *Jewish Social Service Quarterly* XXIV, no. 4 (June 1948): 408–411.

64. ORT offered classes to DPs in Europe to train for employment. Vocational schools were established across postwar Europe, with the first opening in Landsberg DP camp in August 1946. Classes ranged from metal machining, shoemaking, and carpentry to automobile motor repair, typesetting, watch repair, and agricultural training. Other nonsectarian groups, such as Save the Children, had similar sponsorship programs, but I include Foster Parents Plan here because the program appealed to the JDC in Europe to be paired up with Jewish children. In fact, some of its donors asked to be paired with Jewish children specifically. The JDC did not participate in these kinds of sponsorship programs and particularly criticized Foster Parents Plan for only giving the children four dollars per month if they lived in an institution or seven dollars per month if they lived at home. Letter from Lotte

Marcuse, June 22, 1945 and Letter #4565, 45/54, #1625, JDC-NY. "My Four Year Story: 1949–1953" by Mrs. Louis Broido, Box 28, Folder 1, NCJW/AJHS.

65. The JLC's Child Department sponsored a Care for Children Overseas program, but letters refer to an "adoption" program. They employ quotation marks around the word "adoption" to designate the appropriation of the term. The program asked JLC members to give $300 to sponsor a child. Children received $15 per month and packages of clothing, books, and other items. These packages were sent directly from the JLC offices and therefore were not dependent on donors. Letter from Z. J. Lichtenstein and B. Tabachinsky to Mr. Frederichs, April 4, 1949, Box 118, Folder: Sarah Aizenberg, JLC/USHMM.

66. The program was launched in March 1946 and invited B'nai B'rith Lodges or individual members to donate eight dollars per month for at least three months. B'nai B'rith pledged to send packages to the family and asked that the individual keep correspondence with them. Letter from Reuben Frieman to Maurice Bernhardt, March 27, 1946, 45/54, #1517, JDC-NY.

67. Letter dated July 14, 1948, as quoted in ibid.

68. In the first bulletin of the new Friendship Service, Varchaver included the note: "We are glad to find the expression of the very essence of the aim of our Agency; the same aim which animated the former Child Care Division, World Jewish Congress, which originated the 'Correspondence Service for European Jewish Children' immediately after the end of the war." *Quarterly Bulletin: Friendship Service for Jewish Children, Inc.* Vol. 1, No. 1, January 1950, 2, Box D75, File 7, WJC/AJA.

69. Excerpts of letters received by the Child Care Division after the announcement of its liquidation, November 11, 1948, Box D75, File 5, WJC/AJA; Questionnaire from Doris Lesik, Box D80, File 15, WJC/AJA; *Correspondent's Service Bulletin*, 2:1–3, January–March 1947, Box D74, File 10, WJC/AJA.

70. In the later-published letter, Barbara states that she continued to correspond with George, hearing from him almost weekly in January 1948. *Correspondent's Service Bulletin*, 2:1–3, January–March 1947, Box D74, File 10, WJC/AJA.

71. Questionnaire from Doris Lesik, Box D80, File 15, WJC/AJA.

72. Questionnaire from Hilda Herschaft, Box D80, File 15, WJC/AJA.

73. Cohen, *Case Closed*.

74. Language barriers were addressed by a large number of volunteers working at the Child Care Division office in New York. Material for the Correspondents' Service indicates that correspondents should write their first letter in English and then ask what language was best for continued communication.

75. Bulletin for the Correspondents' Service for European Jewish Children, 1:1, January 1946, Box D74, File 10, WJC/AJA. The original translation of Robert's letter reads, "I am a Jewish boy of 16 years of age who has gone through terrible experience and whose parents both, unfortunately, have been deported by the Nazis. As

174 NOTES TO PAGES 119–122

I have no one left, my most ardent desire is to belong to a family again. This is the reason why I write to you today and I am sure you will give me a favorable answer." Letter from Robert S., Limoges, November 11, 1945, Box D78, Folder 9, WJC/AJA.

76. Bulletin for the Correspondents' Service for European Jewish Children, 1:1, January 1946, Box D74, File 10, WJC/AJA.

77. "Let Us Help Jewish Boys and Girls Who Want to Study!" May 28, 1947, Box D74, File 10, WJC/AJA.

78. Bulletin for the Correspondents' Service for European Jewish Children, 1, Vol. 3, No. 1–4, October 1948, Box D74, File 10, WJC/AJA.

79. The letter, which was copied and sent around to publicize the expansion of the program to Australia, included a note that Mrs. R. had learned about the Correspondents' Service from an article in *Aufbau* from May 1946. "Correspondents' Service for European Jewish Children Extended to Australia!" Box D80, File 8, WJC/AJA.

80. To prove that Oskar's letter fulfilled the mission of the Correspondents' Service, Mrs. R.'s letter also included a request for a longer list of names of boys and girls to distribute to friends who had been inspired by Oskar's story. Ibid.

81. Varchaver, "Rehabilitation for European Jewish Children," 410.

82. "Correspondents' Service for European Jewish Children Extended to Australia!" Box D80, File 8, WJC Records, AJA.

83. Oskar wrote of the reunion with his mother: "No novelist would be able to describe our reunion." Ibid.

84. Catherine Varchaver, "The Letters of European Jewish Children," *Jewish Social Service Quarterly* 23, no. 2 (December 1946): 119–124, 120.

85. In an additional example, Tamara B. wrote from the Otwock Home in Poland, "We are pleased when packages arrive, not because they bring us clothing, but because they tell us that you remember us, and it makes us feel less lonely." Bulletin for the Correspondents' Service for European Jewish Children, 1:3–4, March–April 1946, 6, Box D74, File 10, WJC/AJA.

86. Varchaver, "Rehabilitation of European Jewish Children," 411.

87. An additional voice echoing Rose's sentiments about Americans and Jewish solidarity, twelve-year-old Adam S. wrote to his correspondent Mrs. H. on October 27, 1946: "I was very happy to receive your letter, not only because I saw that the American heart sends the words of affection even to such a far country, but also for I realize that there is human solidarity in the world." Bulletin for the Correspondents' Service for European Jewish Children, 2:1–3, January–March 1947, Box D74, File 10, WJC/AJA.

88. The term *She'erit Hapletah* translates as "the surviving remains," "the remnant," or "the surviving remnant." Here, Rose uses the term to indicate a wider community of surviving Jews of Europe, as she was living in Budapest outside any formal DP administration.

NOTES TO PAGES 123–126

89. For more about Vaad Hatzala, see Alex Grobman, *Battling for Souls: The Vaad Hatzala Rescue Committee in Post-Holocaust Europe* (Jersey City, NJ: KTAV, 2004).

90. Letter from Herbert Tenzer, undated, 1, Box 14, Folder 6, RCP/Yeshiva.

91. Clippings from *Herald-Tribune*, Box 2, Folder 296, RCP/Yeshiva.

92. 1947. Dinner Transcript, Box 3, RCP/Yeshiva.

93. Clipping of *New York Times*, July 4, 1947, Box 14, Folder 9, RCP/Yeshiva.

94. "Orphans Clothed," *Life*, November 17, 1947, 57–60.

95. Ibid., 57, 58.

96. Irene and Charles served as representatives of the hundred children sponsored by Busy Buddies through Rescue Children and were meant to bring "with them the heartfelt thanks and best wishes of the children who had to remain behind." Annual Luncheon Brochure, Box 15, Folder 4, RCP/Yeshiva.

97. "They Can't Talk for Looking," *New York Post*, October 21, 1947; "War Orphans from Czechoslovakia and Poland," *New York Times*, October 21, 1947; "Sprucing up for Their Visit to President Truman," *New York Times*, October 22, 1947; Letter from William Novick to Mrs. Magda Bierman, November 4, 1948, Box 15, Folder 4, RCP/Yeshiva.

98. "Orphans Clothed," 57.

99. All accompanying articles noted that B. Altman and Company had donated the new clothes Irene and Charles wore.

100. The short article in *Life* does not mention Rescue Children at all, focusing on Busy Buddies as the sponsoring organization. In fact, Busy Buddies organized the trip, but Rescue Children took on responsibility for both Irene and Charles during and after the ten-day tour. "Orphans Clothed," 57.

101. Annual Luncheon Brochure, Box 15, Folder 4, RCP/Yeshiva.

102. Interview with William Z. Novick in *Rene and I*, film, directed by Gina M. Angelone, produced by Gina M. Angelone, Leora Kahn, and Zeva Oelbaum, 2005.

103. Charles Karo Bio, Box 14, Folder 7, RCP/Yeshiva.

104. Charles sent Bar Mitzvah invitations to Rescue Children board members, including Tenzer, William Novick, Magda Bierman (Busy Buddies director), and Kate Diamant, the woman who had accompanied him on his initial flight to the US. Letters from Charles Karo (undated); Letter from Herbert Tenzer to Magda Bierman, November 24, 1951; Letter from Herbert Tenzer to Charles Friedman, November 6, 1951; about the bank account, Letter from Herbert Tenzer to Lawrence-Cederhurst Bank, September 18, 1951: "Charles is desirous of transferring his bank account to Lancaster, PA." Letter from Tenzer to Bierman, November 24, 1951, Box 14, Folder 7, RCP/Yeshiva.

105. Box 14, Folder 13, RCP/Yeshiva.

106. A memo sent from the Germany JDC office on June 4, 1948, claims that the shoes sent to Berlin are useless and asks that used shoes stop being sent. Memo,

June 4, 1948, 45/54, #1332, JDC-NY. On September 7, 1948, Mr. Edward M. M. Warburg sent a "personal message" to all SOS chairmen, leaders, and volunteers stating that "no used clothing and no used shoes should be collected." Three days later, Robert Dolins sent a formal memo to SOS committee chairmen and contributing committees, repeating, "No used clothing, no used shoes" should be collected in the fall 1948 campaign. At the same time, new clothing and shoes both were listed as priorities for the Trade and Industry Committee. Memo from Robert Dolins, June 7, 2948, 45/54, #1331, JDC-NY.

107. An image of women at sewing machines was captioned, "11,000,000 pounds of SOS used clothing helped end the days of nakedness. Skilled workers repaired and remodeled garments." "Three Years of Achievement."

108. Levy, *Our Child Survivors*.

109. Advertisement in the *New Orleans Item*, April 9, 1945 (among others), vol. 2, part 5, UNCC/LOC.

110. Memo from Dan West to Financial Advisor, January 12, 1946, Reel GC/3, Folder: Clothing Collection Drive, UNRRA/Columbia.

111. Bauer, *Out of the Ashes*, xxi.

112. USHMM Oral History Collection, interview with Irene Hizme, November 22, 1995, RG-50.549.01*0004, transcript at https://collections.ushmm.org/search /catalog/irn504886, 27.

113. USHMM Oral History Collection, interview with Irene Hizme and Rene Slotkin, April 12, 1992, RG-50.233.0056, transcript at https://collections.ushmm .org/oh_findingaids/RG-50.233.0056_trs_en.pdf; USHMM Oral History Collection, interview with Irene Hizme and Rene Slotkin, April 19, 1995, RG 50.030.0320, viewable at https://collections.ushmm.org/search/catalog/irn504815; USHMM Oral History Collection, interview with Irene Hizme and Rene Slotkin (Guttmann twins), October 12, 2002, RG- 50.718.0005, viewable at https://collections .ushmm.org/search/catalog/irn60513.

114. *Rene and I*, 2005, directed by Gina M. Angelone. For more details, see https://jewishfilm.org/Catalogue/films/reneandi.htm.

Conclusion

1. Föhrenwald DP camp remained open until 1957, passing from US to German administration in December 1951. Those who remained in camps after 1952 were known as the "Hard Core"; many could not leave Germany for a variety of reasons. Most eventually settled in Germany. Brenner, *After the Holocaust*, 41.

2. *This Is Your Life*, Hanna Bloch Kohner, May 27, 1953, UCLA Film and Television Archive, DVD7453T. The show is available on YouTube at http://www.youtube .com/v/m3F9Rc6i_-w. Jeffrey Shandler details this episode in *While America Watches*, 30–37.

3. *This Is Your Life*, Hanna Bloch Kohner.

NOTES TO PAGES 129–135

4. For more about Hanna's story and the transatlantic love story between Hanna and her husband, Walter, see their memoir: Hanna Kohner, Walter Kohner, and Frederick Kohner, *Hanna and Walter: A Love Story* (New York: Random House, 1984).

5. Shandler, *While America Watches*, 36.

6. Shandler notes that the show intended to provoke an "emotional response" and that the tears central to Hanna's episode were a fixture of *This Is Your Life*. Shandler, *While America Watches*, 35.

7. *This Is Your Life*, Hanna Bloch Kohner.

8. In addition to giving Hanna a charm bracelet that marked her life experiences, the company also gave her a jeweled lipstick case as a souvenir of having been on the show. *This Is Your Life*, Hanna Bloch Kohner. For more about the fundraising component of this episode, see Shandler, *While America Watches*, 35–36.

9. "Oh, You Shouldn't Have," March 4, 2011, *This American Life*, audio and transcript at http://www.thisamericanlife.org/radio-archives/episode/428/transcript.

10. In fact, Kohner's daughter, Julie Kohner, remembers happily watching the episode on holidays with her parents and uses the bracelet and a book based on her mother's experience to teach about the Holocaust across the country. Her foundation, Voices of the Generations, has developed curricular materials related to Hanna and Walter's stories: http://vogcharity.org/.

11. In referring to some forms of Holocaust representation as inappropriate, I rely on the discussion documented in Friedländer, *Probing the Limits of Representation*.

12. *The Future Can Be Theirs*, USHMM.

13. Diner writes, "Because the memorial works of the postwar period differed from those of later decades does not mean that they did not exist." *We Remember with Reverence and Love*, 17.

14. Donald L. Niewyk, *Fresh Wounds: Early Narratives of Holocaust Survival* (Chapel Hill: University of North Carolina Press, 1998).

15. Voices of the Holocaust Project, Paul V. Galvin Library, http://voices.iit.edu/; Alan Rosen's 2010 study of Boder's work, *The Wonder of Their Voices*, is the bookend of this renewed attention.

16. The USC Shoah Foundation YouTube channel originally published one thousand full-length testimonies and has since added clips and shorts from survivor testimonies as well as event recordings. The Foundation continues to add contemporary interviews, including testimonies from "Survivors of the Hamas Terror Attack" and the Armenian Genocide Survivor collection. Accessed April 26, 2024. https://www.youtube.com/user/USCShoahFoundation/featured.

17. The Visual History Archive is one part of the USC Shoah Foundation. The archive is available for search at https://vha.usc.edu/home.

18. Shenker, *Reframing Holocaust Testimony*.

19. iWitness, USC Shoah Foundation, https://iwitness.usc.edu/home.

20. Dimensions in Testimony, USC Shoah Foundation, https://sfi.usc.edu/dit.

21. For a detailed assessment of the technology behind Dimensions in Testimony and how to create interactive survivor testimony, see Presner, *Ethics of the Algorithm*, in particular chapter 7, "Cultural Memory Machines and the Futures of Testimony," which I cowrote with Presner.

BIBLIOGRAPHY

Manuscript Collections

American Jewish Archives (AJA), Cincinnati, OH

Herbert A. Friedman Papers, 1940–2005 (HAFP), MS 763
Nearprint Collections: UJA, JDC, UPA
Women of Reform Judaism Records, 1913–2000 (WRJ), MS 73
World Jewish Congress Records, 1918–1982 (WJC), MS 361

American Jewish Historical Society (AJHS), Center for Jewish History, New York, NY

American Jewish Congress Records, 1916–2006 (AJC), I-77
Cecilia Razovsky Papers (CRP), P-290
Collection of Coordinating Committee of National Jewish Organizations for the
 United National Clothing Collection for War Relief (CC-UNCC), I-175
National Council of Jewish Women Collection (NCJW), I-469

Columbia University Manuscripts and Rare Books Collection, New York, NY

United Nations Relief and Rehabilitation Administration Records (UNRRA),
 microfilm copy of United Nations Archive, RG 17

Hadassah Archive, Center for Jewish History, New York, NY

Hadassah Newsletters, 1945–1953 (HN), RG 17
Operations and Functions/Public Affairs Series (OFPA), RG 15
Youth Aliyah Papers (YAP), RG 1

JDC Archives (JDC-NY), New York, NY

New York Headquarters Records, AR 45/54:
Subjects: Displaced Persons: Children, 1944, Jan–June 1945, #1032–#1038

180 BIBLIOGRAPHY

Subjects: Relief Supplies: Donations, 1945–1948, #1268
Subjects: Relief Supplies: S.O.S., 1949, #1330–#1345
Orgs: B'nai B'rith, 1945–1946, #1517
Orgs: Foster Parents Plan for War Children, #1625
Orgs: Free Synagogue Child Adoption Committee (New York), 1948, #1628

Library of Congress (LOC), Washington, DC

Collection of clippings and other miscellaneous material on the United National
Clothing Collection, 1945–1946 (UNCC), D809.U5 A14
National Council of Jewish Women Papers (NCJW), Manuscript Division 0806A

New York Public Library Manuscript Division, New York, NY

Koppel Pinson Collection, Mss 2429

UCLA Special Collections, Los Angeles, CA

David P. Boder Papers (DPB), Collection 1238

United States Holocaust Memorial Museum (USHMM), Archival Branch, Washington, DC

Holocaust Era Records of the Jewish Labor Committee, Child Adoption Case
Files (JLC), RG 67.002M (Reels 1–24)
International Tracing Service (ITS)
Oral History Collection
Selected records from the American Jewish Joint Distribution Committee Archives, Jerusalem, 1937–1966 (JDC-J), RG 68.066M

Wisconsin Historical Society, Madison, WI

Historical Society Library Pamphlet Collection (HSLPC):
A radio forum conducted by the American Federation of Labor on: should
America open its doors to displaced persons of Europe?, 54–1506
Citizens Committee on Displaced Persons, "A Brief Statement of Aims," 54–1522
Displaced Persons Digest, 54–1507

Yeshiva University Special Collections, New York, NY

Rescue Children Papers (RCP), 1985.024
Vaad Hatazala Papers (VHP), 1969.099

YIVO Archive, Center for Jewish History, New York, NY

American Jewish Committee Papers, Subject Files (AJC), 347.17.10, Gen 10
Records of the American Jewish Joint Distribution Committee, Landsmanshaftn
Department, RG 335.7
Records of the American ORT Federation (ORT), RG 380

Records of the Labor Zionist Organization of America Collection (LZOA), RG 606
United States Territorial Collection (USTC), RG 117

YIVO Library, Center for Jewish History, New York, NY

Hillel Guideposts, 015007722
JDC Digest, 015005140
Levy, Adele. *Our Child Survivors*. New York: United Jewish Appeal, 1946, 000119904
Maps of Destiny, brochure, 000043096
What Are the Facts? The Basis for the $170,000,000 United Jewish Appeal in 1947, brochure, 000119906

Film Archives

YIVO Film Archive, YIVO Archives, NY

Placing the Displaced, HIAS, 1948, Tape 101, v. 184
Untitled Rochester SOS film, JDC, Tape 101

Steven Spielberg Film and Video Archive of the United States Holocaust Memorial Museum

Battle for Survival, UJA, 1946, RG 60.2632, Tape 2296 and RG-60.2521, Tape 2293
Dollars for Destiny, UJA, 1948, RG 60.2660, Tape 2298
The Future Can Be Theirs, JDC, 1947, RG 60.2616, Tape 2311
ORT documentary footage, ORT, RG 60.0082
Seeds of Destiny, UNRRA, RG 60.1017, Tape 928
UJA Report from Israel, UJA, 1950, RG 60.1348, Tape 2924

Spielberg Jewish Film Archive, Hebrew University

Hadassah, *Tomorrow's a Wonderful Day*, Spielberg Jewish Film Archive, http://www.youtube.com/watch?v=9iXkhML3MHk

UCLA Film and Television Archive

This Is Your Life, Hannah Bloch Kohner (May 27, 1953), DVD 7453T

Sound Archives

YIVO Max and Frieda Weinstein Archives of Recorded Sound, Center for Jewish History

"The Arrival of Delayed Pilgrims," YIVO 42.01
"Delayed Pilgrims Dinner," United Service for New Americans (November 27, 1947), YIVO 17.51–17.52

BIBLIOGRAPHY

"Displaced," YIVO 28.01A
Golden Door, "Case History" (June 8, 1947), YIVO 17.40A
Golden Door, "Joseph in America," YIVO 41.01 A/B
"Escape from a Dream" (May 18, 1947), YIVO 17.34
The Eternal Light, "The Late Comers" (November 23, 1947), YIVO 25.01–25.02
"JDC Interview with a Czech Refugee" (June 27, 1950), YIVO 37.08 A
"Out of the Wilderness," USNA (April 6, 1947), YIVO 17.10–17.12
"Sadie Sender for JDC" (June 6, 1946), YIVO 37.12
SOS Radio Ads, YIVO 37.11

Marr Sound Archive, University of Missouri-Kansas City

"An American with a Mission," Citizen's Committee for Displaced Persons, 1948, Goldin 42,727
"Displaced," Goldin 42,883
Golden Door, "A Parable for Easter," Goldin 42,643
Golden Door, "I Am a Displaced Person," Goldin 42,643

Online Resources

American Presidency Project Digital Archive, UC Santa Barbara (https://www.presidency.ucsb.edu)
"Harry S Truman, Letter to Henry J. Kaiser Calling upon Him to Head the Second United National Clothing Collection Campaign." (September 23, 1945)
"Harry S Truman, Radio Report to the American People on the Potsdam Conference." (August 9, 1945)
"Ephemera," Library of Congress Collections Policy Statements, https://www.loc.gov/acq/devpol/ephemera.pdf

USC Shoah Foundation

iWitness, USC Shoah Foundation, http://sfi.usc.edu/teach_and_learn/iwitness
Shoah Foundation YouTube Channel, https://www.youtube.com/user/USCShoahFoundation
Visual History Archive, https://vha.usc.edu/home
"Voices of the Holocaust Project." Illinois Institute of Technology, http://voices.iit.edu/

Yad Vashem

Documentation of the Central Historical Commission (CHC) of the Central Committee of Liberated Jews in the American Occupied Zone, Munich, M.1, https://collections.yadvashem.org/en/documents/4019540
Oyneg Shabes Archive, https://www.yadvashem.org/yv/en/exhibitions/ringelblum/index.asp

BIBLIOGRAPHY 183

Photo and Film Archive

Righteous Among the National Database, https://collections.yadvashem.org/en/righteous

Published Works

"$10,000 Food Goal for Friendship Train." *Ames Daily Tribune*, November 4, 1947.

Anderson, Mark M. "The Child Victim as Witness to the Holocaust: An American Story?" *Jewish Social Studies* 14, no. 1 (fall 2007): 1–22.

Angelone, Gina M. *Rene and I.* 2005. http://www.jewishfilm.org/Catalogue/films/reneandi.htm.

Baldwin, Peter. *Reworking the Past: Hitler, the Holocaust, and the Historians' Debate*. Boston: Beacon Press, 1990.

Baron, Lawrence. "The First Wave of American 'Holocaust' Films, 1945–1959." *American Historical Review* 115, no. 1 (February 2010): 90–114.

Bauer, Yehuda. *American Jewry and the Holocaust: The American Jewish Joint Distribution Committee, 1939–1945*. Jerusalem: Institute of Contemporary Jewry, 1981.

———. *Flight and Rescue: Brichah*. 1st ed. Contemporary Jewish Civilization Series. New York: Random House, 1970.

———. *My Brother's Keeper; A History of the American Jewish Joint Distribution Committee, 1929–1939*. 1st ed. Philadelphia: Jewish Publication Society of America, 1974.

———. *Out of the Ashes: The Impact of American Jews on Post-Holocaust European Jewry*. 1st ed. Oxford: Pergamon Press, 1989.

Benjamin, Ludy T. "David Boder's Psychological Museum and the Exposition of 1938." *Psychological Record* 29 (1979): 559–565. https://doi.org/10.1007/BF03394644.

Berenbaum, Michael. *After Tragedy and Triumph: Essays in Modern Jewish Thought and the American Experience*. Cambridge: Cambridge University Press, 1990.

Berman, Lila Corwin. *The American Jewish Philanthropic Complex: The History of a Multibillion-Dollar Institution*. Princeton, NJ: Princeton University Press, 2020.

———. *Metropolitan Jews: Politics, Race, and Religion in Postwar Detroit*. Chicago: University of Chicago Press, 2015.

Boder, David P. "The Displaced People of Europe: Preliminary Notes on a Psychological and Anthropological Study." *Illinois Tech Engineer*, March 1947, 18–34.

———. *I Did Not Interview the Dead*. Urbana: University of Illinois Press, 1949.

———. *Topical Autobiographies of Displaced People: Recorded Verbatim in Displaced Persons Camps: With a Psychological and Anthropological Analysis.* Chicago: n.p., 1950.

Boum, Aomar, and Sarah Abrevaya Stein, eds. *The Holocaust and North Africa.* Stanford, CA: Stanford University Press, 2019.

Bremner, Robert H. *American Philanthropy.* Chicago: University of Chicago Press, 1960.

Brenner, Michael. *After the Holocaust: Rebuilding Jewish Lives in Postwar Germany.* Princeton, NJ: Princeton University Press, 1997.

Brodkin, Karen. *How Jews Became White Folks and What That Says about Race in America.* New Brunswick, NJ: Rutgers University Press, 1998.

Browning, Christopher R. *Collected Memories: Holocaust History and Postwar Testimony.* Madison: University of Wisconsin Press, 2003.

———. *Remembering Survival: Inside a Nazi Slave-Labor Camp.* New York: W.W. Norton, 2010.

Cesarani, David. "Introduction." In *After the Holocaust: Challenging the Myth of Silence*, edited by David Cesarani and Eric J. Sundquist, 1–14. London: Routledge, 2012.

Cesarani, David, and Eric J. Sundquist, eds. *After the Holocaust: Challenging the Myth of Silence.* London: Routledge, 2012.

Cohen, Beth B. *Case Closed: Holocaust Survivors in Postwar America.* New Brunswick, NJ: Rutgers University Press, 2007.

Cohen, Michael J. *Truman and Israel.* Berkeley: University of California Press, 1990.

Crago-Schneider, Kierra Mikaila. "A Community of Will: The Resettlement of Orthodox Jewish DPs from Föhrenwald." *Holocaust and Genocide Studies* 32, no. 1 (spring 2018): 93–110. https://doi.org/10.1093/hgs/dcy007.

Cramsey, Sarah A. *Uprooting the Diaspora: Jewish Belonging and the "Ethnic Revolution" in Poland and Czechoslovakia, 1936–1946.* Bloomington: Indiana University Press, 2023.

Curti, Merle. "American Philanthropy and the National Character." *American Quarterly* 10, no. 4 (December 1, 1958): 420–437.

———. "Forward." In *Fund Raising in the United States, Its Role in America's Philanthropy*, edited by Scott M. Cutlip. New Brunswick, NJ: Rutgers University Press, 1965.

Cutlip, Scott M. *Fund Raising in the United States, Its Role in America's Philanthropy.* New Brunswick, NJ: Rutgers University Press, 1965.

Deblinger, Rachel. "Holocaust Memory in DP Camps: David P. Boder." In Cesarani and Sundquist, *After the Holocaust*, 115–126.

Des Pres, Terrence T. *The Survivor: An Anatomy of Life in the Death Camps.* New York: Oxford University Press, 1976.

BIBLIOGRAPHY

Diner, Hasia R. *The Jews of the United States, 1654 to 2000*. Berkeley: University of California Press, 2004.

———. "Origins and Meanings of the Myth of Silence." In Cesarani and Sundquist, *After the Holocaust*, 192–201.

———. *We Remember with Reverence and Love: American Jews and the Myth of Silence after the Holocaust, 1945–1962*. New York: New York University Press, 2009.

Dinnerstein, Leonard. *America and the Survivors of the Holocaust*. New York: Columbia University Press, 1982.

Doron, Daniella. *Jewish Youth and Identity in Postwar France: Rebuilding Family and Nation*. Bloomington: Indiana University Press, 2015.

Dulles, Foster R. *The American Red Cross: A History*. New York: Harper & Brothers, 1950.

Ellis, Carolyn, and Jerry Rawicki. "More Than Mazel? Luck and Agency in Surviving the Holocaust." *Journal of Loss and Trauma* 19, no. 2 (2014): 99–120.

"An End to the Darkness." *Chicago Sentinel*, June 13, 1946, 143:11.

Erbelding, Rebecca. *Rescue Board: The Untold Story of America's Efforts to Save the Jews of Europe*. New York: Doubleday, 2018.

Faure, Laura Hobson, and Veerle Vanden Daelen. "Imported from the United States? The Centralization of Private Jewish Welfare after the Holocaust: The Cases of Belgium and France." In *The JDC at 100: A Century of Humanitarianism*, edited by Avinoam Patt, Atina Grossmann, Linda G. Levi, Maud S. Mandel, Mikhail Mitsel, and Elissa Bemporad, 279–314. Detroit: Wayne State University Press, 2019.

Felman, Shoshana. "The Return of the Voice: Claude Lanzmann's Shoah." In Felman and Laub, *Testimony*, 204–283.

Felman, Shoshana, and Dori Laub, eds. *Testimony: Crises of Witnessing in Literature, Psychoanalysis, and History*. New York: Routledge, 1992.

Fermaglich, Kirsten Lise. *American Dreams and Nazi Nightmares: Early Holocaust Consciousness and Liberal America, 1957–1965*. Waltham, MA: Brandeis University Press, 2006.

Fine, Ellen S. *Legacy of Night, the Literary Universe of Elie Wiesel*. Albany: State University of New York Press, 1982.

Finkelstein, Norman G. "Daniel Jonah Goldhagen's 'Crazy' Thesis: A Critique of Hitler's Willing Executioners." *New Left Review* 224 (August 1997): 39–87.

———. *The Holocaust Industry: Reflections on the Exploitation of Jewish Suffering*. London: Verso, 2000.

Flanzbaum, Hilene. *The Americanization of the Holocaust*. Baltimore: Johns Hopkins University Press, 1999.

Fogu, Claudio, Wulf Kansteiner, and Todd Samuel Presner, eds. *Probing the Ethics of Holocaust Culture*. Cambridge, MA: Harvard University Press, 2016.

"Forty Jewish Leaders Leave by Plane for Europe and Palestine on U.J.A. Mission." *Jewish Telegraphic Agency*. Accessed April 18, 2014. http://www.jta
.org/1948/01/28/archive/forty-jewish-leaders-leave-by-plane-for-europe-and
-palestine-on-u-j-a-mission.

Friedländer, Saul, ed. *Probing the Limits of Representation: Nazism and the "Final Solution."* Cambridge, MA: Harvard University Press, 1992.

———. *The Years of Extermination: Nazi Germany and the Jews, 1939–1945.* 1st ed. New York: Harper Collins, 2007.

Friedländer, Saul, and Martin Broszat. "A Controversy about the Historicization of National Socialism." *Yad Vashem Studies* 19 (1988): 1–47.

Gallas, Elisabeth, and Laura Jockusch. "Anything but Silent: Jewish Responses to the Holocaust in the Aftermath of World War II." In *A Companion to the Holocaust*, edited by Simone Gigliotti and Hilary Earl, 311–330. Chichester: John Wiley & Sons, 2020.

Garbarini, Alexandra. "Document Volumes and the Status of Victim Testimony in the Era of the First World War and Its Aftermath." *Études arméniennes contemporaines* vol 5 (June 2015): 113–138.

———. *Numbered Days: Diaries and the Holocaust.* New Haven, CT: Yale University Press, 2006.

Garland, Libby. *After They Closed the Gates: Jewish Illegal Immigration to the United States, 1921–1965.* Chicago: University of Chicago Press, 2014.

Glaser, Zhava Litvac. "Laura Margolis and JDC Efforts in Cuba and Shanghai: Sustaining Refugees in a Time of Catastrophe." In *The JDC at 100: A Century of Humanitarianism*, edited by Avinoam Patt, Atina Grossmann, Linda G. Levi, Maud S. Mandel, Mikhail Mitsel, and Elissa Bemporad, 167–204. Detroit: Wayne State University Press, 2019.

Goldin, Milton. *Why They Give: American Jews and Their Philanthropies.* New York: Macmillan, 1976.

Goldstein, Eric L. *The Price of Whiteness: Jews, Race, and American Identity.* Princeton, NJ: Princeton University Press, 2006.

Goren, Arthur. "A 'Golden Decade' for American Jews: 1945–1955." In *The American Jewish Experience*, edited by Jonathan D. Sarna, 294–313. New York: Holmes & Meier, 1986.

Greenberg, Marian G. *There Is Hope for Your Children: Youth Aliyah, Henrietta Szold and Hadassah.* New York: Hadassah, the Women's Zionist Organization of America, 1986.

Greene, Daniel. *The Jewish Origins of Cultural Pluralism: The Menorah Association and American Diversity.* Bloomington: Indiana University Press, 2011.

Greenspan, Henry. "The Awakening of Memory: Survivor Testimony in the First Years after the Holocaust, and Today." United States Holocaust Memorial

BIBLIOGRAPHY

Museum, Monna and Otto Weinmann Lecture Series, May 17, 2000. http://www.ushmm.org/m/pdfs/Publication_OP_2001-02.pdf.

———. *On Listening to Holocaust Survivors: Recounting and Life History.* Westport, CT: Praeger, 1998.

Greenspan, Henry, Sara R. Horowitz, Éva Kovács, Berel Lang, Dori Laub, Kenneth Waltzer, and Annette Wieviorka. "Engaging Survivors: Assessing 'Testimony' and 'Trauma' as Foundational Concepts." *Dapim: Studies on the Holocaust* 28, no. 3 (2014): 190–226. https://doi.org/10.1080/23256249.2014.951909.

Grobman, Alex. *Battling for Souls: The Vaad Hatzala Rescue Committee in Post-Holocaust Europe.* Jersey City, NJ: KTAV, 2004.

Gross, Jan T. *Fear: Anti-Semitism in Poland after Auschwitz: An Essay in Historical Interpretation.* New York: Random House, 2006.

———. *Neighbors: The Destruction of the Jewish Community in Jedwabne, Poland.* Princeton, NJ: Princeton University Press, 2012.

Grossmann, Atina. *Jews, Germans, and Allies: Close Encounters in Occupied Germany.* Princeton, NJ: Princeton University Press, 2007.

Harrison, Earl G. *The Plight of the Displaced Jews in Europe: A Report to President Truman.* New York: Reprinted by United Jewish Appeal for Refugees, Overseas Needs and Palestine on behalf of Joint Distribution Committee, United Palestine Appeal, National Refugee Service, 1945.

Hartman, Geoffrey H. *Holocaust Remembrance: The Shapes of Memory.* Oxford: Blackwell, 1994.

———. *The Longest Shadow: In the Aftermath of the Holocaust.* Bloomington: Indiana University Press, 1996.

Helmreich, William B. *Against All Odds: Holocaust Survivors and the Successful Lives They Made in America.* New York: Simon & Schuster, 1992.

Heymont, Irving. *Among the Survivors of the Holocaust, 1945: The Landsberg DP Camp Letters of Major Irving Heymont, United States Army.* Cincinnati, OH: American Jewish Archives, 1982.

Horten, Gerd. *Radio Goes to War: The Cultural Politics of Propaganda during World War II.* Berkeley: University of California Press, 2002.

Jick, Leon. "The Holocaust: Its Uses and Abuses in the American Public." *Yad Vashem Studies* 14 (1981): 301–318.

Jockusch, Laura. *Collect and Record! Jewish Holocaust Documentation in Early Postwar Europe.* New York: Oxford University Press, 2012.

Kadosh, Sandra Berliant. "Ideology vs. Reality: Youth Aliyah and the Rescue of Jewish Children during the Holocaust Era, 1933–1945." PhD diss., Columbia University, 1995.

Karp, Abraham J. *To Give Life: The UJA in the Shaping of the American Jewish Community.* New York: Schocken Books, 1981.

Kassow, Samuel D. *Who Will Write Our History? Emanuel Ringelblum, the Warsaw Ghetto, and the Oyneg Shabes Archive.* Bloomington: Indiana University Press, 2007.

Kavanaugh, Sarah. *ORT, the Second World War and the Rehabilitation of Holocaust Survivors.* London: Vallentine Mitchell, 2008.

Kelman, Ari Y. *Station Identification: A Cultural History of Yiddish Radio in the United States.* Berkeley: University of California Press, 2009.

Kirshenblatt-Gimblett, Barbara, and Jeffrey Shandler, eds. *Anne Frank Unbound: Media, Imagination, Memory.* Bloomington: Indiana University Press, 2012.

Klapper, Melissa R. *Ballots, Babies, and Banners of Peace: American Jewish Women's Activism, 1890–1940.* New York: New York University Press, 2012.

Kliger, Hannah, ed. *Jewish Hometown Associations and Family Circles in New York: The WPA Yiddish Writers' Group Study.* Bloomington: Indiana University Press, 1992.

Kobrin, Rebecca. "American Jewish Internationalism, Laura Margolis and the Power of Female Diplomacy, 1941–1943." *Journal of Modern Jewish Studies* 21, no. 2 (2022): 234–252.

Kochavi, Arieh J. *Post-Holocaust Politics: Britain, the United States & Jewish Refugees, 1945–1948.* Chapel Hill: University of North Carolina Press, 2001.

Kohner, Hanna, Walter Kohner, and Frederick Kohner. *Hanna and Walter: A Love Story.* New York: Random House, 1984.

Kohner, Hanna Bloch. *This Is Your Life.* May 27, 1953. NBC, Ralph Edwards. https://www.youtube.com/watch?v=m3F9Rc6i_-w.

Krah, Markus. "Role Models or Foils for American Jews? *The Eternal Light*, Displaced Persons, and the Construction of Jewishness in Mid-Twentieth-Century America." *American Jewish History* 96, no. 4 (2010): 265–286.

LaCapra, Dominick. *History and Memory after Auschwitz.* Ithaca, NY: Cornell University Press, 1998.

———. "Revisiting the Historians' Debate: Mourning and Genocide." *History and Memory* 9, no. 1/2 (October 1, 1997): 80–112.

Lang, Daniel. "Displaced." *New Yorker,* September 13, 1947, 100–111.

Langer, Lawrence L. *Admitting the Holocaust: Collected Essays.* New York: Oxford University Press, 1995.

———. *Holocaust Testimonies: The Ruins of Memory.* New Haven, CT: Yale University Press, 1991.

Lania, Leo. *The Nine Lives of Europe.* New York: Funk & Wagnalls in association with United Nations World, 1950.

Laub, Dori. "Bearing Witness or the Vicissitudes of Listening." In Felman and Laub, *Testimony,* 57–74.

———. "An Event without a Witness: Truth, Testimony, and Survival." In Felman and Laub, *Testimony,* 75–92.

Lavsky, Hagit. *New Beginnings: Holocaust Survivors in Bergen-Belsen and the British Zone in Germany, 1945–1950.* Detroit: Wayne State University Press, 2002.

Lawrence, Jerome. *Actor, the Life and Times of Paul Muni.* New York: Putnam, 1974.

Levi, Primo. *Survival in Auschwitz: The Nazi Assault on Humanity.* Translated by Stuart Woolf. New York: Touchstone, 1996.

Levitt, Laura. *The Objects That Remain.* University Park: Pennsylvania State University Press, 2020.

Lilienheim, Henry. "Mine Eyes Have Seen." In *The Root and the Bough: The Epic of an Enduring People,* edited by Leo W. Schwarz, 3–11. New York: Rinehart, 1949.

Linenthal, Edward Tabor. *Preserving Memory: The Struggle to Create America's Holocaust Museum.* New York: Viking, 1995.

Little, Stuart J. "The Freedom Train: Citizenship and Postwar Political Culture 1946–1949." *American Studies* 34, no. 1 (April 1, 1993): 35–67.

Los Angeles United Jewish Welfare Fund. *1947 Year Book.* Los Angeles: Los Angeles Jewish Community Council, 1947.

———. *1948 Year Book.* Los Angeles: Los Angeles Jewish Community Council, 1948.

Lustig, Jason. *A Time to Gather: Archives and the Control of Jewish Culture.* New York: Oxford University Press, 2022.

Mankowitz, Zeev W. *Life between Memory and Hope: The Survivors of the Holocaust in Occupied Germany.* New York: Cambridge University Press, 2002.

Marziali, Carl. "Uncovering Lost Voices: 1946 David Boder Tapes Revived." *American Libraries* 34, no. 2 (February 1, 2003): 45–46.

Matthäus, Jürgen, ed. *Approaching an Auschwitz Survivor: Holocaust Testimony and Its Transformations.* Oxford: Oxford University Press, 2009.

McCarthy, Kathleen D. "Parallel Power Structures: Women and the Voluntary Space." In *Lady Bountiful Revisited: Women, Philanthropy, and Power,* edited by Kathleen D. McCarthy, 1–33. New Brunswick, NJ: Rutgers University Press, 1990.

———, ed. *Lady Bountiful Revisited: Women, Philanthropy, and Power.* New Brunswick, NJ: Rutgers University Press, 1990.

Medoff, Rafael. *The Deafening Silence: American Jewish Leaders and the Holocaust.* New York: Carol, 1986.

———. *The Jews Should Keep Quiet: Franklin D. Roosevelt, Rabbi Stephen S. Wise, and the Holocaust.* Lincoln: Jewish Publication Society, 2019.

Mintz, Alan L. *Popular Culture and the Shaping of Holocaust Memory in America.* Seattle: University of Washington Press, 2001.

Moore, Deborah Dash. *To the Golden Cities: Pursuing the American Jewish Dream in Miami and L.A.* New York: Free Press, 1994.

Morton, David. *Off the Record: The Technology and Culture of Sound Recording in America.* New Brunswick, NJ: Rutgers University Press, 2000.

Mott, Robert L. *Radio Sound Effects: Who Did It, and How, in the Era of Live Broadcasting.* Jefferson, NC: McFarland, 1993.

Newman, Roberta. "Delayed Pilgrims: The Radio Programs of the United Service for New Americans, 1947–48." MA thesis, New York University, 1996.

Nichanian, Marc. "Catastrophic Mourning." In *Loss: The Politics of Mourning*, edited by David L. Eng and David Kazanjian, 1st ed., 99–124. Berkeley: University of California Press, 2003.

Niewyk, Donald L. *Fresh Wounds: Early Narratives of Holocaust Survival.* Chapel Hill: University of North Carolina Press, 1998.

Norich, Anita. *Discovering Exile: Yiddish and Jewish American Culture during the Holocaust.* Stanford, CA: Stanford University Press, 2007.

Novick, Peter. *The Holocaust in American Life.* Boston: Houghton Mifflin, 1999.

"Oh You Shouldn't Have." *This American Life.* March 4, 2011. http://www .thisamericanlife.org/radio-archives/episode/428/oh-you-shouldnt-have.

"Orphans Clothed." *Life*, November 17, 1947.

Ozick, Cynthia. "Who Owns Anne Frank?" *New Yorker* 73, no. 30 (October 6, 1997): 76.

Patt, Avinoam J., and Kierra Crago-Schneider. "Years of Survival: JDC in Postwar Germany, 1945–1957." In *The JDC at 100: A Century of Humanitarianism*, edited by Avinoam J. Patt, Atina Grossmann, Linda G. Levi, Maud S. Mandel, Mikhail Mitsel, and Elissa Bemporad, 361–420. Detroit: Wayne State University Press, 2019.

Pearson, Drew. "The Washington Merry-Go-Round." October 11, 1947. American University online archive of Drew Pearson's Washington Merry-Go-Round. http://hdl.handle.net/1961/2041-21899 (Local Identifier: b08f05-19471011-z.

Pinchevski, Amit. "The Audiovisual Unconscious: Media and Trauma in the Video Archive for Holocaust Testimonies." *Critical Inquiry* 39, no. 1 (autumn 2012): 142–166.

Pinson, Koppel. "The Jewish Spirit in Nazi Germany." *Menorah Journal* 24, no. 3 (autumn 1936): 235–238.

Prell, Riv-Ellen. "Triumph, Accommodation, and Resistance: American Jewish Life from the End of WWII to the Six-Day War." In *The Columbia History of Jews and Judaism in America*, edited by Marc Lee Raphael, 114–141. New York: Columbia University Press, 2008.

Presner, Todd. *Ethics of the Algorithm: Digital Humanities and Holocaust Memory.* Princeton, NJ: Princeton University Press, 2024.

"Rabbi Heller Is Back." *New York Times*, August 18, 1945.

Raider, Mark A. "From Immigrant Party to American Movement: American Labor Zionism in the Pre-state Period." *American Jewish History* 82, no. 1/4 (1994): 159–194.

Raphael, Marc Lee. *A History of the United Jewish Appeal, 1939–1982*. Chico, CA: Scholars Press, 1982.

Reinharz, Shulamit, and Mark A. Raider. *American Jewish Women and the Zionist Enterprise*. Waltham, MA: University Press of New England, 2005.

Rosen, Alan. *The Wonder of Their Voices: The 1946 Holocaust Interviews of David Boder*. New York: Oxford University Press, 2010.

Rosenfeld, Alvin H. "The Americanization of the Holocaust." *Thinking about the Holocaust: After Half a Century*, edited by Alvin Rosenfeld, 119–150. Jewish Literature and Culture. Bloomington: Indiana University Press, 1997.

———. "The Assault on Holocaust Memory." *American Jewish Year Book* 101 (2001): 3–20.

———. *The End of the Holocaust*. Bloomington: Indiana University Press, 2011.

Sarna, Jonathan D. "The Cult of Synthesis in American Jewish Culture." *Jewish Social Studies*, n.s., 5, no. 1/2 (October 1, 1998): 52–79.

Schwartz, Joseph J. *Testimony before the Anglo-American Committee of Inquiry*. New York: American Jewish Joint Distribution Committee, 1946.

Schwarz, Leo W. *A Golden Treasury of Jewish Literature*. New York: Farrar & Rinehart, 1937.

———. *The Jewish Caravan: Great Stories of Twenty-Five Centuries*. New York: Farrar & Rinehart, 1935.

———. *The Root and the Bough: The Epic of an Enduring People*. New York: Rinehart, 1949.

Segal, Eli. *The Eternal Light: An Unauthorized Guide*. Newtown, CT: Yesteryear Press, 2005.

Segev, Zohar. "Rethinking the Dilemma of Bombing Auschwitz: Support, Opposition, and Reservation." *Jewish Quarterly Review* 111, no. 2 (2021): 265–288. https://doi.org/10.1353/jqr.2021.0011.

Seidman, Naomi. "Elie Wiesel and the Scandal of Jewish Rage." *Jewish Social Studies*, n.s., 3, no. 1 (October 1, 1996): 1–19.

Seldes, Gilbert. *The Great Audience*. New York: Viking Press, 1950.

Seymour, Harold J. *Design for Giving: The Story of the National War Fund, Inc., 1943–1947*. New York: Harper, 1947.

Shandler, Jeffrey. "Di Toyre Fun Skhoyre, or, I Shop Therefore I Am: The Consumer Cultures of American Jews." In *Longing, Belonging, and the Making of Jewish Consumer Culture*, edited by Gideon Reuveni and Nils Roemer, 183–200. Leiden: Brill, 2010.

———. *Jews, God, and Videotape: Religion and Media in America*. New York: NYU Press, 2009.

———. *While America Watches: Televising the Holocaust*. New York: Oxford University Press, 2000.

Shandler, Jeffrey, and Elihu Katz. "Broadcasting American Judaism: The Radio and Television Department of JTS." In *Tradition Renewed: A History of JTS*, edited by Jack Wertheimer, volume 2: Beyond the Academy, 363–402. New York: Jewish Theological Seminary, 1997.

Shapiro, Edward S. *A Time for Healing: American Jewry since World War II*. Baltimore: Johns Hopkins University Press, 1992.

Shenker, Noah. *Reframing Holocaust Testimony*. Bloomington: Indiana University Press, 2015.

Shephard, Ben. *The Long Road Home: The Aftermath of the Second World War*. New York: Alfred A. Knopf, 2011.

Siepmann, Charles A. *The Radio Listener's Bill of Rights: Democracy, Radio and You*. New York: Anti-Defamation League of B'nai B'rith, 1948.

Smith, Mark L. "No Silence in Yiddish: Popular and Scholarly Writing about the Holocaust in the Early Postwar Years." In Cesarani and Sundquist, *After the Holocaust*, 55–66.

"SOS Collected over 26,300 Pounds of Relief Supplies During Past Three Years." *Jewish Telegraphic Agency*. Accessed September 1, 2024. https://www.jta .org/archive/sos-collected-over-26300-pounds-of-relief-supplies-during -past-three-years.

Soyer, Daniel. *Jewish Immigrant Associations and American Identity in New York, 1880–1939*. Cambridge, MA: Harvard University Press, 1997.

Srole, Leo. "Why the DPs Can't Wait: Proposing an International Plan of Rescue." *Commentary* 3 (1947): 13–47.

Stahl, Ronit Y. *Enlisting Faith: How the Military Chaplaincy Shaped Religion and State in Modern America*. Cambridge, MA: Harvard University Press, 2017.

Stein, Sarah Abrevaya, and Aomar Boum, eds. *Wartime North Africa: A Documentary History, 1934–1950*. Stanford, CA: Stanford University Press, 2022.

Stier, Oren Baruch. *Holocaust Icons: Symbolizing the Shoah in History and Memory*. New Brunswick, NJ: Rutgers University Press, 2015.

Stone, Amy. "The Locked Cabinet." *Lilith Magazine*, December 4, 1976. https:// lilith.org/articles/the-locked-cabinet/.

Subak, Susan Elisabeth. *Rescue & Flight: American Relief Workers Who Defied the Nazis*. Lincoln: University of Nebraska Press, 2010.

Sundquist, Eric J. "Silence Reconsidered." In Cesarani and Sundquist, *After the Holocaust*, 202–216.

Sutzkever, Avrom. "A Load of Shoes." In *The Literature of Destruction: Jewish Responses to Catastrophe*, edited by David G. Roskies, 493. Philadelphia: Jewish Publication Society, 1988.

Syrkin, Marie. *Blessed Is the Match: The Story of Jewish Resistance*. Philadelphia: Jewish Publication Society of America, 1976.

Tolleris, Beatrice Klein. *Radio; How, When and Why to Use It*. New York: National Publicity Council for Health and Welfare Services, 1946.

BIBLIOGRAPHY

Trachtenberg, Barry. *The United States and the Nazi Holocaust: Race, Refuge, and Remembrance*. London: Bloomsbury Academic, 2018.

"United Jewish Appeal Raised Total of $150,000,000 in 1948, National Chairmen Report." *Jewish Telegraphic Agency*. Accessed April 18, 2014. http://www.jta .org/1949/01/03/archive/united-jewish-appeal-raised-total-of-150000000-in -1948-national-chairmen-report.

Varchaver, Catherine. "The Letters of European Jewish Children." *Jewish Social Service Quarterly* 23, no. 2 (December 1946): 119–124.

———. "Rehabilitation for European Jewish Children through Personal Contact." *Jewish Social Service Quarterly* XXIV, no. 4 (June 1948): 408–411.

Wall, Wendy. *Inventing the "American Way": The Politics of Consensus from the New Deal to the Civil Rights Movement*. Oxford: Oxford University Press, 2008.

Waxman, Zoë. *Writing the Holocaust: Identity, Testimony, Representation*. Oxford: Oxford University Press, 2006.

Weinstein, David. *The Eddie Cantor Story: A Jewish Life in Performance and Politics*. Waltham, MA: Brandeis University Press, 2018.

Weissman, Gary. *Fantasies of Witnessing: Postwar Efforts to Experience the Holocaust*. Ithaca, NY: Cornell University Press, 2004.

Wenger, Beth S. "Jewish Women and Voluntarism: Beyond the Myth of Enablers." *American Jewish History* 79, no. 1 (1989): 16–36.

Wiesel, Elie. "Remarks at the Dedication Ceremonies for the United States Holocaust Memorial Museum, April 22, 1993." April 22, 1993. "Elie Wiesel," United States Holocaust Memorial Museum website. https://www.ushmm.org /information/about-the-museum/mission-and-history/wiesel.

———. "Why I Write: Making No Become a Yes." *New York Times*, April 14, 1985, section 7, page 13.

Wieviorka, Annette. *The Era of the Witness*. Ithaca, NY: Cornell University Press, 2006.

Winkler, Allan M. *The Politics of Propaganda: The Office of War Information, 1942–1945*. New Haven, CT: Yale University Press, 1978.

Wishengrad, Morton. *The Eternal Light*. New York: Crown, 1947.

"World Relief Is America's Job." *Saturday Evening Post* 218, no. 25 (December 22, 1945): 112.

Wyman, David S. *The Abandonment of the Jews: America and the Holocaust, 1941–1945*. New York: Pantheon Books, 1984.

———. *Paper Walls: America and the Refugee Crisis, 1938–1941*. New York: Pantheon Books, 1985.

Wyman, David S., and Charles H. Rosenzveig. *The World Reacts to the Holocaust*. Baltimore: Johns Hopkins University Press, 1996.

Young, James Edward. "The Biography of a Memorial Icon: Nathan Rapoport's Warsaw Ghetto Monument." *Representations* 26 (1989): 69–106.

———. *Writing and Rewriting the Holocaust: Narrative and the Consequences of Interpretation*. Bloomington: Indiana University Press, 1988.

Zahra, Tara. *The Lost Children: Reconstructing Europe's Families after World War II*. Cambridge, MA: Harvard University Press, 2011.

Zucker, Bat-Ami. *Cecilia Razovsky and the American Jewish Women's Rescue Operations in the Second World War*. London: Vallentine Mitchell, 2008.

Zunz, Olivier. *Philanthropy in America: A History*. Princeton, NJ: Princeton University Press, 2012.

Zuroff, Efraim. *The Response of Orthodox Jewry in the United States to the Holocaust: The Activities of the Vaad Ha-Hatzala Rescue Committee, 1939–1945*. Booklyn, NY: Ktav Publishing House, 2000.

INDEX

Italicized words denote images

Adopt-A-Family Plan (World Jewish Congress), 116–17

aid workers: American, 59, 64–65, 70, 75–77, 84, 91, 100; emotional appeals of, 99; and immigration reform, 91; as secondary witnesses, 75–78 (see also chapter 3). *See also* Friedman, Herbert; Razovsky, Cecilia; Sender, Sadie

Allied Zones of Postwar Europe, 10–11, 35, 56, 78–79, 82, 88, 96

American Council for Judaism, 56

American Jewish Committee (AJC), 56

American Jewish Conference, 92

American Jewish Congress, 98

American Jewish Joint Distribution Committee (JDC): 1945 annual report, *39*; 1948 annual report, *114*; and aid workers, 76–81, 84, 86; and direct aid, 101–4, 107–9, 126–27, 11–17; and film, 29, 37–38; and fundraising, 24–28, 35, 39, 76 (see also chapter 1); Operation Ezra, 46; Operation Magic Carpet, 46; Operation Open Sesame, 46; *Out of the Ashes*, 26–27; and radio, 53, 110; *Report on the Living*, 29; and secondary witnesses, 89, 94; *The Future Can Be Theirs*, 36–38; and the UJA, 21–22, 24–26; and the UNCC, 107; women as leaders,

108; and Zionism, 132. *See also JDC Digest*; Supplies for Overseas Survivors (SOS); United Palestine Appeal (UPA)

American Red Cross, 26, 52, 121

"An American with a Mission," 2–3, 5, 7, 17, 55

Anne Frank's Diary, 8

archives (archival): booklets, 34–35, 42–44; brochures, 3, 7, 16–17, 21–22, 27, 34, 37, 44–45, 48, 56, 60, 66–71, 75, 102–4, 110; ephemera, 4, 7, 14–18, 21, 23, 47, 134; Holocaust archive, 7–9, 19; JDC, 108; National, 114; posters, 3, 7–8, 16–17, 102, 110; USC Shoah Foundation, 6, 7, 134–35; Yad Vashem 8; Yale Fortunoff Video Archive of Holocaust Testimony, 4, 7. *See also* documentaries; film

atomic war (nuclear disaster), 106, 109

Auschwitz concentration camp, 2, 5, 17, 31–32, 57–61, 113, 119, 129

Australia, 120, 135

Austria, 64, 82, 86, 116

B'nai B'rith, 89, 103, 107, 117: Adopt-a-Family Abroad, 117

Baerwald, Paul (JDC), 101

Bassfreund, Jürgen (Boder testimony), 97–98

Battle for Survival (UJA), 30–33, 36, 62

195

INDEX

Bauer, Yehuda, 16, 25–26, 127
Bergen-Belsen concentration camp, 5, 10, 31–32, 53
Berman, Lila Corwin, 13, 28
Bernstein, Phillip (Rabbi), 82
Boder, David, 17, 49–51, 62, 72, 77, 93–100, 134
Brazil (fundraising tour), 81
Bronfman, Samuel (United Jewish Relief Agency of Canada), 33
Browning, Christopher, 61
Buchenwald concentration camp, 5, 17, 32, 34, 57–60, 72, 76
Bulgaria, 84, 107
Burkenwald, Israel, 2–5, 13, 55
Busy Buddies, 125

Canada, 33, 89, 122
Cantor, Eddie, 110
Central Committee of Liberated Jews, 31
Cesarani, David, 4–5
Chanukah, 116, 128: Chanukah Campaign for European Jewish Children, 116
chaplains, 17, 75, 77, 81, 101. *See* individual chaplains by name
children: aid for, 101–2; American Committee for the Rehabilitation of European Children, 13; Chanukah Campaign for European Jewish Children, 116; Children for Palestine, 91; DPs, 13, 78; Correspondent's Service for European Jewish Children, 116–22, 128; in Europe, 29, 46–47, 67; and film, 29–30, 33–34, 37; and Jewish women's organizations, 13; orphans, 3, 11, 13, *44*, 46, 67, 91, 102, 109, 119, 123–26; *Our Child Survivors*, 109; and Palestine, 39–44, 50–51, 68–71, 92; in radio appeals, 3, 54, 62, 66; US Children's Bureau, 78, 92; Vaad Hatzala's Children's Homes, 105, 122; WJC Child Care Division, 103–5, 116–19. *See also* Rescue Children (Vaad Hatzala); Youth Aliyah (Hadassah)
Children for Palestine, 91. *See also* Sharp, Martha
Chochema, Minnie, 118
Christians (Christian), 56, 116, 121: Protestants, 52, 64. *See also* Roman Catholicism (Roman Catholic)

Chwojnik, Avraham, 95
Citizen's Committee on Displaced Persons (CCDP), 2–3, 13, 17, 50, 55–59, 65–66, 72, 85, 122, 133
clothing drives, 12, 18–19, 99, 102–12, 116, 123–28, 132
Cohen, R., 20–23, 33, 47
Cold War, 9, 16, 18, 66, 92, 114, 116, 131
concentration camps: and American aid workers, 76, 92–95; in American media, 125, 129 ; as death camps, 27, 67, 129; DP camps created on grounds of, 10; and film, 31–32, 72; fundraising for survivors, 25, 67–68, 119, 132; gas chambers, 2, 5, 27, 34, 60–61; in radio depictions, 2, 5, 57–62; as symbol, 61, 111–13; tattoos, 5, 12, 17, 37–38, 47–48, 71–72, 104, 120; uniforms, 31, 111; work camps, 80, 127. *See individual camps by name*
Congregation Emanuel (Denver, CO), 82–83
consumerism, 18, 125, 133
Correspondent's Service for European Jewish Children (World Jewish Congress), 116–22, 128
Cuba, 78, 81
Cyprus, 90
Czechoslovakia (Czech), 11, 25, 35, *41*, 57–60, 68, 83, 129, 131

Dachau concentration camp, 32, 76, 94–97, 113
Dautmergen concentration camp, 94
de Sola Poole, Tamara, 90–91
DeLacy, Hugh, 106
"Delayed Pilgrims Dinner," 1–3, 7, 17, 55–58
Denmark, 82
Des Pres, Terrance, 80-81
Diner, Hasia, 4, 15, 37, 134
Dinnerstein, Leonard, 11
"Displaced," 17, 50–51, 55–58, 61–66, 70, 73, 80
displaced persons or displaced Persons camps (DP): and direct aid, 101, 104, 108–13, 126; Displaced Persons Act of 1948, 46, 56; Displaced Persons Act of 1950, 11; *Displaced Persons Digest*, 56; fundraising campaigns related to, 9, 19, 26–38, 42–46; and immigration, 11; and Jewish women's

INDEX

organizations, 13, 26, 50–53, 67, 78, 101, 103, 107–8, 117, 119, 132; and represented on radio, 1, 17, 49–66, 70–73; and secondary witnesses, 77, 80–99; *She'erit Hapletah*, 15, 122; Truman directive on, 11; and UNRRA, 10

documentaries, 29–30, 111, 128. *See individual productions by name*

Dolins, Robert (Supplies for Overseas Survivors), 107–8

Dollars for Destiny (UJA), 35

Edwards, Ralph, 129–31

Egypt (Egyptian), 37, 46

Eisenhower, Dwight D., 31

English (language), 2–3, 32, 49–52, 55, 58–59, 62, 78, 96–97, 129

Estonia (Estonian), 65

Fabian, Bela (testimony), 61, 79–81

Federal Communications Commission (FCC), 52

Felman, Shoshana, 76

film: *Battle for Survival*, 30–33, 36, 62; compared to radio, 52; distribution by OWI, 12; documentaries, 29–30, 111, 128; *Dollars for Destiny*, 35; *March of Time*, 55; and material aid, 104, 111; and narrative strategy, 3, 7, 16–17, 21–22, 27–38, 46–47, 67, 75; *Our Child Survivors*, 109; *Placing the Displaced*, 29, 113; *Report on the Living*, 29; *Seeds of Destiny*, 30; *Shoah*, 112; *The Future Can Be Theirs*, 36–38; *They May Live Again*, 29; *This Is Your Life*, 129–31, 136; *UJA Report from Israel*, 46–47; US Army, 72

Finkelstein, Norman, 4

Flanzbaum, Hilene, 23, 47

Forshee, Peter, 3, 5, 13, 55

Foster Parents' Plan (World Jewish Congress), 116–17

Foster Parents Plan for War Children, 117

Founding Fathers, 17, 57

France (French), 10, 78–79, 90, 96, 102, 113–19, 123–27: French language, 8, 50, 96

freedom: 18, 65–66, 77, 91–92, 106; America as land of, 2–5, 54–58, 133; as Jewish story,

37–38; in Palestine, 39–42; from religious persecution, 3, 13; in survivor narratives, 17, 51, 54–58, 93; symbols of, 113–16

Friedman *or* Karo, Charles, 105, 123–26

Friedman, Helen and Ernst, 125–26

Friedman, Herbert (Rabbi), 17, 75–77, 81–92, 96, 99

Friendship Service for Jewish Children Inc., 117

fundraising (fundraisers): annual reports, 7, 21, 52, *39*, 90, 109, 112, *114*; and displaced persons, 9, 19, 26–38, 42–46; financial goals, 24, 26, 28, 35–36, 42, 47, 67, 78, 120, 132; and Hadassah, 16–18, 26, 66–73, 108, 122; and immigration, 22–25, 44–47; and the JDC, 24–28, 35, 39, 76; and Jewish futurity, 16, 21–27, 30–31, 34–38, 41–45, 66, 71, 116, 132; and Palestine, 34, 36, 39–44; and radio, 28, 48, 66–72; related to displaced persons, 9, 19, 26–38, 42–46; and the UJA, 16, 21–47, 65–66, 76. *See organizations and fundraisers by name*

futurity *or* future (Jewish): and aid workers, 79, 84–85, 92; American Jews held responsible for, 109; defined after the Holocaust, 24–27; and fundraising, 16, 21–27, 30–31, 34–38, 41–45, 66, 71, 116, 132; and Passover, 54; and survivor narratives, 92, 95, 98, 128, 132–33; *The Future Can Be Theirs*, 36–38; and trains, 113, 115. *See also* fundraising; survival (Jewish)

Germany (German): and American aid workers, 78, 82–87, 90; and American Jewish fundraising, 24, 47; Berlin Olympics (1936), 20; and DP survivors, 113–16; and Boder, 50, 96; Nuremberg Laws, 20; and radio, 56, 64. *See also* Nazism (Nazis)

ghettos, 8, 31, 38, 46–47, 58–61, 68–70, 94–95, 112, 121, 128

GI Bill, 13

Gilman, Blanche (Supplies for Overseas Survivors), 107–8

Great Britain (British), 10, 35, 92, 110

Greece, 116

Greenspan, Henry, 14, 61, 63, 80

Grobe, Albert, 46–47
Guttman, Irene. *See* Hizme, Irene Guttman
Guttman, Rene. *See* Slotkin, Rene Guttman

Hadassah: "Case History #20,000," 17, 50–51, 55, 66, 70–73; and film, 29–30; fundraising, 16–18, 26, 34, 66–73, 108, 122; *Hadassah Headlines,* 90, 112; Hadassah Medical Organization, 67; "Hannah", 17, 50, 66–73; Henrietta Szold (Founder), 66–67; and radio, 50–53, 66–73; and secondary witnessing, 76–77, 89–91; slideshow, 34; *They May Live Again,* 29; Youth Aliyah, 18, 51, 66–71, 90
Harrison, Earl G. (Harrison Report), 10, 31, 56
Hartman, Geoffrey, 72–73
Hass, Irene, 5
Hebrew Immigration Aid Society (HIAS), 13, 16, 29–30, 113, 133: *Placing the Displaced,* 29, 113
Heller, James G. (United Palestine Appeal), 15, 24–25
Hillel International, 89
Hitler, Adolph, 15, 33, 37, 47, 66, 77, 83, 93, 110, 114
Hizme, Irene Guttman, 105, 123–28: *Rene and I,* 128
holidays (Jewish), 37–40, 46, 53–57, 85
Holocaust narratives: defined, 6. *See also* survivors (Holocaust); testimony; witnessing *or* witnesses
Holocaust: Americanization of "Holocaust" as term, 15–16; archives, 7–9, 19; and Jewish futurity, 9, 24–27; and material aid, 5, 100–5, 109–16, 126–28, 133; and memory, 4–7, 14–19, 32, 51, 61, 73, 105, 128–31, 134–35; never again rhetoric, 81; symbols, 17, 37, 41, 61, 71–72, 100, 104, 111–16, 120, 123–26; US Holocaust Memorial Museum (USHMM), 7, 72, 111–13, 127–28; what it meant to be Jewish in America in light of, 19. *See also* concentration camps; narratives (Holocaust); survivors (Holocaust)
Hungary (Hungarian), 25, 35, 80, 92, 107, 118–21
hunger, 5, 11, 27, 36, 42, 78, 87, 106

Illinois Institute of Technology (IIT), 49, 96, 99, 134: Voices of the Holocaust Project, 49, 96, 134
immigration (immigrants): and Americanization, 1–2, 30, 129–33; estimated number of Holocaust immigrants to US, 10–11; and fundraising, 22–25, 29, 44–47, 113; to Palestine, 10–11, 44; and pen pals, 118; quotas, 10–11, 16, 42, 55–57, 92, 133; and radio, 50–66, 73–74; reform, 50–51, 55–56, 66, 77, 91–92, 131, 133; and refugee policies, 11–19, 50–51, 56–57, 77, 91–92; and Rescue Children, 126; and secondary witnesses, 77–78, 91–92; symbols of, 41–44, 113–14. *See also* Hebrew Immigration Aid Society (HIAS); United Service for New Americans (USNA)
Intergovernmental Committee on Refugees, 10
International Refugee Organization (IRO), 10, 86, 102
Iraq (Iraqi), 46
Israel *or* Israeli (Jewish state), 11, 23–26, 35–38, 41–48, 66–67, 113–14, 132, 135. *See also* United Israel Appeal (UIA)
Italy (Italian), 11, 82, 90, 96, 116

JDC Digest, 24, 113, 115
Jewish Agency, 67, 86, 90
Jewish Charities of Chicago, 98
Jewish Federations, 14, 76, 107
Jewish Labor Committee (JLC), 13, 103, 117: Child Adoption Program, 103, 117
Jewish Publication Society (JPS), 98
Jewish Telegraphic Agency, 90
Jick, Leon, 4
Joint Distribution Committee (JDC). *See* American Jewish Joint Distribution Committee (JDC)
Joycrafter Group, 117–20

Kaiser, Henry, 106
Kaplan, Eliazer (Jewish Agency), 86
Karo, Charles. *See* Friedman *or* Karo, Charles
Katz, Elihu, 55
Kielce Pogrom (Poland), 11, 81–82, 87–88
Kobrin, Rebecca, 78

INDEX

Kohner, Hanna Bloch, 129–33, 136: *This Is Your Life*, 129–31, 136
Kosher (kashrut), 1, 13, 122
Krah, Markus, 53
Kramarsky, Lola (Hadassah), 18, 70

labor camps. *See individual camps by name*
Landsberg DP camp, 10, 91
Lang, Daniel, 58–65, 80
Langer, Lawrence, 33, 62–63, 72–73, 84
Lania, Leo, 77, 89, 99
Latvia (Latvian), 49–50, 96
Leavitt, Moses A. (JDC), 36
Lehman, Herbert H. (JDC), 36, 92–93
Levi, Primo, 32
Levitt, Laura, 111
Levy, Adele (UJA), 33–34, 109, 126
Levy, Henry (JDC), 84–85
Levy, Raphael (JDC), 109–10, 113
liberation of *or* liberated Jews (from concentration camps): 10, 12, 31, 60 132; in edited collections, 94; failed promise of, 27–28, 33, 77, 83, 91; images from liberation, 12, 25, 72; as letter writers, 120–21; and material aid 104, 108; note on terminology, 15; precarity of, 9–12; as remnant, 15, 27, 30, 35, 76, 92; survivor voices recorded following, 14, 49, 128; by US soldiers, 12
Life Magazine, 105, 123–28
Lilienheim, Henry, 94–95
Linder, Harold (JDC), 36
Linenthal, Edward, 112
Lithuania (Lithuanian), 50, 96
Lustig, Jason, 8

Maier, Kurt, 17, 50, 54, 57–66, 72
Maldist, Silva, 65
Manischewitz, D. Beryl, 1–2
March of Time, 55
Margolis, Laura (JDC), 78
marketing (public relations), 21, 29, 45, 123
Massey, Raymond, 1–2, 58
material aid: 100–5, 126–28; donation of fur coats, 126–27; financial aid, 119–20; food collection and distribution, 1, 10, 12, 18–19, 24, 27, 32, 36, 43, 87, 97, 99, 102–11, 116, 128; fundraising, 15–18, 23, 27, 36–38;

and Holocaust memory, 5, 109–16; and Holocaust narratives, 100–5, 126–28, 133; humanitarian aid, 6–10, 18–19, 22, 26–27, 46–47, 84, 101, 104, 106, 116–17, 120, 131–32, 136; medical, 34; and radio promotion, 52–55, 73; *See also* clothing drives; *individual organizations by name*
Mauthausen concentration camp, 129
McNarney, Joseph (General), 82, 86
melting pot (metaphor), 3, 116
memory: Holocaust, 4–7, 14–19, 32, 51, 61, 73, 105, 128–31, 134–35; and materiality, 109–16; memory making, 63, 66, 72
Mennonites, 96
Michaelis, Eva (Hadassah), 70
Mintz, Alan, 4, 15
Montor, Henry (UJA), 25–26
Morgenthau, Henry Jr. (UJA), 34, 82, 86–87
Morocco (Moroccan), 46
Muni, Paul, 57, 62, 65–66

Nadich, Judah (Rabbi), 31
National Community Relations Advisory Council (NCRAC), 92
National Conference of Jewish Social Welfare, 121
National Council of Jewish Women (NCJW), 26, 50–53, 67, 78, 103, 107–8, 117, 132
National Jewish Welfare Board, 108
National Refugee Service (NRS), 13
Nazism (Nazis): Berlin Olympics (1936), 20; non-Jewish victims of, 49; Nuremberg Laws, 20; symbols of, 5, 12, 17, 37–38, 41, 47–48, 61, 71–72, 100, 104, 111–16, 120, 123–26; war crimes, 12, 31, 37, 72. *See also* concentration camps
networks: of communal organizations, 17–18, 47, 99; and fundraising, 28–29, 42, 76–77; of pen pals, 120; and secondary witnesses, 75–78, 89–93, 99; of SOS committees, 102, 111; speaking tours, 81, 89–93
New Americans (discourse of), 13, 15, 22–23, 39, 42–45, 54, 118, 131, 133, 135
newsreels, 12, 37, 72, 111
New York City, 1–2, 45, 46, 59–60, 67, 82, 90, 93–94, 101, 116, 123–24, 127
Nichanian, Marc, 14–15

Niewyk, Donald, 134
Nordhausen concentration camp, 32
North Africa, 46–47
Norway, 116
Novick, Peter, 4
Novick, William (Rescue Children), 4, 126

O'Dwyer, William, 1–2, 58, 123
Office of War Information (OWI), 12
Ohrdruf concentration camp, 57, 60, 64
Opatovska, Helen, 53–54
Organization for Rehabilitation and Training (ORT), 13, 29, *43–45*, 66, 103, 107, 117
orphanages (orphans), 3, 11, 13, *44*, 46, 67, 91, 102, 109, 119, 123–26
Orthodox Jews (orthodoxy), 4, 122–23. *See also* Rescue Children (Vaad Hatzala); Vaad Hatzala
Oskar L. (testimony), 120–21
Our Child Survivors, 109
"Out of the Wilderness" (USNA), 54–59, 62

Palestine (Palestinian): and fundraising, 34, 36, 39–44; immigration to, 10–11, 21–22, 25, 30, 51–52, 56, 66–71, 91–92, 113, 132; Jewish National Home in, 15, 24; and radio, 66–71; and secondary witnesses, 90–92; and the UN, 35. *See also* United Palestine Appeal (UPA)
Passover, 37–40, 54–57: Seder Ritual of Remembrance, 37
Pearson, Drew (and Merry-Go-Round), 115–16
pen pals, 103–5, 108, 116–23 128
pilgrims (narratives of), 1–3, 7, 9, 13, 17, 51, 55–59, 133; as "delayed" pilgrims, 1–3, 7, 9, 13, 17, 55–59, 133
Pinson, Koppel, 20
Pioneer Women, 16, 38
pioneers (Holocaust survivors as), 17, 22, 39–44, 48, 133
Placing the Displaced (HIAS), 29, 113
poetry (poems), 32, 54, 111–12
Poland (Polish), 31, 64, 76, 83–84, 87–88, 123: Kielce Pogrom, 11, 81–82, 87–88; Polish language, 50, 96
Prell, Riv-Ellen, 94

President's War Relief Control Board, 106
Protestants. *See* Christians (Christian), Protestants

Rabbis (Rabbinic), 23, 88, 101, 122–23: Union of Orthodox Rabbis, 122. *See individual rabbis by name*
Rackovsky, Isaiah (Rabbi), 81
radio: and aid, 106, 110; "An American with a Mission," 2–3, 5, 7, 17; audio, 50–55, 58, 64, 67, 72–73; "Case History #20,000," 17, 50–51, 55, 66, 70–73; "Delayed Pilgrim Dinner," 1–3, 7; FCC Communications Act of 1934, 52; and fundraising, 28, 48, 66–72; "Hannah", 17, 50, 66–73; holiday specials, 53; "I am a Displaced Person", 65; and immigration, 91; "Joseph in America", 65; and knowledge dissemination, 16, 129, 136; "Look at Their Faces," 34; one-off events, 52–53; and optimism, 85; "Out of the Wilderness", 54–59, 62; "Parable for Easter," 56, 59, 65; scripts, 17, 50, 53–55, 65–66, 70–71; and sharing Holocaust narratives, 48, 50–55, 72–75, 80, 129, 136; "The Arrival of Delayed Pilgrims," 56; "The Late Comers", 56; *This American Life*, 130–31; and voicing displacement, 57–66; Yiddish, 8
Razovsky, Cecilia, 17, 62, 77–81, 91, 96, 99–100, 121–22
refugees: after 1953, 129, 133, 135; and citizenship, 45; as delayed pilgrims, 1–3, 7, 9, 13, 17, 55–58, 133; European refugee crisis, 11, 30, 55, 57, 59, 73, 77; and fundraising, 42, *44*; non-Jewish, 65, 95–96; *Placing the Displaced*, 29; on radio, 5, 55–59, 65; refugee policies, 11–19, 49–51, 56–57, 77, 91–92; and secondary witnesses, 78–79, 83. *See also* immigration (immigrants); National Refugee Service (NRS); United Nations Relief and Rehabilitation Administration (UNRRA)
Report on the Living (JDC), 29
Rescue Children (Vaad Hatzala), 103, 105, 122–28
resettlement: and fundraising, 26–27, 34–35; in Palestine, 41, 46; of survivors, 23, 84, 96, 129; in testimony narratives, 9, 133

INDEX

revenge, 60–61
Rhodes, Irving, 90
Riga ghetto, 94–95
Ringelblum Archive (Underground Archive of the Warsaw Ghetto), 8
Roman Catholicism (Catholic), 13, 52, 64
Romania (Rumania), 102, 107
Rose D., 119–22
Rosen, Alan, 72–73, 98
Rosenbaum, Charles (UJA), 76
Rosenberg, Julius and Ethel, 131
Rosenfeld, Alvin, 85
Rosensaft, Joseph, 31
Rosenwald, Julius (UJA), 109
Rosenwald, William (UJA), 31
Rosh Hashanah, 85
Ross, Anthony, 3
Russia, 83, 96, 101, 108: Russian language, 50. *See also* Soviet Union

Sachsenhausen concentration camp, 57, 60
Sadie Sender for JDC in Frankfurt, 53–54
Schindler's List, 6
Schwartz, Joseph J. (JDC), 31, 86, 92
Schwarz, Leo, 77, 93–96, 99
Seeds of Destiny (UNRRA), 30
Seidman, Naomi, 61
Sender, Sadie (JDC), 53–54
Shandler, Jeffrey, 55, 130
Shanghai (China), *43*, 78, 127
Sharp, Martha, 90–91: Children for Palestine, 91
Shephard, Ben, 11
Shoah, 112
shoes, 60, 104, 105, 110–12, 126–28
silence *or* silent (myth of): 4–7, 118, 130
Silverman, Allison, 130–31, 136
Slotkin, Rene Guttman, 126, 128: *Rene and I*, 128
Sobel, Louis (JDC), 107
social work (social workers), 17, 62, 75, 78–81, 118, 121
South America, *43*, 81
Soviet Union, 11, 115. *See also* Russia
Spanish language, 50, 96
Srole, Leo, 17, 77, 91–92
Starachowice labor camp, 61

Stier, Oren Baruch, 111–12
Sundquist, Eric, 5
Supplies for Overseas Survivors (SOS), 18, 101–12, 116, 118, 126–28: committees, 102, 110–12; women leaders in, 13, 101–4, 107–9, 118
survival (Jewish): *Battle for Survival*, 30–33, 36, 62; and fundraising narratives, 14–17, 20–23, 27–35, 39–40, 46, 87; image of, 42–43; and Jewish futurity, 24–27, 36–39; and material aid, 109; and narrative framing, 58, 80, 94, 99. *See also* futurity *or* future
survivor narratives: defined, 6. *See also* testimony (Holocaust); witnessing *or* witnesses
survivors (Holocaust): in American media, 125, 129; as destitute, 24, 39, 42, 66, 102; and futurity, 92, 95, 98, 128, 132–33; as New Americans, 13, 15, 22, 39–45, 54, 118, 131, 133, 135; note on terminology, 16; as pioneers, 17, 22, 39–44, 48, 133; and representation, 6, 42–43, 129; and resistance, 94–98, 113; as She'erit Hapletah, 15, 122. *See also* Supplies for Overseas Survivors (SOS); testimony (Holocaust); voices (survivor). *See also* individuals: Bassfreund, Jürgen; Burkenwald, Israel; Chochema, Minnie; Fabian, Bela; Forshee, Peter; Friedman *or* Karo, Charles; Guttman, Irene; Hass, Irene; Kohner, Hannah Bloch; Lilienheim, Henry; Maier, Kurt; Opatovska, Helen; Oskar L.; Rose D.; Rosensaft, Joseph; Slotkin, Rene
Sutzkever, Avrom, 112
Sweden, 82
Switzerland (Swiss), 94, 96
synagogues, 13, 23, 83, 89, 110: Synagogue Council of America: Adopt a Synagogue Program, 117
Szold, Henrietta (Hadassah), 66–67

testimony (Holocaust): authenticity, 54, 73, 76, 120, 135; and Boder: 97, 99; curation of survivor voices, 93–99; defined, 14–15; emergence in the 1970s and 1980s, 4–5, 61; and memory, 5–7; and radio, 62–64, 72–74; as sacred or privileged, 6, 32, 51, 134; and

202 INDEX

secondary witnesses, 17, 79–82, 92, 94; and survival, 80; survivors as "bearers of testimony," 32, 78; USC Shoah Foundation, 6–9, 134–35; USHMM Testimony Collection, 7, 127–28; Yale Fortunoff Video Archive of Holocaust Testimony, 4, 7

Tenzer, Herbert (Rescue Children), 122–23, 126

Thanksgiving, 1–3, 51, 55–56, 133

The Eternal Light, 52–53, 56, 62: "The Arrival of Delayed Pilgrims," 56; "The Late Comers", 56

The Future Can Be Theirs (JDC), 36–38

The Golden Door, 56–57: "I am a Displaced Person," 65; "Joseph in America", 65; "Parable for Easter," 56, 59, 65

Theresienstadt concentration camp, 17, 60–61, 129

They May Live Again (Hadassah), 29

This American Life: "Oh, You Shouldn't Have,"130–31

This Is Your Life, 129–31, 136

Timmons, David, 54–58

Trachtenberg, Barry, 13-14

trains: 104, 111–16; and aid, 111–16; Freedom Train, 114–16; Friendship Train, 106, 114–16; as symbols, 104–5, 112-114; and *Shoah* (film), 112; and US Holocaust Memorial Museum, 112-13

Treblinka extermination camp, 32, 94

Truman, Harry S., 11, 105–6, 125

United Israel Appeal (UIA), 21, 29, 132. *See also* United Palestine Appeal (UPA)

United Jewish Appeal (UJA): 1947 Emergency Conference, 86, 88; and aid workers, 76–77, 81–82, 86–90; annual campaigns, 26–27, 33–35, 38, 46, 113–14; *Battle for Survival*, 30–33, 36, 62; Big Gifts efforts, 28; *Dollars for Destiny*, 35; and film, 62; fundraising, 16, 21–47, 65–66, 76; of Greater New York, 42, 46; greatest homecoming in history campaign, 46–47; and material aid, 109; and material culture, 113; National Women's Division, 109, 126; *Our Child Survivors*, 109; and radio, 50–54, 130; Speaker's Bureau, 27; yearbooks, 113

UJA Report from Israel, 46–47

United Jewish Relief Agencies of Canada, 33

United Jewish Welfare Board, 41–42

United Jewish Welfare Fund (Los Angeles), 42

United National Clothing Collection (UNCC), 18, 105–7, 127

United Nations, 35, *44*, 89

United Nations Relief and Rehabilitation Administration (UNRRA), 2, 10, 30, 79–80, 86, 91–92, 102, 105–7

United Palestine Appeal (UPA), 12, 15, 21–26, 29, 36, 39–40, 43–44, 132: *UPA Reports*, 24. *See also* United Israel Appeal (UIA)

United Service for New Americans (USNA), 1, 13, 21–22, 43–45, 50, 54–59, 133: "Out of the Wilderness," 54–59, 62

US Army, 60, 72, 75–76, 86, 94, 129

US Congress, 55, 65, 77, 92, 106

US Holocaust Memorial Museum (USHMM), 7, 72, 111–13, 127–28

USC Shoah Foundation, 6–9, 134–35: Dimensions in Testimony (DiT), 135–36

Vaad Hatzala: Children's Homes, 105, 122; and fundraising, 26, 34; kosher kitchens, 13; Rescue Children, 103, 105, 122–28

Varchaver, Catherine (WJC), 103, 105, 116–22, 128

Victory Clothing Collection, 105–6

videotape *or* video (as form of testimony), 4, 7, 51, 63, 72–73, 81, 135

Vilna Ghetto, 94–95, 112

voices (survivor), 7, 14–17, 49–55, 71–73, 93–100, 129, 134–35

Voices of the Holocaust Project, 49, 96, 134

volunteerism *or* volunteers, 2, 18, 21, 27, 38, 50, 71, 75, 100–4, 107, 111, 116, 119–20, 132. *See also* women volunteers (Jewish)

Wall, Wendy, 115

War Refugee Board, 1

Warburg, Edward M.M. (JDC), 28, 31, 36

Warburg, Frieda Schiff (JDC), 107

Warsaw Ghetto, 8, 38, 61, 94, 113: Ringelblum Archive (Underground Archive of the Warsaw Ghetto), 8

Weissman, Gary, 16

INDEX

Welles, Orson, 30–33
Westerbork transit camp, 129
White Papers (Great Britain), 10
Wiesel, Elie, 32
Wieviorka, Annette, 6
Wise, Jonah (Rabbi) (JDC), 24–25
witnessing *or* witnesses: of aid workers, 74–78, 99–100; and archives, 5–8, 135; bearing witness, 14, 80; edited volumes of survivor narratives, 93–99; eyewitness accounts: 5–8, 49–50, 68, 76, 83, 89, 94–95, 98, 119, 135; and listening, 50–53, 72, 78–81; in *New Yorker*, 60, 63; objects as, 111; and radio, 67–68, 73; secondary witnesses, 17–18, 76–82, 86, 89–93, 96–100; and survivors, 6-8
women volunteers (Jewish): create narratives, 13, 77; as leaders, 108; and material aid, 13, 101–9; as secondary witnesses, 77–81, 90. *See also* Hadassah; National Council of Jewish Women (NCJW); Pioneer Women; *individual women by name*
World Jewish Congress (WJC), 12, 66, 103, 105, 120, 122, 132: American Jewish Congress, 98; Chanukah Campaign for European Jewish Children, 116; Child Care Division, 116–19; Correspondent's

Service for European Jewish Children, 116–22, 128
world peace, 106-07
World War II, 1–3, 8–9, 12–13, 18, 21–24, 46, 52, 56, 78, 136
Wyzanksi, Gisela (Hadassah), 18, 90

Yale Fortunoff Video Archive for Holocaust Testimonies, 4, 7
Yemen (Yemeni), 46
Yiddish (language), 8, 50, 52, 54, 58, 62, 96, 110
Young, James, 72–73
Youth Aliyah (Hadassah), 18, 51, 66–71, 90: Advisory Council of the Hadassah National Youth Aliyah Committee, 18
YouTube, 134–35

Zeilsheim DP camp, 53
Zionism (Zionist): and fundraising, 22, 25, 35, 42; and immigration, 56, 66; Labor Zionist, 38; and material aid, 108; non-Zionist, 25, 108; in radio broadcasts, 66. *See also* Hadassah; Pioneer Women; United Israel Appeal (UIA); United Palestine Appeal (UPA); World Jewish Congress (WJC)

Rachel Deblinger is Director of the Modern Endangered Archives Program (MEAP) at the UCLA Library, a granting program that supports digitization, preservation, and access to at-risk cultural heritage materials from around the world. She is a member of the UCLA Holocaust Research Lab and continues to research and write about Holocaust memory in America and digital archives.

For Indiana University Press
Sabrina Black, Editorial Assistant
Lesley Bolton, Project Manager/Editor
Dan Crissman, Editorial Director and Acquisitions Editor
Anna Francis, Assistant Acquisitions Editor
Anna Garnai, Editorial Assistant
Katie Huggins, Production Manager
Dan Pyle, Online Publishing Manager
Pamela Rude, Senior Artist and Book Designer
Stephen Williams, Assistant Director of Marketing